"Is This Thing On?"

A Computer Handbook for Late Bloomers, Technophobes, and the Kicking & Screaming

Abby Stokes

Illustrations by Michael Sloan and Susan Hunt Yule

WORKMAN PUBLISHING • NEW YORK

Library of Congress Cataloging-in-Publication Data is available.
ISBN-13: 978-0-7611-4619-3

Author photo © 2000 by Laura Straus, NY

Trademarks: All brand names, product names, and logos used or illustrated
in this book are trade names, service marks, trademarks, or registered
trademarks of their respective owners. Neither Workman Publishing Co., Inc.,
nor Abby Stokes is associated with any of such owners and no endorsement
by such owners has been made or is implied.

Workman books are available at special discounts when purchased in bulk
for premiums and sales promotions as well as for fund-raising or educational
use. Special editions or book excerpts also can be created to specification.
For details, contact the Special Sales Director at the address below.

Design: Janet Vicario; layout: Lidija Tomas

WORKMAN PUBLISHING COMPANY, INC.
225 Varick Street
New York, NY 10014-4381
www.workman.com

Printed in the United States of America
First printing July 2008
10 9 8 7 6 5 4 3 2 1

For Nancy
I dedicate this book to my mother . . .
who tried and succeeded.

Thank You, Thank You, Thank You

I thank my lucky stars every day for the incredible group of family and friends that I am privileged to call my loved ones. My lucky stars also have me dividing my time between the most exciting city in the world and a little piece of heaven on the water. Above and beyond my lucky stars I thank the following people: Mom, Eve, and Sherri, whose unwavering support is always felt and appreciated; Dan Tucker, Judy Hirsch, and the late Henry Hirsch, whose sage advice guided me through every aspect of the book; Peter Workman, Suzie Bolotin, and Margot Herrera, who welcomed me back to Workman for the second time; Justin Nesbit, Amy Lewis, Anastasia Fuller, and Jay Fienberg, who designed *abbyandme.com;* Janet Vicario, Lidija Tomas, Michael Sloan, Susan Hunt Yule, Cassie Murdoch, Tom Boyce, Beth Doty, Amy Corley, Andrea Bussell, and the entire team at Workman; all of my students, who make going to work a pleasure; and above all you, the reader, for having enough faith in this book to open your wallet or being smart enough to know someone who would buy it for you.

Let the Shopping Begin

Baby's First Day Home

The Newlywed Game

Welcome to the Neighborhood

A Word Before You Begin

When I was in second grade, I proudly went to the library to sign out my first book with chapters. After finishing the book, I confessed to my older sister, Eve, that I found it a bit confusing. She pointed out what was supposed to be obvious, but obviously wasn't to me—the chapters were meant to be read in sequence. Who knew?

Read this book in sequence at your own pace and it will take you from the basics—what you need to know to make a sound computer purchase, set it up in your home, and connect to the Internet—and then on to how to master e-mail attachments, online shopping, scanners, cell phones, and much more. This book is intended to demystify the computer, not to explain the gory inner workings of the machine. Every day we use devices such as a car, the telephone, and the TV, but have no idea how they really work. Nonetheless, we do work them. The computer is no different.

Be forewarned that once you arrive at Chapter 10, it is all hands-on instruction and will definitely be overwhelming if you try to visualize what is being discussed rather than actually seeing it in front of you. If you haven't bought a computer by then, make sure that you're sitting in front of someone else's before you continue. If you're looking at a computer screen and you find that what's described in the book differs a bit from what you see, don't panic. Websites and computer software change over time, so we'll figure it all out together.

Take a deep breath and begin your journey. You're going to be pleasantly surprised at how much easier it is than you anticipated. Before you know it, you'll be skillfully "surfing the net," e-mailing all your friends, and conquering your fear of technology!

Abby

P.S. For the mighty faithful who have read *It's Never Too Late to Love a Computer* and are back again, you may see familiar material in the first chapters of this book, but read very carefully as there is new information throughout those early chapters and plenty to keep you on your toes as you read on.

THERE IS NOTHING TO FEAR BUT TECHNOLOGY ITSELF

CHAPTER 1

Bring the World to Your Fingertips

Research, find, and buy anything you can imagine, and communicate with loved ones, without leaving home—what a computer and the Internet offer

My mother still can't reset her car's clock after daylight saving time. She just adds or subtracts an hour until I come home for a visit. Even better, for the first week after she buys a new car, she'll only drive it in the Stop & Shop parking lot. Once she feels comfortable enough to take it on the road, it's still a few months before the windshield wipers stop being activated whenever she means to signal a right turn. All that said, I am incredibly proud of her for joining the community of the computer savvy. Mom had never shown any interest in computers, but like so many seniors, she knew she was missing out on something when she began to notice that every article she read ended with "For more information go to *www.[insert almost anything here].com.*"

"Peach, what is a website?" she asked me.

"I had no idea what the computer could do for me, but I knew that if I didn't try it soon, I never would. Now I use it for everything. . . . I write the newsletter and maintain the mailing list for my church. I love finding out all kinds of information on the Internet and I'm a big fan of e-mail."
—*Marsha*

"Think of the computer as a combination television set and typewriter. Then think of the Internet as a library. You can find information on absolutely anything you can dream up on the Internet by accessing different websites—as you would books in a library. Just type in what you want to learn about, and it will appear in front of you in the form of pictures, text, and sound" was my answer.

A website is like a book. Instead of going to the library and looking up a title in the card catalog, you go to the computer and type in a website address.

Because there can be more than one website for a given subject, you'll have many choices available to you. Each website is designed individually, just as books are written individually by different authors.

Anyone can have a website—even you. All that is needed is the desire to convey information and the willingness to pay a small annual fee to a company to register the name of your website. If you don't mind piggybacking on another website or having advertisements on your site, you may be able to have a website at no cost.

A few months after my mother first asked me about the Internet, she visited me in New York and wanted to see a Broadway musical. This was the perfect opportunity to show her what a computer can do, what the Internet has to offer, and how I make my living (I teach computer skills to seniors and others). I turned on my computer, connected to the Internet, and then typed in *www.playbill.com* (the website address of a company that sells theater tickets), and like magic, their website appeared on my screen. I picked the show we wanted to see and the date that was best for us. Next, the seating chart appeared on the screen and we chose our seats. Then I ordered the tickets and typed in my e-mail address where I would receive the e-tickets and then print them on my printer at home.

Mom was impressed. I've been teaching people how to maneuver around the Internet for over a decade now, and it continues to amaze me with the infinite ways that it can benefit those who use it. The Internet allows you to track investments, research family genealogy, contact buddies, purchase a new car, auction a coin collection, search for the best deal on airline tickets, and so much more.

Convincing Mom Continues . . .

The ease with which we were able to purchase the theater tickets via the computer had my mother intrigued.

"What else can the Internet do?"

"I can't tell you everything it can do, Mom, because it's constantly evolving. I don't think anyone really knows its full capabilities. But I'll give you some examples of what I think is fun and practical about it."

Mom had lost track of a dear friend of hers several years ago and, after much effort, sadly gave up on finding her. I signed on to the Internet and typed in *www.switchboard.com* (a website where you can search for people and businesses). A form appeared on the screen of my computer, into which I typed her friend's name and some additional information. Within a few seconds there were seven listings of people with the same name as Mom's long-lost friend. The listings that appeared included telephone numbers, street addresses, and e-mail addresses. The happy ending is that Mom found her friend. From that moment on, she was sold on the computer.

Shirley, one of my mother's friends, suffers from a very rare cancer. After she became hooked on the computer, not only did she find detailed information about her specific form of cancer and alternative treatment ideas, but she also found a group of people with the same condition. She now communicates with some of them daily. All of this is done through her computer, which enables her to be involved in the world around her even when she is housebound.

To say that the Internet can give you information on anything you can dream up may sound like a huge overstatement, but it's true.

A Taste of What Some People Do with the Internet

Sophie always has an interesting list of things she wants to find out about on the Internet. During one of our lessons we visited websites that gave information about renting a house on Martha's

"The Internet allows us to get up-to-date stock quotes, access detailed information on a company of interest, and directly buy and sell stocks any time we want. We even access *The Wall Street Journal* online. All this has increased our enjoyment and the value of our investments. Who can argue with that?"

—*Cy and Ruth*

Vineyard, tracked down an artist whose work she wanted to buy, and found a doormat with Jack Russell terriers emblazoned on it.

By typing *Martha's Vineyard rentals* in a search engine (which I'll explain to you later), we came upon more than a dozen websites, many of them with photos of the interiors and exteriors of the houses available. While looking at a photo of one of the rentals, we noticed the words "how to get here" on the screen. We clicked on the words and a different website appeared that offered us driving directions and a map that showed the best route. Sophie printed the directions and set them aside to put in her car's glove compartment.

Then came the mission of tracking down the artist whose work she liked. First we typed in the artist's name, but that didn't work. Then she remembered what gallery showed his work and typed that in. Not only did it give us contact information, but one of his paintings was featured on the website as well.

On to the doormat. That took a little ingenuity. We searched for "doormats" and "doormats with dogs." We found tons of doormats and a surprising number of doormats with dogs, but not the right kind of dog. Then we searched for "Jack Russell terriers." We found a great-looking doormat and bought it over the Internet with her credit card. It was delivered the next week. We both had ear-to-ear grins of satisfaction.

What More Does the Internet Offer?

Another really great feature of the information superhighway is that you can communicate inexpensively with other people all over the world. I remember when we would call my grandparents and have just enough time to say, "Hello. How are things?" before my grandfather would say, "Okay. Enough, ladies. This is long distance. Say good-bye now." I don't mean to make light of the cost of a telephone call or how hard my grandfather worked for his money, but wasn't that why they invented long distance, so we could talk to each other? Well, thank heaven for computer technology. I have students who communicate with friends and family across the globe everyday. If it wasn't for the Internet, this would be financially impossible for most of us.

E-mail = ?

E-mail, or electronic mail, is the same idea as sending a letter (now lovingly referred to as snail mail), but rather than waiting for it to go from a mailbox to your local post office, get sorted, sent to another post office, and then delivered by foot to the recipient, you send your message through the computer by way of your phone line or a high-speed connection to the Internet. This all happens in a matter of seconds rather than days.

Still confused? Well, e-mail confused me too until I could actually see how it all worked. So if things in this book get a bit murky, have faith that when you get in front of a computer and see what I'm talking about, it will all make sense.

What Else Can a Computer Do for Me?

It cannot be denied that along with all the other things you can accomplish on a computer, it is the Internet, with its access to the information superhighway, that has made computers a must-have in the last few years.

However, having a computer offers you much more than the Internet. You will have the ability to organize your address book, create a family newsletter, and, if you want to, simulate flying a plane and master chess. Some of my students track their frequent-flier miles, inventory their collectibles, and design their own stationery. The computer can consolidate your paperwork, create order in your life, and track your finances.

There is no end to how a computer can organize, simplify, and enhance your life. But first you need to learn a bit more about computers, decide what you want to buy, and get it up and running. The whole undertaking of buying a computer can seem very overwhelming, but don't get discouraged. This book will guide you through the entire process. You will be pleasantly surprised by how easy it will be to make an educated purchase and how quickly you will learn to use and love your computer.

"I'm sure when my son gave me the computer he thought I might never use it. I guess I wasn't sure either. But I've always been a tinkerer, and the computer became a new challenge. Last month I gave my son advice about websites to check out for buying a new car. That felt good."
—*Peter*

"The computer is such a part of my grandchildren's lives—I wanted to know what it was about. Once I got online, they started to send me weekly e-mails. We used to see one another only at holidays and talk only on birthdays. It's the last thing I expected, but it has brought us closer together."
—*Jon*

In Conclusion

Mom now e-mails me every day. She sends and receives attachments (which I'll describe to you later in the book) from the various committees she volunteers on. When my brother was looking into summer camp for his four kids, Mom did all of the research for Jeff online. She even made the reservations and received confirmations by e-mail, which she forwarded to him. Next she investigated the location of each camp and gave my brother printouts from the local chamber of commerce and tourism websites with hotel and restaurant recommendations, highlighting the best places to buy a lobster roll! All things she found surfing the web.

This world that you keep hearing about is not passing you by—it's just waiting for you to come along. What computers can offer you is amazing and boundless, but you're not alone if it seems elusive and intimidating. Most of my students are over 50, and I can't explain to you how exciting it is for them (and me) when they start to zoom around the Internet.

Before you know it, the world will be your oyster. Trust me, if my mother can do it, you can too! (I'm only teasing you, Mom.)

Q: I've just bought a computer for my parents. What things should I avoid discussing so I don't confuse them?

A: There are no topics you need to avoid discussing with them. What you need to avoid is using computer jargon. You'll know when you've done it because their eyes will start to glaze over. The other crucial thing is to take your time. You may be in a rush, but they are not. Rushing people who are fearful or overwhelmed only makes them retreat. Good luck!

Q: What's the difference between the World Wide Web and the Internet, if there is one?

A: The Internet contains the World Wide Web in the same way that the United States contains Vermont. The World Wide Web is actually a subnetwork of the Internet.

Q: **What is an e-ticket?**

A: E-ticket means "electronic ticket." Rather than have an actual ticket in your hand, a record of your ticket is in the computer system of the company you bought the ticket from. E-tickets are used for airline reservations, theater, and other entertainment venues. It is smart to print the record of your e-ticket as proof of your purchase.

Q: **Where can I test a computer before deciding to buy one?**

A: Your local library should offer free access to computers. If the computers at the library are very busy, there may be a sign-in sheet where you can reserve a time slot. Ask the librarian if they offer any computer classes. If they don't, contact your nearest community center about classes. A lot of adult education programs offer computer classes as well. Any of these are good options for playing around on a computer and see if you might want to venture further. Senior Net has Senior Learning Centers all over the country. Call 408-615-0699 to find one near you.

CHAPTER 2

Hardware:
The Thigh Bone's
Connected to the . . .

A simple introduction to the parts
of a computer and how they
relate to one another

D o you remember the first time you got behind the wheel of a car when you were 16? You weren't concerned with how the engine worked or what all the parts were called. What was important was that you learned to drive yourself to the movies (without crashing into anything). The same can be said for the computer. The focus should not be on how it works but on how to get where you want to go.

Computers are very much like cars—they come in different sizes, styles, and colors, but they all have the same basic components and do the same thing. A car under your control gets you from one place to another. By performing the tasks you command, a computer gets you from one piece of information to another. In the same way that you decide where to go for a Sunday drive, you decide where to go on the computer and, before long, you'll enjoy yourself along the way. But first let's get familiar with the machine.

The Hardware of the Computer

Hardware is the machinery of the computer. Whatever your motivation is to learn how to use a computer, the basic parts of the machine and what they do will be the same for everyone. You do not need to understand how the parts of a computer work to use a computer, but it can be helpful to know what they are called. Just read through the information below and know that it is here for you to refer to if you need it later.

"I have an enormous family, and come Christmas my computer is my personal assistant. It keeps a list of who I sent cards to and who I get them from. It also keeps track of what gifts I gave to my 13(!) grandchildren and, of course, who has been naughty and who has been nice."
—*Joan*

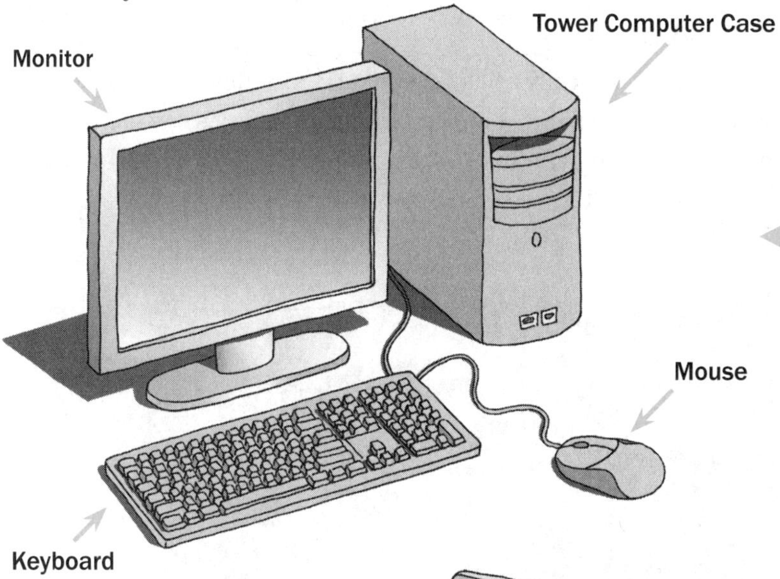

Monitor

Tower Computer Case

DESKTOP

Mouse

Keyboard

Monitor

Keyboard

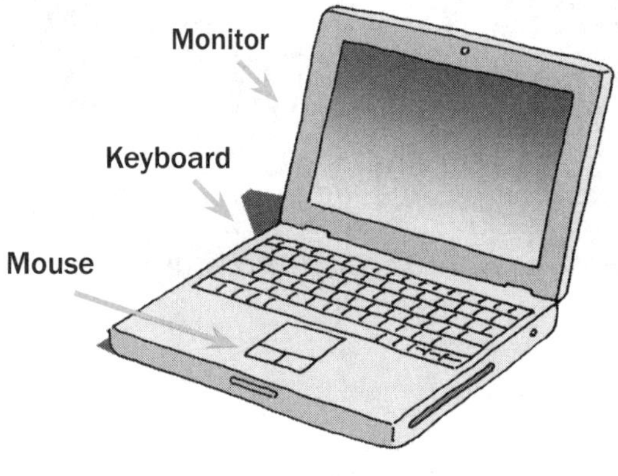

LAPTOP

Mouse

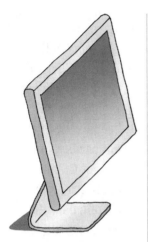

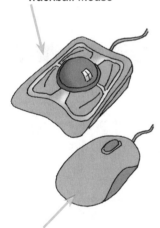

The Monitor

The monitor houses the screen of the computer. It is where any information in your computer is viewed. For example, as you type a letter using the keyboard of your computer, the words will appear on the screen of your monitor.

You can get monitors in as many different sizes as you can buy television sets, but you probably don't want a monitor that's too large. For most, a monitor somewhere between 14 and 20 inches is sufficient. The monitor size is measured in diagonal inches from a top corner to the opposite bottom corner of the screen itself. When we narrow down what is the best computer for you, we'll talk more about screen options.

■ Monitors come in a variety of styles and sizes, including this flat-screen model.

Trackball Mouse

The Mouse

A mouse is basically a hand-operated device that controls the movement of a pointer that appears on your monitor's screen. This pointer can appear in different shapes depending on what its function is at a given time. It can also be referred to as the arrow, mouse arrow, or cursor.

Mouse Arrow

Standard Mouse

■ The mouse controls the pointer that appears on the computer screen. You can choose from several types of mouse styles.

A mouse can come in a variety of shapes and sizes, but all perform in the same way. You rest your hand or finger on the mouse, and when you move your hand, a ball on the bottom of the mouse moves. Or, with more recent models, a light on the bottom of the mouse detects your movements. When you move the mouse, it sends a message through a cable to the brain of the computer, and the pointer or arrow on your screen moves accordingly. You press and release a button (or buttons) on the top of the mouse to perform an action. A slight click might be heard when you do this, so people often refer to the motion as "clicking the mouse."

Sometime in the 1970s, Xerox researchers invented computer icons. Icons are pictures on your computer screen that you click on to take an action rather than typing in a text command. Shortly afterward, a device was created that would move about on tiny wheels to control the clicking action used to activate icons. The original name for the mouse was "X-Y position indicator for a display system." What a mouthful! It didn't take long for the little gray device with the long tail (a cord connected to the computer) to be renamed a mouse. Eureka!

> "The hardest part for me was learning to use the mouse. I never thought I would figure it out. But I kept practicing and making mistakes and practicing some more. It isn't quite second nature yet, but I'm getting there."
> —*Martin*

NO CABLES, NO PROBLEM
Nowadays you can buy a mouse, keyboard, and even a printer that will work wirelessly (no cables to be seen) with your computer.

The Keyboard

The keyboard on a computer is very similar to the keyboard on a typewriter. The alphabet and number keys are set up in exactly the same pattern as on your old Smith-Corona and function in the same way. Whatever you type on the keyboard will appear on your monitor's screen.

However, the computer keyboard is not used just for typing. There are several other keys beyond the numbers and the letters, such as arrow keys that allow you to move around the screen, much as you do with the mouse. There is either an **Enter** key, on a PC, or **Return** key, on a Mac, as well as some additional keys that are called function keys.

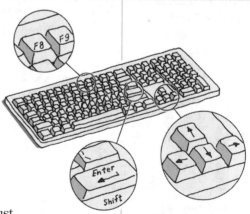

■ A computer keyboard is set up much like a standard typewriter, with additional keys that perform specific tasks.

The **Enter** and **Return** keys are significant because through them you can instruct the computer to carry out a task. These keys are similar to the addition and subtraction keys on a calculator. With a computer you can depress a keyboard key to tell the computer to move a paragraph, delete a sentence, or access a piece of information. *A word of caution:* You don't want to use the **Enter** or **Return** keys without knowing what the result will be. Enough said on that. It is hard to visualize this without having a computer in front of you. You'll see what I mean when you start working with an actual keyboard.

Even though the mouse and keyboard are physically very different, many functions can be carried out by using either of them. For example, if you want to move from the top to the bottom of a page, you can use either the keyboard or the mouse to get the job done. When you are on the Internet, most of your activity will be controlled by the mouse, but the keyboard will remain essential for typing information.

The monitor, keyboard, and mouse are the most straightforward parts of a computer. Each of them plays a major role in allowing you to view, access, and manipulate information.

One other thing worth mentioning: I don't know how to type. I use the "Columbus Method"—find the key and land on it. I am sharing this with you in case you think that you can't use a computer if you don't know how to type. Poppycock. It's how I make my living.

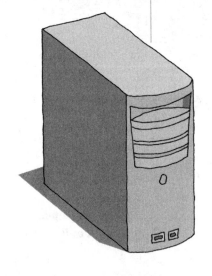

■ The computer case houses the brain of the computer. Cases come in various shapes and sizes. This vertical box is called a tower case.

The Brain of the Computer

Several components make up the brain of the computer, all of which work together to gather, identify, move, and store information.

The Computer Case

A computer case is nothing more than a plastic box, but it houses the most important and most expensive part of your computer—the central processing unit (CPU), the hard drive (C:), and the random access memory (RAM). (In a laptop, these components are inside the laptop itself.)

Sounds complicated already, doesn't it? Fear not. This combination of CPU, hard drive, and RAM is simply the brain of your machine. Some users refer to the computer case as a BUB (big ugly box)!

The Central Processing Unit (CPU) is the pathway for all of the information in your computer. The CPU is to information on the computer what the post office is to a letter. The information has to go through the CPU to get to its proper place. When you hear references to megahertz or gigahertz, people are talking about the speed of the CPU, or how quickly it moves information through your computer. The more megahertz, the faster the computer will operate. It's not unlike your car—the more horsepower it has, the faster it goes from 0 to 60.

The Hard Drive (C: Drive) is the permanent memory of your computer. The information that you type into the computer lives on the hard drive, as does the software that has been installed. (I'll explain software in the next chapter.) Even when your computer is turned off, the information remains stored in the hard drive.

Random Access Memory (RAM) is the memory used to open up programs or images only while the computer is on. The size of the RAM is important when we get on the Internet. Websites are made up of pictures, and to help those pictures appear on the screen, your computer uses the power of the RAM.

In summary, the CPU is the organizer and messenger of all information in the computer. The hard drive and RAM both store information. The hard drive is your permanent memory, and RAM is the temporary memory used only when the computer is on.

How Does It Measure Up?

Hertz

(Mega or Giga) is a measurement of speed. The CPU (central processing unit) has a speed measured in hertz—the more (i.e., faster) the better.

Bytes

(Mega or Giga) is a measurement of space. The hard drive and the RAM (random access memory) are storage spaces measured in bytes—the more the better.

Don't get bogged down if you don't quite grasp the concept of bytes or hertz. It's not necessary to understand either to use the computer.

■ A peek inside a standard computer case . . . eek!

The Brain's Memory

Information stored in a computer takes up space. This space is measured in bytes. Both the hard drive and the RAM are measured in bytes.

- A megabyte can store about as much text as *Moby Dick*.
- A gigabyte is capable of storing about 1,000 copies of *Moby Dick*.

So if you're planning to write a fat book about a whale and follow up with 999 sequels, you'll want a computer with a hard drive of at least a gigabyte! I'll explain how many bytes you'll really need for your hard drive and RAM when we're closer to shopping for your machine.

Other Parts of the Computer

Here we'll review some other essential parts of the computer. Each of the components described in this section transfers information onto the brain of the computer.

■ The A: drive is where a floppy disk is inserted. The D: drive is for a CD or DVD. These may be located differently on your computer.

Additional Drives

As I said before, the hard drive, also sometimes referred to as the C: drive, is where all information is permanently stored on your computer. The A: and D: drives (on some computers the D: drive is referred to as the E: drive) are where information can be fed or "installed" into the computer. A CD or DVD is inserted into the D: or E: drive in the same way you put a CD into a compact disc player.

This is all theoretical at the moment, but when you get near a computer, whether it's in a store, at a friend's, or at your local library, take a look at these drives. You'll see that it's really quite simple.

A: drive

D: drive

Modem

A modem is a device that connects your computer to the Internet, which in turn connects your computer to the outside world. This allows you to access websites and send e-mail. You *cannot* access the Internet or send e-mail without a modem.

A Note When You're Shopping

Most computers come with a CD and/or DVD drive. Without at least one of these drives, you would have no way to install software onto your computer. I recommend you get a computer with both a CD-RW and DVD drive.

If you've been given a hand-me-down computer, you may have a floppy disk drive. If you have a floppy disk drive, a floppy disk is inserted into the A: drive in the same way you put a cassette tape into a car stereo.

Most computers have a modem inside the computer case, along with the CPU, hard drive, and RAM.

Internet connections come in different speeds. The speed of the connection will affect how quickly or slowly transmission happens to the Internet. The slowest means of connecting to the Internet is a dial-up connection where a telephone line is plugged into the modem of your computer and the other end of the phone line is plugged into your phone jack. When you connect to the Internet, the computer will actually call the Internet using your telephone line. Most people nowadays opt to use DSL or cable connections to the Internet because they are faster and don't tie up the phone line. Your local telephone company probably offers DSL (digital subscriber line). Your cable TV provider almost certainly offers a cable connection to the Internet.

DSL or cable connections are referred to as high-speed or broadband connections. With a high-speed connection, your e-mail or an image on the Internet arrives more quickly. A high-speed connection, even if it is a bit more expensive, relieves you of the frustration of waiting and waiting for information to appear on the computer's screen as you would if it were a dial-up connection. (The World Wide Web can seem more like the World Wide Wait.) Ask family and friends, already surfing the net, which Internet service they recommend.

Without adding to your possible confusion, you should also know that you can connect to the Internet wirelessly. Almost all new laptops offer this feature. Wi-fi (wireless fidelity) is discussed in greater detail in Chapter 16. Hang tight and it will all make sense to you as you keep reading.

NO BUSY SIGNALS
A DSL or cable connection to the Internet will not cause your phone to be busy and will provide a faster connection.

How Does It All Get Connected?

L et's review the hardware on a desktop computer before we get into how it is connected. There is a monitor, mouse, and keyboard. There is also the computer case, which houses the brain of the computer, the modem, and the disk drives. The pieces of hardware must be connected to have information conveyed from one part to another.

■ The monitor, like the keyboard and mouse, is connected to the computer case by a cable.

Ports

Desktop computers have a bunch of ports at the back of the case where the cords that connect each piece of hardware are plugged in. For example, the monitor must be connected to the case before you can view the information that your computer has stored. The connection between the monitor and the computer case is made by way of a port. A cable coming from the back of the monitor is plugged into a port on the computer case. The same is true for the keyboard, mouse, and any additional equipment you may choose to have, such as a printer. On the computer case there is also a place to plug in an electrical cord to bring electricity to the computer.

■ The cables that connect the various parts of the computer are plugged into ports in the back of the computer case. Thank heaven the ports have different shapes. It makes plugging in cables a whole lot easier.

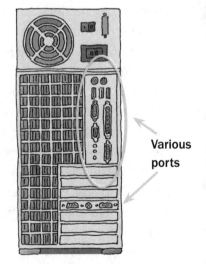

Various ports

Each piece of hardware has a different-shaped plug to match a specific port. This makes it difficult to plug things in incorrectly, which makes connecting the parts of a computer easier than you would expect. Laptop computers have fewer ports because most pieces are already connected, but what ports there are are on the side or back.

Peripherals

P eripherals are pieces of hardware that you can add to your computer above and beyond the basic pieces of hardware discussed (e.g., scanner, webcam, etc.). These can be added at any time, so there is no urgency to buy them when you make your computer purchase. But a printer is pretty essential and I think you'll regret not having one from the get-go.

Printer

The printer will print whatever you ask it to print from the computer. For example, you can print the letters or recipes you've written or an e-mail you've received. You can also print the information from the websites that you've pulled up on the Internet or a photo you're taken digitally or received in an e-mail. Perhaps you have accessed a website that sells antique weathervanes. Before you make your purchase, you might print out several that appeal to you so your spouse can have a say in the decision.

"With every e-mail from my kids that I print out for my mother, she gets closer and closer to wanting a computer of her own."
—*Evelyn*

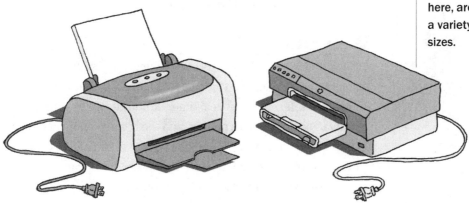

■ Printers, like the two here, are designed in a variety of styles and sizes.

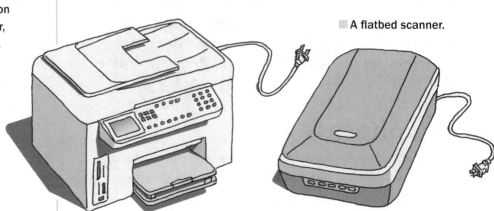

■ A combination printer, scanner, copier, and fax.

■ A flatbed scanner.

Scanner

A scanner is a bit like a photocopier. It scans an image and sends a copy of that image to your computer. Once the image is in your computer, you can make changes to it, print it, or even send it as e-mail. I have a student who is building a new house. She scanned her first pictures of the construction crew's progress into her computer. Then she wrote an e-mail to each of her children and attached the pictures to the e-mails so they could see the house. It was really exciting and not very hard to do.

A scanner can also scan documents. This same student scanned all of the letters her husband had sent her when he was stationed in Europe during World War II. The letters were beginning to fall apart and she didn't want to risk losing them forever.

■ A webcam.

Webcam

A webcam records sounds and moving images like a video camera, but it sends the video spontaneously over the Internet in what is referred to as "real time." It boils down to your ability to see and hear a person, and the reverse, in the moment that it is really happening. If you have relatives or friends who live far away and you rarely get to see one another, a webcam can bring everyone into the same room at the same time.

Let's Review

A: drive
the place to insert floppy disks

arrow keys
features of the keyboard; allow movement of the cursor around the screen

bytes
measurement of space

CD
contains software to be installed, documents, images, or music to listen to on the computer

click
depressing the mouse button to take an action

computer case
contains the CPU, hard drive, RAM, modem, and disk drives

CPU (central processing unit)
the processing part of the computer

D: drive (or E: drive)
the place to insert CDs or DVDs

DVD
contains software to be installed, documents, images, music to listen to, or a movie to watch on the computer

Enter or Return and function keys
features of the keyboard; perform actions

hard drive (or C: drive)
where information is permanently stored

hertz
measurement of speed

keyboard
used to type information into the computer

modem
communicates through a phone line to connect to the Internet

monitor
houses the screen where information is viewed

mouse
device to move the pointer on the screen

peripherals
additional pieces of hardware such as a printer or scanner attached to the computer

pointer
appears on the screen and moves according to the manipulation of the mouse; also referred to as the cursor

port
where cords that connect the different computer parts are plugged in

printer
allows you to print information from the computer

RAM (random access memory)
temporary memory used when the computer is on

scanner
copies images and text into the computer

wi-fi (wireless fidelity)
allows access to the Internet without wires or cables

webcam
sends and receives video of users through the Internet

Don't fret if you feel overwhelmed by the technical aspect of this information. How many of us can actually describe how our telephone works? Do you have any problem using a telephone? I don't think so!

Q: **Can I use my TV set instead of buying a monitor?**

A: Some new TVs allow you to use them as a computer monitor, and some computer monitors allow you to watch TV on them. But keep in mind: Where is the TV is in relationship to your using it as a computer? Can you really read an e-mail comfortably from your sofa?

Q: **Is there a keyboard designed for the visually impaired?**

A: Yes, there are keyboards designed to make viewing and use easier for the visually impaired. Contact the American Foundation for the Blind (1-800-232-5463) or the American Council of the Blind (1-800-424-8666) for advice about where to order or buy exactly what you require.

Q: **I'm not sure I can use a mouse because of my Parkinson's. Are there any other options?**

A: Yes, you do have options. Computers didn't always use a mouse to navigate. Before the mouse came along, the keyboard was used for all tasks on the computer. There are keyboard shortcuts that allow you to use a mouse-free computer. In the back of the book is a list of shortcuts and some recommended websites where you can find even more shortcuts.

CHAPTER 3

Software: Feeding the Computer Brain

An explanation of software and how it is used

For a computer to function, it must have software added to the brain. Think of it this way: Hardware is the machinery and brain of the computer. The machinery and brain are useless unless intelligence or information is added to it. Software is the information or intelligence of the brain. Without software, a computer is nothing more than an oversized chunk of plastic. It's like the telephone: The phone is the hardware; our voices are the software.

You do not need to completely understand software to be able to use a computer. My guess is that, unless you are a brain surgeon, you've been using your brain all this time without really understanding how it works in any detail. Again, the goal is to be able to use the computer, not dismantle and reassemble it!

WHY CAN'T I STICK WITH MY OLD UNDERWOOD?

If you make a mistake on a typewriter, you have to remove the error with correction tape or Wite Out, or, even worse, type it all again. With a computer you can make tons of changes on a document and view it in its entirety on the screen to make sure it's just the way you want it before you print it out. The computer will even check the spelling and grammar for you.

Operating Software vs. Application Software

There are two types of software: operating software and application software. Your computer will come with operating software already stored on the hard drive. (Remember, the hard drive is the permanent memory of the computer.) Operating software organizes and manages your computer. Think of it as the computer's filing system and library.

In Chapter 2 we became familiar with the central processing unit (CPU)—the hardware that organizes the flow of information. Well, the operating software works hand in hand with the CPU. A computer would not be able to function without operating software. It would be like having the lumber (hardware) to make a house, but no foundation and no blueprints (operating software).

Application software, with the help of the operating software, enables you to perform certain tasks (e.g., type a letter, design a website, chart your family genealogy). For example,

---

Different Kinds of Application Software

Word Processing
lets you type and edit letters, recipes, a novel

Financial Management
helps you track accounts, print checks, pay bills, figure out taxes

Organizational
helps you maintain a calendar, address book, home inventory

Communication
enables you to send e-mail, travel the Internet

Educational
offers you typing instruction, language lessons, reference materials, and much more

Graphics
lets you create pictures and design cards, invitations

Entertainment
games, music, photographs, video

word-processing application software allows you to use the computer as a typewriter with advanced editing tools. Other application software teaches you to speak Spanish, set up your taxes, or play chess. There are tens of thousands of different application software programs on the market.

How Does the Software Get into the Computer?

S oftware needs to be transferred to the brain of the computer. This is done by way of a CD or DVD (or sometimes, in the case of older computers, floppy disk). The CD or DVD drives of the computer read the information off these disks and store it in the brain. The CD or DVD drives are the bridge between software and the computer.

CDs and DVDs

Regardless of which type of application software interests you, it will now come in the form of either a CD or DVD. A CD and DVD look just like a compact disc for a stereo. However, unlike a compact disc for your stereo, which contains only sound, a CD and DVD are capable of holding sound, text, and images (even moving images), which we can access on our computer's monitor and speakers. A CD can store the equivalent of an entire set of encyclopedias, about 400 times the information on a floppy disk—its predecessor. A DVD can store up to 26 times the information on a CD. By the way, CDs and DVDs aren't just for installing software. A CD can also hold music for your listening pleasure or photographs for you to see. A DVD can do all that and let you watch movies on your computer.

CDs, DVDs, and floppy disks all store information. A CD stores 400 times as much as a floppy. A DVD stores 26 times as much as a CD.

It used to be that a CD or DVD drive was considered a luxury add-on, but this is no longer the case. Although it is still possible to buy a computer without both, I wouldn't advise it. Why? More and more software is being offered only on CD or DVD, not on a floppy disk. In some cases, the manufacturer has to be contacted

A THING OF THE PAST
The floppy disk is going the way of the wooly mammoth. Expect its extinction.

directly to get their software on floppy disks. Also because a CD stores so much more than a floppy, it may require several floppy disks to get the same job done as one CD or DVD. In short, a CD or DVD is easier, more convenient, and, now, more widely used.

Installing Software

Before you can use application software, it needs to be added to the brain of the computer. To add software to your computer, your computer transfers the information stored on a CD or DVD onto the hard drive. This process of transferring the software to the hard drive is referred to as "installing" software. Once the software has been installed, it is stored permanently on the hard drive.

To install software, you first insert either the CD or DVD into its proper drive (see the illustration to the left).

The drive for the CD or DVD works one of two ways. There may be a button you push to open the drive. What looks like a shallow cup holder in your car will slide out. You will place the CD or DVD on this tray, label side up, and push the button again to close the tray. This particular piece of the computer can be quite fragile. *You never want to force the CD or DVD tray to close. Always use the open and close button.* Or your computer may not have a button to open the drive but instead a slot where you insert the CD or DVD (label side up). After part of the disk is inserted, the computer will grab the CD or DVD. You don't need to use any force.

Open Drive

■ A CD or DVD is inserted into the D: drive. Once the disk is inserted, the computer can read its contents.

Once the disk is inserted, you will either follow the instructions that will automatically appear on the screen of your computer or the written instructions included with the software. Through this process the hard drive will transfer and store the information from the CD or DVD into the brain of the computer. You may also hear people refer to this transferring of data as "reading" the software onto the computer.

Where to Buy Software

Mail-Order Catalogs

- Often have competitive prices.
- Generally have well-informed salespeople.
- Be sure to ask if they have a money-back guarantee!

Software Stores

- Often have competitive prices.
- The good ones have informed salespeople.
- Offer face-to-face contact.
- Generally have a fair return policy, but do check it out.

Online

- You can often sample the software on your computer.
- Can be purchased and transferred from the Internet onto your hard drive.

Pirating

- Accepting unauthorized copies of software is unlawful.
- You will not get technical support from the manufacturer.

How Else Can a CD or DVD Be Used?

We've discussed putting information into the computer, but what if you want to take information out of the computer? A CD or DVD can work in two ways. Information can be transferred from the CD or DVD onto the computer. The reverse is also true; you can take information from the computer and store it on a CD or DVD.

Let's say that you want to give your publisher a copy of the autobiography you've typed on the computer. You could print out the whole book and lug it to the publisher's office. Or you could copy it (aka burn it) onto a CD, slip the disk into your pocket, and stroll over to deliver it. At that point your publisher would copy the information from the CD onto the hard drive of their computer.

On an older computer the CD is a one-way operation. Information can be transferred from a CD onto your computer, but the old ones do not let you transfer information onto the CD or DVD. Now there are writable CD and DVD drives on the market that allow information to be transferred onto them both.

Upgrading Software

As you purchase your new software, a group of diligent computer researchers (aka computer geeks) are fast at work improving that software. So within a relatively short period of time, there may be a new and improved version of what you have purchased. This is true for application and operating software. Both are constantly being improved and changed to better meet your needs. It may be that the upgrade (another term used for an upgrade is update) is just cosmetic or that the company corrected glitches people complained about. Rather than buying a whole new version of the software, you can buy an upgrade from the manufacturer. Some manufacturers offer their upgrades at a greatly reduced price; others may offer them for free.

An update or upgrade can come in the form of either a CD or DVD and is installed on the computer as you would install any application software. Alternatively, some upgrades can even be installed directly to your computer from a website. Once you install the upgrade, it will automatically make changes to the existing software on your hard drive to reflect the improvements.

You do not need to upgrade your software unless you need to or want to. When the time comes, you will know whether you are interested in the improvements that are being touted. If there is any uncertainty, ask a friend with more computer experience for his or her advice or experience with upgrading.

REGISTER YOUR GOODS

It is important that you fill out and send in the product registration information that comes with your software. This way the manufacturer can reach you to notify you of an upgrade for their product, and it may be for free!

When purchasing software, look to buy from a company that isn't going to disappear into the sunset. Buy only from a manufacturer with a good reputation and a solid track record.

Let's Review

application software

lets you perform specialized tasks, such as word processing

CD

contains software to be installed, documents, images, or music to listen to on the computer

CD-R (writable)

a blank CD you can use to copy information from your computer

CD-RW (rewritable)

a blank CD you can use over and over again to copy information from your computer

DVD

contains software to be installed, documents, images, music to listen to or a movie to watch

DVD-R (writable)

a blank DVD you can use to copy information from your computer

DVD-RW (rewritable)

a blank DVD you can use over and over again to copy information from your computer

installing process

where software is read and stored on the hard drive

operating software

the system that organizes and manages your computer

upgrade

new and improved generation of an existing software program

Q: **How expensive is most software?**

A: That's kind of like asking "how expensive is a car?" The price varies depending on what you're buying. I would say the cheapest personal software is as little as $19.99, and the highest I've run across is close to $400.

Q: **Will the store where I buy my computer or software install it on my computer?**

A: The store where you buy your computer may be willing to install the software you purchased from them onto your computer at the time of purchase. Because you're making a fairly large purchase, they should do it for free. It is certainly worth asking.

Q: **My son bought Microsoft Office for his computer. Can I borrow it and install it on mine?**

A: Using software that you have not paid for is called "pirating software" and is technically against the law. Many software manufacturers protect their product so it can be installed only once and then never again. Some programs allow for several installations. If the latter is the case with your son's software, then you can install it without a problem on your coomputer (providing your computer is compatible to that version of software—ask your son to check).

WHERE WILL IT SLEEP AND HOW OFTEN DO I NEED TO WATER IT?

CHAPTER 4

There's No Place Like Home vs. Taking Your Show on the Road

Desktop vs. laptop

Can you picture yourself sitting in your backyard watching the roses bloom while "surfing the net"? Or perhaps you're traveling on a plane with your computer tucked into your carry-on luggage. Maybe you're even snuggled up all comfy in your bed answering e-mails. On the other hand, you might be sure you'll use the computer only in the warmth of your den and have no intention of moving it. This chapter will help you decide whether a desktop or laptop best suits your needs, based on how you think you might want to use it. If at the end of this chapter you're still on the fence, don't lose hope; we'll be test-driving both options after Chapter 8. I know that when it is time to acquire your computer you'll have all the information necessary to make the perfect purchase.

■ Desktop and laptop computers do the same things. The main difference is size and portability.

How Are Desktops and Laptops Alike?

First, let's discuss the similarities. A desktop and a laptop function in exactly the same way, using the same software and allowing you to access the Internet. They both have the same basic hardware (monitor, keyboard, and mouse) and they think alike—using the CPU (central processing unit), hard drive, and RAM (random access memory). Both use the drives to read CDs and DVDS. Software is installed on both types of computers in the same manner. They also have the capability of being linked to a printer or other peripherals using ports. (If these parts of the computer are still vague, just look over the "Let's Review" section at the end of Chapters 2 and 3 to refresh your memory.)

KEEPING THE BATTERY CHARGED

A laptop computer's battery recharges when you plug the machine into an electrical outlet, not unlike your DustBuster. The computer doesn't need to be turned on to recharge (but your surge protector does). For maximum battery life, let the battery fully run down every month.

■ The average laptop is about the same size as a small stack of magazines and weighs between 4 and 7 pounds. Some swankier designs are even smaller and lighter.

How Is a Laptop Different from a Desktop?

Laptops aren't so very different from desktop computers. Laptops were given their name because they are small enough and light enough to sit comfortably on your lap when you use them. Although, actually having your laptop on your lap for an extended period of time isn't a great idea. A laptop can get hot because there isn't enough circulation around the computer. It's always best to have the computer on a tabletop. A laptop can also be referred to as a "notebook" because it's about the same size as a notebook. To be realistic, most laptop (or notebook) computers are a little too big and heavy to slip under your arm as you would a real notebook, but they continue to get smaller and lighter every year. There are no cables connecting the monitor, keyboard, and mouse on a laptop because these parts are all contained within the laptop.

The sarifice that you make for something so portable is that everything is smaller. Both the monitor and keyboard on a laptop are usually smaller than on a desktop—in fact, you may find some laptop screens difficult to view. And if your hands are large, you may feel cramped using the keyboard or mouse. But for some people it is infinitely more important that they can take the computer with them, even if it is a little less comfortable to use. Read on—there are some other things to consider.

Freedom of Movement

Laptops can be plugged into a wall outlet or they can run off a battery. On average, laptops run for a few hours on a fully charged battery. This is wonderful for people who want to use a computer while en route and don't have access to a wall outlet. Another battery bonus: If you are plugged into a wall outlet and you lose electricity, the machine won't shut down (potentially losing the document you are working on). Instead, the battery will kick in automatically and the computer will keep going and going and . . .

The Cost of Freedom

The weight of laptop computers varies. The lightest one out now is about 2 pounds, but most average about 6 pounds and may be too heavy to carry around for very long. Remember, when you transport your computer, you will also have to take along the electrical cord and a case to carry it all.

There are other possible disadvantages to taking your computer with you. You risk dropping it, losing it, or having it stolen. To be on the safe side, my laptop is covered under my renter's policy in case it disappears while I'm on the road.

Space Saving/Visual Appeal

A laptop may appeal to you even if you're not thinking of traveling with it. It will take up less space in your home than a desktop computer. There is a big difference between the look of a monitor, keyboard, and bulky computer case with all their messy cable attachments and that of a box the size of a small stack of magazines.

"Within a few months we both loved the computer so much that we decided to buy a laptop so we could take it with us when we travel and so when we're home we don't fight over whose turn it is to use the desktop computer!"
—*Marie and Larry*

▒ Unlike a desktop computer, a laptop doesn't come with an external mouse. A laptop mouse is usually either a touch pad or touch point.

Touch Pad

Touch Point

Mouse Types for a Laptop

A desktop comes with a standard external mouse. This is not true of a laptop. Laptops usually come with either a touch pad or a touch point. You won't necessarily be able to choose which one will be on your laptop.

Some manufacturers have just one type of mouse, and others offer a choice. If you're interested in purchasing a laptop, it is vital that you try out each type of mouse to see how it feels. By no means should you expect to find it easy to manipulate any of these mouse options without practice, but you may favor one over the other by its feel. Be assured that over time you will be able to use whichever mouse you choose with great dexterity.

Expense

At the moment, laptops are more expensive than desktops. Smaller parts = more technology = more $$$. Over time this may level off. There is a waiting game that some people play with computers: "If I wait long enough, will they get cheaper?" The answer is probably yes, but as long as you shop wisely, it is very possible to buy something now and not feel like a fool in a few years (or months!).

Questions to Ask Yourself

1. Do you want to be able to use your computer anywhere?

2. Do you want a large screen?

3. Do you need a standard-size keyboard?

4. Do you have a very limited amount of space at home?

5. Do you want to spend as little as possible for as much speed and power as you can get?

6. Do you have a bad back and shouldn't carry anything heavy?

Answers: 1. Laptop 2. Desktop 3. Desktop 4. Laptop 5. Desktop 6. Desktop

Having Said All This . . .

I didn't mean to hold out on you, but I wanted you to really weigh your basic options before I tell you how you can have it both ways. If you want to buy a laptop because it's portable, but you're concerned about the comfort of working on a laptop while at home, you could plug a larger monitor and a standard keyboard into your laptop through ports in the back of the machine for home use. And if you don't like the mouse on your laptop, you can even attach an external mouse.

You may now know which type of computer (laptop or desktop) is best for you. But if you don't, have no fear. Once you've seen and touched a variety of computers, you will instinctively feel what is right for you. Just keep reading and we'll get there together. For those of you who already know what kind you want to buy, stick with us—there's still more to consider.

■ It is possible to attach an external mouse, keyboard, and/ or monitor to a laptop so you can enjoy the larger features of a desktop.

Q: What if I buy a laptop and decide later I really want a desktop?

A: Well, you could decide you want to own two computers, but that may seem a little extravagant. Or you could make your laptop feel like a desktop. You can plug a full-size monitor, mouse, and keyboard into your laptop, making it seem like a desktop.

Q: Is there a better time of year to buy a computer?

A: That's a very good question. My experience is that after Christmas computer salespeople are often willing to negotiate prices.

Q: Is it wrong to buy a laptop if I'm never going to move it from my desk?

A: No, not at all. A laptop takes up less space than a desktop. If space is at a premium, buy whatever fits into your home and lifestyle.

Creating a Computer Comfort Zone

Tips on finding a comfortable and safe work area

Some people have the luxury of an entire room dedicated to their computer; others need to be more resourceful. One of my students whose space is limited converted a closet into a small home office; she opens the closet door and pulls up a chair to work on the computer. Another student utilizes an old armoire. When she's done working she just closes the doors and her "little secret" is hidden in the living room. There are many factors that affect your decision in selecting the best place to set up your computer. Setting up shop inside an extra closet may work for one person but may not be very pleasant for another.

Assuming you can use the dining room table and move all your things in time for dinner isn't realistic. Using that spare storage room may seem like a great idea, but if you leave all those musty boxes in there with you, you're probably not going to want to spend much time there either. Take a few minutes to stroll around your home. Scan the space for possible work areas. Ideally, where you put your computer will be a space where you like to be.

What You Need to Check Out

Y ou'll want to choose a spot near an electrical outlet. If your setup is not near an electrical outlet, you will end up with extension cords for the computer, as well as whatever peripherals you may buy, snaking all over the floor.

If you choose a dial-up connection, you will need to be near a phone jack for your modem. If you decide on a high-speed connection, the company that provides the service should be able to install the high-speed modem wherever you decide is the best location for your computer. If you choose to utilize wi-fi in your home, your computer won't be tethered to anything except the electrical source and can be used all over your home and maybe even in the backyard depending on the strength of the signal.

> **THE THREE LITTLE BEARS TEST**
> Set a chair where you think you might like to put your computer workstation. Sit in the chair for a bit—read a chapter of this book, check out the sports section, or browse a magazine. Does the space feel right to you? Is it too noisy? Is it too drafty? Or is it just right?

The Computer Desk

Even though a laptop is smaller than a desktop, it, too, needs a happy and safe home. One of my students confessed that she sits on the sofa with her computer on her lap while watching television. (It *is* called a laptop, isn't it?) This is fine every once in a while, but even a laptop should have a designated work area. It will make your time at the computer more efficient and enjoyable.

■ Tower computer cases are designed to stand vertically under a desk.

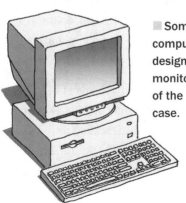

■ Some desktop computers are designed so the monitor sits on top of the computer case.

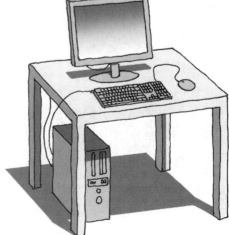

If your computer is a desktop, you'll need a table or desk large enough to hold the computer case, monitor, and keyboard. Make sure there is space so the computer case can be positioned within reach (not a big stretch) from where you will sit. You don't want to have to get out of your seat to insert a CD or DVD.

Tower computer cases, a standard design of computer case, stand vertically and can fit under a desk, thereby saving a great deal of desktop space. There are more and more computers being offered where the components in the computer case are housed within the body of the monitor or on the base that holds the monitor. Whether you choose a laptop or a desktop, you'll also need to have enough empty space on your desk to hold a book or any papers you might refer to while you're at the computer.

A standard desk is usually too high for proper computer posture. Ideally, your thighs should be at about a 90-degree angle to your calves and, with your hands resting on the keyboard, your elbows should be at a 90-degree angle as well. This can be solved in three different ways:

1. If possible, adjust the height of your chair to put your body higher than you would normally sit at the desk. Unfortunately, this may cramp your leg space.

2. Invest in a computer desk or workstation. Not only is it designed to accommodate peripherals (such as your printer), thereby giving you a single unit where all the parts of your computer can be together, but your keyboard will be at the proper height in a holder attached below the desktop. The position of the keyboard is significant because you will prevent wrist injury when you maintain a straight line from elbow to fingertips.

3. If you don't want to invest in a special computer desk, you can buy a keyboard holder that can be installed under your current desk. This will put the keyboard at a healthier height and free up more desk space.

■ Watch your posture and your distance from the screen. Your elbows, knees, and hips should be at 90-degree angles.

90°

You don't have to have your computer space set up perfectly in the beginning. I'm just letting you know that the more you use the computer, the more you'll have to be careful not to strain yourself in any way. If all you have at the moment is a card table in the corner of your living room, start there. My computer is set up on an antique tea cart in my dining room with the printer on the shelf below. I use a dining room chair with two pillows on it. Because this is not the best arrangement for my back, I make sure to get up and walk around every half hour or so.

■ A retractable keyboard shelf fits under a desk or computer table.

Some Other Things You Need to Consider

Certain health issues should not be ignored with regard to choosing where you set up your computer. "Ergonomically correct" is a phrase becoming almost as popular as "politically correct." It refers to creating a healthy work environment and positioning your body properly to accomplish the task at hand without injury.

Monitor: Your monitor should be at a 15-degree angle below your sight line. Flat-panel monitors often have an adjustable neck to allow you to find the perfect height. If you set the monitor on the computer case, that may or may not bring it to the correct height. If it doesn't, try setting the monitor on a large phone book or a dictionary instead. Be sure the monitor is stable.

Chair: The chair you sit on is extremely important. Make sure you have proper back support. If you want to make the investment, an adjustable office chair is the best choice. Used office furniture can often be found through your local classified section or online if you have a friend or family member to help you shop on the Internet.

Footrest: You also want to make sure you don't cut off circulation in the back of your legs. If you need to raise your feet, an open file drawer, a wastebasket, or a couple of books make great inexpensive footrests.

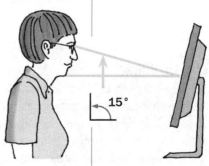

15°

■ To avoid eyestrain, it is essential to position the monitor properly.

Glasses: If you wear glasses (especially bifocals), you may want to visit your eye doctor to be sure your prescription will be accurate for the computer. I have several students who have a separate pair of glasses that they use exclusively for the computer.

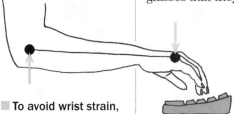

■ To avoid wrist strain, keep a straight line from your elbow to your fingertips.

Keyboard: Your keyboard should be at a height where your elbows are at a 90-degree angle and there is an unbroken line from your wrist to your fingertips. Try adding a cushion to your chair, if you need to sit higher.

Injuring yourself while sitting at a computer may seem a bit odd to you, but it's not uncommon. Bad posture, repetitive motion, and eyestrain can take a real toll. Many people lose track of time when they're in front of a computer. Before they know it, they've been staring at the screen for two solid hours without ever moving their body from its slightly slumped position.

We'll review safety issues again when you are actually using the computer.

A Few Don'ts

Besides making sure you're physically comfortable at the computer, there are a few potential problems to watch out for when setting things up.

Don't place the computer in too tight a space. A computer generates a fair amount of heat, and you want to make sure that air can circulate around it.

BUILD IN BREAKS

The National Institute of Occupational Safety and Health recommends that you take at least one 15-minute break for every hour that you are at the computer. You need to relax your eyes and move your body a bit. Something as simple as going to the kitchen to get a drink of water is enough to ease strain.

Don't place the computer by an open window. The glare from the sun may make it difficult to view the screen. Also, constant direct sunlight on the computer can make the computer too warm when in use. And all of the microscopic things that blow in the window (whether it is grit in New York City or pollen in Nebraska) can eventually damage the inner workings of the computer.

Don't let your animals get too friendly with your computer. Cats in particular are attracted to the heat emitted by the computer case and monitor. Unfortunately, animal fur can really muck up your system.

Don't put your computer equipment in a room with thick carpeting. Very thick carpeting can conduct excessive static electricity, which can be harmful to the computer. If you choose to get a tower computer case, do not set it directly on carpeting. There are trays you can buy to hold it, or simply set it on a wooden board.

Don't place any magnets near the computer or the software. Magnets have been known to damage the monitor. Crazy, but true.

Don't place any kind of liquid near the computer. Spilling fluids on the keyboard can cause serious and expensive damage. This includes cereal and milk. I had to have my computer repaired after breakfast didn't make it from the bowl to my mouth. If my computer hadn't still been under warranty, I'd have been crying over spilt milk.

It's important to set your computer up properly to avoid strain or injury.

What Else?

You've chosen your work area and decided the best way to arrange everything once you make your purchase. Be sure to measure your workspace before you go computer shopping. Bring the measurements with you and refer to them to ensure a perfect fit.

There is another thing to do to get completely prepared for bringing your new computer home. You will need to have a small amount of easy-access storage space near your work area. A shelf in a bookcase or a file box will do. You'll want to store assembly instructions, instructional manuals (although, regrettably, instructional manuals are rarely included anymore), installation CDs and DVDs, as well as other office supplies, such as paper and replacement ink cartridges for your printer.

Addressing the issues of your workspace before you go into a store ensures that your computer will have a good home. Now we can get to the business of deciding what kind of computer is right for you.

Q: **What are some tips for preventing back pain and other discomfort when using a computer?**

A: The best thing you can do is take a 15-minute break every hour. Walk around and stretch before you sit down again. Be very aware of your posture as well. Visit the back of the book for some recommended exercises to help computer users.

Q: **My cat loves to sleep on top of the CPU. Is that bad?**

A: Yes that's bad! It isn't good for your computer *and* I doubt it is healthy for your cat. Set a large bowl on top of the CPU to dissuade the cat from curling up there. Just don't put anything liquid into the bowl. That would be dangerous near the equipment.

Q: **Can I put my computer in front of my air conditioner?**

A: The real enemy of a computer is heat, not cold. Nonetheless, my concern is the air blowing onto the computer. I'd imagine unwanted particles would be more apt to get into your computer. Try to find a spot that's not directly in front of your AC.

GO FOR
A TEST-DRIVE

CHAPTER 6

Apples and Oranges

Macintosh vs. PC

Perhaps you've decided whether a desktop or a laptop computer best meets your needs. And you've scoped out your home for the perfect place to set up shop. The next big question is—should you buy a Mac or a PC?

The Apple Macintosh computer is referred to as a Mac or an Apple and has, as you have probably seen, an apple as its logo. Macs were the first computers designed for personal use that used visuals (or icons) as a way to get from one piece of information on the computer to another. They also introduced the mouse and menus (lists of options). These innovations were designed to make the Mac easy and fun to use and less confusing (aka user-friendly).

In the 1980s, IBM came out with a model called the IBM PC (IBM Personal Computer). For a while people referred to other non-Mac brands as IBM-compatible, but that didn't make for catchy advertising, so the partial name PC (Personal Computer) stuck.

"I had no idea that my daughter used a different type of computer than I did. I thought they all worked the same. When I called her in a panic and she couldn't help me, I felt lost. Luckily, my neighbor also has a PC, and he came to my rescue."
—*Dan*

Technically, a Mac is also a personal computer (PC), but it has the prestige of carrying its own brand name. For our purposes a Macintosh is a Mac or an Apple, and a PC is everything else.

Many companies followed in the footsteps of the original IBM PC and actually surpassed IBM in sales. Some of the manufacturers' names might be familiar to you: Hewlett-Packard (HP), Dell, and Toshiba, among others.

What Makes a PC and a Mac So Different?

When the Macintosh hit the market in 1984, the differences between its system and that of the PC were enormous. Mac had an incredibly easy operating system (remember, the operating system is what manages the information you have in your machine) and became known as the company that made computers user-friendly. That translates to being easy to use, less intimidating, and more fun. They accomplished this through creative graphic design and the use of visual cues to access information on the computer.

Macintosh made the decision not to share its operating system with any other manufacturers. Think of it this way: Macs speak a special language all their own. The pickle is that Macs and PCs have different operating systems. When software is designed, it needs to be designed in one version for Macs to understand and in another version for all other PCs to understand.

When Mac decided *not* to share its operating system, this left the door open for someone else to enter the market. That is exactly what Microsoft did when it came out with Windows 95 (an ancestor of Windows XP and the great, great, great grandfather of Vista). Microsoft designed a PC operating system based on a lot of Mac's original ideas. The creation of Windows 95 gave PCs an operating system as straightforward and user-friendly as the Mac's.

At this time PCs dominate the market. There are close to eight PC owners for every Mac owner. If the majority of people are buying software for a PC, naturally the priority for manufacturers is to create software for the majority. Until recently a lot of computer software came out in a PC version long before the Mac version hit the stores, and in some cases it was never designed for Macs at all. Now, however, there is software that allows a Mac to run most PC applications. It doesn't always run perfectly, but with a bit more time it should smooth out.

The Pros and Cons of Macs and PCs

Pros	Cons
Macs	**Macs**
• still considered more user-friendly	• more expensive, but prices are dropping
• great service record	• not always compatible with non-Mac software
• used most by graphic designers	• software can be delayed
PCs	**PCs**
• less expensive	• design is still catching up to the Mac
• software hits the market first	• operating system is more vulnerable to
• more brands available	viruses

From a teaching and learning point of view, this translation software will make life so much easier. That way we can all speak the same language. You'll see what I mean later when I describe how to use a computer if you have a PC, then how to use it if you have a Mac. It would be much more efficient to have only one system to explain.

The basic pieces of hardware are the same on both systems. However, the ports where you plug in the monitor, keyboard, printer, and other peripherals in the back of the computer case can be different. That means that you can't always plug a Mac keyboard into a PC computer case and vice versa without some kind of adapter unless it is a USB port. This is another reason why the division between the

PC   **MAC**

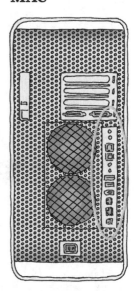

■ Some of the ports at the back of an Apple/ Mac computer (right) are different from those on a PC (left).

USB = UNIVERSAL SERIAL BUS
Universal is the key word. A USB cable will plug into both a Mac and a PC.

two is hard to bridge. You really need to commit to one or the other—they don't mix well.

The dispute between Mac users and PC users is legendary. If you haven't experienced it, just ask Mac users if they would change to a PC, and they will more than likely square their shoulders and give you a powerful "never." A PC user might even offer you a knuckle sandwich. I know it sounds ridiculous, but it's true.

▬ **USB Cable.**

Enough Already. Which Should I Buy?

One big consideration is what your friends and family have—not because you can't march to a different drummer, but because if you find yourself calling someone at 3 o'clock on a Sunday afternoon with a computer problem, if that person has a different operating system than you, his or her ability to advise you will be limited. What if your daughter wanted to give you her old monitor or share some software, but she has a Mac and you have a PC? You'd be out of luck.

That said, don't make a mountain out of a molehill. You will learn to use and love whatever computer you decide to buy. This is a win-win situation. There are more happy PC users in the world than blades of grass in your backyard, and the same is true for Mac users.

Let's Review

Mac	Apple	PC	Windows Vista or XP
brand of personal computer with a unique operating system	synonym for a Mac	personal computer; used as a name for any computer other than a Mac	the operating systems currently used on most PCs

Q: If I learn on a Mac, will I be able to use a PC at some point?

A: Sure. You can learn anything. There are some differences in how things look on the screen and how to organize documents, but I have total faith that you can make the transition. And once you're on the Internet there are very few differences between the two.

Q: How can I tell an Apple computer from a Mac computer?

A: You can't tell one from the other because they are one and the same. Apple and Mac are two names for the same brand of computer.

Q: What if I don't want to buy an Apple *or* a PC?

A: At this point in time, that would mean you wouldn't be buying a computer. I don't know of a computer store that sells any computers that are not either a Mac/Apple or a PC.

POPULARITY CONTEST

If all your friends have Macs, get a Mac. If they all have PCs, get a PC, but don't limit yourself to purchasing the same brand as all your friends. All PCs work the same way, no matter who manufactures them.

CHAPTER 7

Would You Buy a Car Without Test-Driving It?

What to look for when you get behind a keyboard

On more than one occasion I have received calls from students who want me to "choose whatever computer you think is best for me." For the same reasons that it is unwise to buy a car without a test-drive, it is unwise to buy a computer without taking a few different models for a spin. As with a car, you're looking for comfort, ease, speed, and quality at the best price possible. How can you know about comfort and ease until you actually touch the machine? Speed and quality, however, can be determined through research, which includes talking with computer-using friends and family.

What makes one person buy a Cadillac and another a VW bug? I can tell you what kind of computer I like, but my hands may be smaller, my eyesight worse, and my needs entirely different from yours. No matter how tempting it is or how much easier it seems, *don't have someone else make your computer-*

buying decisions for you. An experienced computer user can give you great advice, but you have to get your hands on the machine before you make the final decision. Your adviser is not the one who is going to sit in front of the machine and use it. You are. Would you buy a pair of shoes without trying them on?

Preparation for Your Test-Drive

H ere is a little homework that you need to do before you step into a store to test-drive computers:

Try out the computers of your friends and family. Keep in mind that people are usually very loyal to the computer they use and think it is the *only* choice. For your research assignment, the more variety, the better. If no one you know has a computer, go to your local library, community center, or even the high school. I guarantee you'll find someone around who is proud of his or her computer skills and eager to show them off.

Do research. An eager salesperson can send you reeling with too much information, so it's best to go into the store with a few computer brands in mind. The salesperson might very well show you a gem that you didn't know about, but you're always better off having done some research on your own.

Look through computer magazines to get an idea of what computers you're interested in seeing. Call the magazine publisher and see which issue has the most recent list of the top-ten computers to buy. Get a copy of that issue and narrow your choice to three or four of their top recommendations. Mark the articles so that you remember which computers you want to see. Don't try to read the entire magazine unless you're very interested. It can be confusing (and boring) and may put you off buying a computer.

You might want to call several computer mail-order stores listed in the back of this book. Feel free to ask whatever questions you have. The telephone salespeople are usually very helpful and informative. Give them a call, but do not make a purchase yet. It is

> "I think I was more scared buying my first computer than when I went in for surgery. So, I brought a friend for support. In the end it wasn't that bad."
> —*Eliza*

> "I can't remember what book I read last week. Without my notes I would never have been able to make the right computer choice."
> —*Claire*

still important that you go into a store and test-drive different machines—although you may ultimately decide to buy your computer through the mail.

Prepare notes. It's so easy to become confused or forget details. Write down the size of your available workspace, the components you know you're interested in, what information you would like explained, and the brands you want to test-drive. It is a great way to keep organized, and it may make a salesperson stand a little bit more at attention.

In addition to the marked articles, you'll want to take a note like the one below with you.

Be prepared to take notes. There is nothing worse than spending a whole day shopping for a new apartment or house, seeing a half-dozen possibilities, and then returning home and not being able to remember one from the other. You definitely don't want to have that happen. There's a form on page 56 that you can use to take down information that you've gathered on your expedition. Later you will be able to review your notes and discuss your choices with others without mixing up the details.

What I Want My Computer to Have

Must-haves:

- No less than 512MB of RAM, more than 2GB unnecessary
- Scanner (may be included with printer)
- Bare-bones word-processing software

Questions:

- Is there an extended warranty policy?
- Can someone come to my house and set it up? How much will that cost?

Workspace:

- Old teacher's desk with space underneath:
  24 inches high X 30 inches wide

The task at hand is to find out what feels and looks right to you. You are on an information-gathering mission.

If You Haven't Decided Between a Desktop or a Laptop . . .

If you still haven't decided which is best for you, go to the computer store solely to help you determine whether you should buy a desktop or a laptop. Try a couple of models of each type. While you're doing so, think again about your workspace and how you're planning to use the machine. Keep in mind that all the basic hardware components are the same on a laptop or a desktop. What you're comparing is how the size of the machine suits your needs and whether you want something portable. Once you've made a choice, leave the store. Either go have lunch and return in the afternoon or come back another day to continue your field trip. This is to be sure that you don't experience information overload. If you feel you've absorbed all you can, take a break. This is an important decision and you want to make a thoughtful choice. If you're still confused after your trip, take another look at the questions in Chapter 4 to help you decide.

It's Only a Test-Drive

Before we prepare for your excursion, I want to make sure you're clear about the purpose of this adventure. Test-driving is not the same as buying. No matter how tempting, *do not buy* your computer the same day that you test-drive. We still have more to learn. At the end of Chapter 8 you can put this book down and go shopping.

My mother has friends who have gone through a whole course of computer lessons at her senior center and still haven't bought a computer because they're intimidated by the computer store. The sad thing is that without a computer to practice on, they have forgotten all they had learned. Promise yourself that you will go to the store before finishing the entire book. This way you will make the trip, realize it

"Laptop. Desktop. I had no idea what I wanted. The moment I saw them both in the store, I knew a laptop was for me."
—*Mario*

isn't such a big deal, and continue learning more about the computer before you make your investment.

You are empowered with knowing this is nothing more than a research expedition. No obligation, no financial outlay, no decision making. If you don't want to go back, there is always the option of mail order or purchasing from the store by phone so you never have to reenter the place. And remember, if the salesperson you are dealing with really doesn't appeal to you, give him the brushoff, let him get out of sight, smile sweetly at another salesperson, and watch her come running.

Initially the computer store can sometimes add to any confusion you might have, especially after you get home and try to remember all you saw. The Test-Drive Form that follows will give you a written record to reference at your own pace in your own home. You will find an additional form in the back of the book that you can tear out to bring along with you.

Test-Drive Form

1. Store: _____

Salesperson: _____

Note the address and phone number of the store and the name of the salesperson you spoke with.

2. Brand & Model of Computer: _____

Include any numbers that follow the brand name—this will indicate the model. For example: Dell Dimension 966.

3. Cost: _____

Note the basic cost and any additional costs. For example: $499 plus $50 for RAM upgrade = $549.

SYSTEM INFORMATION

4. Computer Case: ☐ Standard ☐ Tower

Is the computer case a standard model or a tower model that will go on the floor?

5. CPU Speed: _____   Upgradable   ☐ Yes   ☐ No

Remember, the central processing unit (CPU) speed is measured in gigahertz (GHz). You will need a CPU with at least 1 GHz, but if you want to splurge, you could go as high as 2 GHz, or even higher.

6. RAM: _____   Upgradable   ☐ Yes   ☐ No

The Random Access Memory (RAM) size is measured in megabytes (MB). You will want a RAM size of at least 1 GB—but 2 GB is more fun.

7. Hard Drive: _____   Upgradable   ☐ Yes   ☐ No

The hard drive size is also measured in megabytes or gigabytes (GB). I recommend that you start with at least 40 GB. There is no need to exceed 160 GB, since that will suffice for almost anything you could think of doing on the computer.

8. Monitor Size: _____

Monitor size is measured in diagonal inches from a top corner to the opposite bottom corner of the screen itself. For most, a bigger screen is better, but you can judge what suits you best by checking out several different sizes. A flat-panel screen takes up less space on your desk and has better resolution but is more expensive.

9. CD-RW Drive: ☐ Yes   ☐ No

CD-RW stands for "Compact Disc Re-Writable." Information can be brought onto the computer using a CD. You can take information off the computer as well—it could be that you want to have a backup of all the information you have on your computer. With a CD-RW drive, you can copy, or "burn," information onto a CD from your computer.

10. DVD-RW Drive: ☐ Yes   ☐ No

DVD stands for "Digital Versatile Disc" and/or "Digital Video Disc." Whatever the name, you may want to strongly consider having a DVD drive. For most of us layfolk, we'll use a DVD drive to watch movies. If you don't already have a DVD player in your home, now is your chance to be able to watch DVDs on your computer! Another compelling reason to consider a DVD drive is that some software comes on a DVD rather than a CD, so you won't be able to install it without a DVD

"Even with all the choices in the store, there were only a couple of computers that appealed to me. My son helped me decide which of these few was the best."
—*Bert*

drive. With a DVD-RW drive, you can copy, or "burn," information onto a DVD from your computer.

---

11. Number of USB ports: _____

USB stands for "Universal Serial Bus." It is today's most commonly used type of computer port to plug in a mouse, keyboard, printer, or scanner. You want to be sure your computer has at least two USB ports. With one USB port you can purchase a USB hub, which offers additional USB ports off of the hub, but a computer with additional USB ports would be preferred.

---

12. Ethernet: ☐ Yes   ☐ No

This port is used to connect your computer to an external DSL or cable modem for a high-speed Internet connection. An Ethernet port looks like a regular phone jack, but it is slightly wider. Even if you aren't interested in a high-speed Internet connection at the moment, you'll want your computer to have the option for it down the road.

---

13. Wireless Network Card: ☐ Yes   ☐ No

A wireless network card allows your computer to connect to the Internet without needing to be plugged into anything. It works in a similar fashion to a cell phone, which doesn't need to be plugged into a phone jack. Again, even if this technology doesn't interest you now, you want to keep your future options open.

---

14. Speakers Included: ☐ Yes   ☐ No

---

15. Type of Mouse: _____   **Notes on Feel:** _____

If you are buying a desktop, it will come with a standard mouse. If you are buying a laptop, note which kind of mouse it comes with (touch pad or touch point). Jot down some notes on the feel of each. Remember, you can't be expected to master the mouse at this point, but you will have an impression of how it feels. Is the mouse positioned in a place that seems easy to access or is your hand cramped while using it? Your mouse will be your constant companion when you're on the computer, so it must be comfortable to access and control. But generally speaking, control will come with practice.

16. **Notes on Keyboard:** _____

Note the feel of the keyboard. Do the keys feel mushy? Are they too resistant? Or are they just right?

17. **How Will It Fit in Your Workspace?** _____

Take notes on how you picture your computer system in your home.

SUPPORT

18. **Warranty:** _____

The length of the warranty will be in months. What parts fall under warranty?

19. **Extended Warranty:** _____ **Cost:** _____

It's more than likely that the computer store where you make your purchase will offer you an extended warranty. This is an agreement with the store or mail-order company, not the manufacturer. The agreement is valid only if the store is still operational for the duration of the extended warranty—a good reason to make sure you are shopping at a reputable store. Because a single repair on a computer can run into the hundreds of dollars, consider a warranty.

20. **Money-Back Guarantee:** ☐ Yes ☐ No

This may be an agreement with the manufacturer that you have a certain number of days to return the machine—kind of like the lemon law. Beware: Some manufacturers will not exchange a computer even if it is defective. They may only offer to repair the machine. In that case you may want to engage your credit card company as an advocate for you. Or, before contacting the manufacturer, call the store you purchased it from and ask if it is willing to exchange the defective computer.

21. **Technical Support:** ☐ Yes ☐ No

This is crucial. You want to make sure that the store or mail-order company you purchase from has technical support. The last thing you want to have to do is pack up your computer and mail it to the manufacturer.

"I was apprehensive about our class field trip to a nearby computer store. It seemed much more than I could handle. But once I tried a couple of different computers, I knew that it was the right thing to do. I still wouldn't stroll into a computer store for fun, but it helped me make a more informed decision."
—*Vance*

It is irritating enough to have to bring it to the store for repairs. Ask specifically about telephone technical support. A lot of questions or problems can be answered by a telephone call to a technician.

You should be getting free support for the length of your warranty, whether you have a problem with your computer or you have a question about how to use the machine.

If the manufacturer, not the store, provides the technical support, ask your salesperson for the technical repair number of the manufacturers you are considering. When you are home, call the number and see how long it takes for you to speak to a technician. I've been on hold with some for over 20 minutes. This could be a deciding factor in determining which computer you purchase.

---

22. On-Site Repair: ☐ Yes ☐ No **Cost:** _____

Can someone come to your home to repair your computer? How much will it cost if it is still under warranty? What if the warranty has expired?

---

23. On-Site Installation: ☐ Yes ☐ No **Cost:** _____

Can someone come to your house to install your system?

SOFTWARE

24. Operating System: _____

   Preinstalled Software: _____

Note the operating system in your computer (Windows Vista, XP, Mac OSX, other) and any preinstalled application software.

---

25. Additional Software: _____ **Cost:** _____

Additional Software: _____ **Cost:** _____

You may want to buy word-processing software or some other software based on your interest. We talk about this choice in Chapter 8.

PRINTER

26. Brand Name & Model: _____

Include any numbers that follow the brand name—they will indicate the model.

27. Cost: _____

28. Type of printer: ☐ Ink-jet   ☐ Laser-jet

An ink-jet printer is less expensive at purchase time, but a laser printer proves cheaper over the long term because it uses toner cartridges, which last much longer than ink cartridges purchased for the ink-jet. However, that only proves true if you're doing a large volume of printing. Most individuals opt for an ink-jet printer, and most businesses purchase a laser-jet.

29. Features: ☐ Color   ☐ Black & White Only
                     ☐ FaxCopy   ☐ Scanner

You will choose features based on your specific needs. A color printer and scanner might be helpful if you decide to do something like a family newsletter or making your own greeting cards. Color is definitely fun if you're printing from a website or want to print pictures. With a color printer, you have to purchase both a black ink cartridge and a color ink cartridge. Be prepared; cartridges can be pricey.

30. Paper Loading: ☐ Top   ☐ Front

It is important to note whether the printer is front or top loading so you can arrange your workspace accordingly.

31. Wireless: ☐ Yes   ☐ No

Some newer printers don't require a cable between computer and printer.

32. Number of Pages Printed per Minute: _____

If you are anticipating a lot of printing, how quickly the printer works may be quite important to you.

33. Number of Pages Printed per Ink Cartridge: _____

This is an important issue. I have a student who was interested in having a small portable printer. She was unpleasantly surprised when her ink cartridge ran out after fewer than 50 pages were printed and a replacement cartridge cost over $20.

"I almost skipped class the day of the field trip. It made me think of going to the dentist. But it wasn't that bad at all. I've already gone back twice on my own to ask more questions."
—*Nicole*

34. Cost of Ink Cartridge Replacements: _____

35. Length of Warranty: _____

36. Extended Warranty: _____ **Cost:** _____

To repeat point 19, it's more than likely that the computer store where you make your purchase will offer you an extended warranty. This is an agreement with the store, not the manufacturer. The agreement is valid only if the store is still operational for the duration of the extended warranty—a good reason to make sure you're shopping at a reputable store.

37. Money-Back Guarantee: ☐ Full refund ☐ Store credit ☐ Other

Again, this is an agreement with the manufacturer that you have a certain number of days to return the machine. Ask the store if you get a full refund or just a store credit.

38. Toll-Free Support: ☐ Yes ☐ No

Remember, this is crucial. You want to make sure that the store you purchase from has technical support. You should be getting free support for the length of your warranty.

39. On-Site Repair: ☐ Yes ☐ No **Cost:** _____

Even with the printer, ask if someone can come to your home to repair it.

40. Did you ask if all of the peripherals are compatible?

Make sure that all the parts you are buying are friendly with each other. Have your salesperson confirm this and note his or her name in case the person is wrong.

Filling out this form may seem like a lot of work—perhaps more work than you've done buying anything else. This isn't just a way to have you make an educated purchase; it is also a way for you to learn about the machine you will be using. By the time you go through this process and get the computer home, you'll be much more knowledgeable than the average consumer. Your friends and family will be calling *you* for guidance!

Think of your first trip to the computer store as a dress rehearsal. What a relief to go in knowing that you don't have to make any big decisions or spend any money. You're just sightseeing. Bask in all the attention from the salesperson and get as much information as you can, but feel no purchase pressure. Remember: This is only a test-drive.

On Your Mark, Get Set, Go!

O kay. Let's make sure you have everything you need for your test-drive.

- You have a copy of the Test-Drive Form from the back of the book. (You may even want to bring this book with you.)
- You have a sense of where you want to set up your computer and a note with any necessary measurements.
- You have thought about whether you want a desktop or a laptop and a Mac or a PC.
- You are equipped with magazine articles in which the computers and software that interest you are marked.
- You have noted the recommendations of friends and family and any questions you may have.
- You have brought something to write with.
- You are in control. You may not completely understand what you're looking at, but that's fine. Make your salesperson prove his or her worth by helping you understand.
- You have chosen a nice place to have lunch. You deserve a lovely treat after all your hard work!

It's helpful to keep in mind that the performance pressure is on the salespeople, not you. When you get inside the store, the responsibility is on them to make you feel at home and to help you decide which computer best meets your needs. All you

SAY CHEESE!

Photo printers aren't an essential, but they're a lot of fun if you're an avid photographer or if your family and friends deluge you with their own fantastic photos (grandkids, pets, vacations).

DON'T BUY BEFORE YOU'RE READY

Carol, one of my students, bought her computer but didn't want to get started for a couple of months. She ran the risk of not being able to use the free assistance the manufacturers offered at time of purchase.

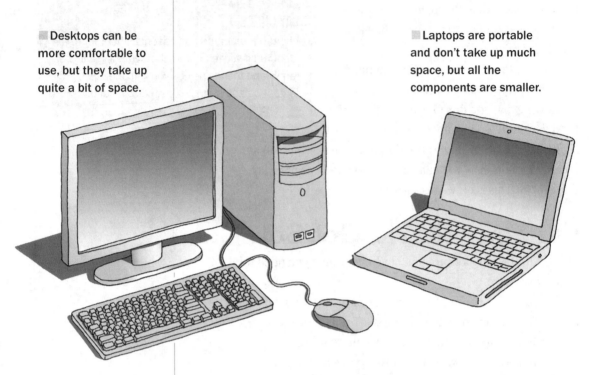

■ Desktops can be more comfortable to use, but they take up quite a bit of space.

■ Laptops are portable and don't take up much space, but all the components are smaller.

have to do is listen, take notes, and ask questions (if you have any). Certainly it isn't necessary, but it wouldn't be a bad idea to bring along a computer-literate friend who can act as a translator if the high-tech jargon gets too thick.

And one last thing: *Enjoy yourself!* Remember, you don't have to make any decisions. Just look, listen, and learn.

Q: How long will I keep my computer?

A: That is a hard question to answer. I had my first computer for nearly ten years and my second for seven. However, the average length of ownership is eighteen months! I think that number is so low because executives trade in their computers when technology makes a new leap. I never really cared about the latest and the greatest. I just wanted a computer that accomplished the tasks I required. Figure you'll be able to keep your computer for at least three years, maybe even five to seven years.

Q: What do you consider the best three laptop companies to do business with?

A: Personally, I'm very fond of Sony, Fujitsu, and Dell. But my preferences are not scientific. Keep your eyes open for computer magazines that have cover stories on the top-ten best computers, and so on. They will have tested all the laptops to make their conclusions.

Q: I really dread going into a computer store. Do you have any suggestions to make it easier?

A: Release yourself from any buying pressure. It is just an outing, nothing more. Bring someone with you for comfort and support.

CHAPTER 8

Choosing
the Best Route

What software and Internet services fit you best

With the test-drive behind you, we can now discuss your software options. However, before we talk further about software, you might want to review Chapter 3, which gives an explanation of software and how it is used.

What Software Will Come with Your Computer?

Regardless of whether you buy a desktop or a laptop, a PC or a Mac, your computer will already have the operating software stored in its brain. Even though the operating software on a PC is different than on a Mac, both offer some features that let you get started right away. However, these are bare-bones features. You will probably want to investigate adding some application software to your computer at the time of purchase or shortly thereafter. (Remember: Application software enables you to type a letter, design a website, chart your family genealogy, and much more.)

The manufacturer of your computer may have already added some application software to your computer. Just to toss some jargon your way, a salesperson might say, "Your computer already has software *loaded* on it." That means some application software has already been installed on your computer.

Each computer is different in what may be preinstalled, but usually there will be some kind of word-processing software. It may not be Microsoft Word, Microsoft Works, or Apple Works, but there should at least be some kind of Notepad program, which allows for simple formatting of a document. Sometimes financial management software (such as Quicken) and often some fun stuff (simulated golf, solitaire, etc.) will also be preinstalled on a new computer. This preinstalled application software is also referred to as "bundled software."

Buyer Beware

When a store offers to sell you a computer "bundled" with software, it may sound convenient, but it does have a downside. When you do not buy the software outright—by that I mean you actually own the installation disk—you may have trouble getting technical assistance if you need it. Each set of installation disks has a serial or registration number. With this number the manufacturer confirms that you have purchased the software and will then offer you technical assistance. This is way manufacturers protect themselves against people who have "pirated" software (not bought, but borrowed and installed).

It is tempting when someone offers to bundle software with your computer purchase. However, I strongly advise that you consider making the extra investment of buying the software to have the security of technical assistance, in case you need it.

Some software manufacturers also offer a "trial version" of their software that is preinstalled on the computer at the time of purchase. At the end of the trial period you sign up and pay for the software online and it is yours to keep on the computer. The downside to this is that when you replace your computer you will have to purchase the software all over again because you don't actually own the installation disks to install it on the new computer.

SOFTWARE INCLUDED
All computers come with preinstalled operating software. The operating software functions as the road map and filing system of your computer. A computer *must* have operating software to function.

"My son bought me software so that I could create a family tree and track our genealogy. It is marvelous. Once I'm done I'll be able to give copies to all the kids."
—*Martina*

"My reason for wanting a computer was e-mail—I had no idea there were so many other things I could do with it."
—*Sonny*

What If You Want to Buy Additional Software?

In addition to what your computer will already have installed in it, you may want to purchase some application software. Whatever application software you may be interested in, here are some things you should check out before you make a purchase.

Compatibility: You *must* make sure that the software is compatible with your computer. On the outside of the software box, it will indicate which operating system it is friendly with (Mac OSX, Windows Vista, Windows XP, etc.). Make sure your operating system is listed. The manufacturer should also post how much space, speed, and RAM it needs to operate properly. (When you buy your computer, you'll record the size of your hard drive and the speed of your CPU. Always have it handy when you go shopping for software.)

A Reminder of Different Kinds of Application Software

Word Processing
lets you type letters, recipes, a novel

Financial Management
helps you track accounts, print checks, pay bills, figure out taxes

Organizational
helps you maintain a calendar, address book, home inventory

Communication
enables you to travel the Internet, send and receive e-mail

Educational
offers you typing instruction, language lessons, reference materials, and much more

Graphics
lets you create pictures, design cards, invitations

Entertainment
offers lots of games, music, photographs, movies

Popularity: It's valuable to find out what the top-selling software is. It still may not be the right choice for you, but there is a reason why it is so popular. Ask your salesperson why a particular software dominates the market.

Pull Out Those Magazines: The same magazines that listed the top-ten computers to buy will also list the top-ten software products.

Friends and Family: Again, if your friends or family have computers, ask which software they're using and why. Have they been happy with it? Can they do a little show-and-tell for you? Keep in mind that people are very loyal to their choice of software. This sense of loyalty should not convince you; the performance of the software should.

> **THE LOWDOWN ON WORD PROCESSING**
>
> Before choosing the word-processing software that is best for you, check it out on someone else's computer. You might be able to try it out at the store, but that is not a common practice.
>
> There is a danger in buying a lesser-known software. You will get very used to how your word-processing software operates. If, over time, the company that manufactured your software goes out of business, you are stuck with that version of software. And as new technology develops, you won't be able to upgrade to a newer version.
>
> Microsoft Word is by far the most dominant word-processing program.

Salespeople: Ask them about software products and have them give you a demonstration. They really do have your best interests in mind. Also ask if they can install it for you and what that will cost. Installing software isn't difficult to do on your own, but if you buy it at the same time you buy your computer, the store may install it for you as a courtesy.

Help: Find out if the software manufacturer offers technical support. Is it free? For how long is it free? Some software manufacturers offer free support for the first 90 days after purchase. If that is the case, it's a good idea to play with the software right away to get out any bugs and take advantage of the free help.

Cost: Some software is surprisingly expensive. If it seems out of your price range, ask your salesperson if he or she can recommend something similar without all the bells and whistles. The same manufacturer that designed the expensive software may offer a pared-down version for substantially less.

Online Services Software

The modem is the hardware that allows you to connect to the Internet, but, if you're using a dial-up connection, you'll also need specific software. Many companies supply software to connect your computer, via the modem, to the outside world. These companies are called "online services," and they provide you with access to e-mail and the Internet.

Your computer manufacturer (for both Mac and PC) may have included application software for several online services preinstalled on your hard drive. Some of the more popular companies may be familiar to you—America Online, Microsoft Network (MSN), EarthLink, and CompuServe, to name a few.

If you've chosen to use DSL or cable for your high-speed connection, the company providing that connection will give you the necessary software or may even come to your home and install it for you. A high-speed connection is much faster than using dial-up, and now the price tag isn't much higher.

When the time comes, you will sign on to one of these providers by using a credit card, which will be automatically charged each month for your subscription to their service unless your phone or cable company adds the cost directly to your monthly bill. Right now the average cost of unlimited use can be as low as $15 a month or as high as $40.

America Online's
(AOL) Welcome Page.

Yahoo's
Welcome Page.

How Will I Know Which Online Service to Choose?

This decision is subjective. There is no dial-up or high-speed service that is "the best." Again, signing on to a service that your friends and family use is always smart in case you need some help.

With any of these services it's a good idea to call their technical support number and see how long you are kept on hold. Inevitably you will need to call them with a question, and if they are impossible to reach, that could be a factor in your decision-making process.

Local Online Services

My mother uses a local online service. AT&T offered her a good deal on a high-speed connection, and she's been very happy with it. Her monthly subscription charges go on her phone bill rather than on her credit card. You may want to call your local phone or cable company to see what they have to offer.

For Now, Keep it Simple

The only application software decision that you need to make soon is which online service you want to use. All other software can be purchased over time. The decision about

DON'T FORGET!

It is very important that you remember to cancel your trial subscription if you no longer want the online service. Even though the company won't bill you for the trial period, they will have asked for your credit card information to start the account. If you forget to cancel the account, they will start billing your credit card when the trial period is over and continue to do so until you cancel your subscription.

your online service isn't such a big deal because that application software will be free and you can change your mind and use a different service at any time. Even if the services suggest it, I don't recommend that you pay for six months or a year in advance in case you do change your mind.

Q: **What does DSL stand for?**

A: Digital subscriber line. DSL offers a high-speed connection to the Internet.

Q: **I get online services and e-mail services mixed up. Please clarify.**

A: An online service connects your computer to the Internet. Some online services also offer e-mail service (e.g., America Online [AOL], EarthLink). An e-mail service (e.g., Yahoo, Gmail, Hotmail) allows you to send e-mail on the Internet, but doesn't connect you to the Internet.

Q: **What if I buy my computer and it doesn't have operating software on it?**

A: Well, if it didn't have operating software on it, it wouldn't turn on. Or, if it turned on, you wouldn't be able to operate the computer. At that point you would return the computer for a replacement. Fortunately, it is extremely unlikely that this would ever happen.

LET THE
SHOPPING BEGIN

CHAPTER 9

Make Your Purchase

Old vs. new, extended warranties, store vs. mail order, and what questions to ask

N
ow that you're armed with the experience of your test-drive and have thought through your application software choices, let's address a few more options before you make your big purchase. Some decisions involve a little gambling, but with careful thought and consideration you'll never have to say, "I can't believe I took such a chance." We'll go over all the bets, sure and otherwise, and I'll tell you what the odds favor. I promise, if you do your homework, you'll love your computer choice.

Hand-me-downs

T
here are always people looking to sell their used computers to finance the purchase of the newest machine on the market. Because technology evolves so quickly, a computer can begin to look like a dinosaur in just a couple of years. However, that's really an issue only for people who

use all the features on their computer to the fullest. For most of us, that's not the case.

People sell perfectly good used machines not because anything is wrong with them but because they want something more. Perhaps they want more speed, more hard drive space, or some new feature their old machine doesn't have. Their old machine may be just right for you. That said, be cautious about whom you purchase used equipment from. You don't want to buy someone else's headache. Never buy a used computer without knowing its history.

It is probably safest to buy only from a friend or family member. If it is one of your kids who wants to buy a new computer and sell the old one, forge ahead! If your local high school is looking to replace its computers, you might get a great deal and personal technical support. Ask if one of the students can set it up for you and give you a demonstration. But if it's someone you don't know who is advertising in the newspaper, think twice. What is your recourse if it breaks down? Probably none. The odds are not in your favor if you buy a computer from a stranger.

MISSING PARTS

When you buy used equipment, be very sure that all the parts end up in your hands. A lot of cables run from one piece of equipment to another, so make a deal with the seller to set up the computer for you. This way you can make sure everything you need is there and that it all works. You must also be sure to get any manuals that came with the equipment and any installation disks for the software on the computer.

Guidelines to Buying Used Equipment

Before you opt to buy a used computer, consider the following:

1. *Is the CPU at least 1.3 GHz?* **Translation:** The CPU, as we have discussed, is what guides everything on your computer. The speed of it should be no less than 1.3 GHz (gigahertz). Anything slower will hinder your use of the Internet, and you might have problems adding software in the future.

2. *Does it have at least 512 MB of RAM?* **Translation:** The RAM is the memory used when the computer is on. To open websites on the Internet and send e-mail, you will need at least 512 MB of RAM.

3. *If it is a PC, does it have Windows XP?* **Translation:** Windows XP is an operating system to help organize your files and documents. You need to have at least Windows XP to buy any software; Windows Vista is even more current.

4. *Is the hard drive at least 40 GB?* **Translation:** The hard drive is where everything on your computer is stored. 40 GB = 40 gigabytes. That is the minimum space you should have. Any less space than that and you'll have problems adding software.

5. *Is the modem at least 56 kbps?* **Translation:** Modems run at a particular speed, measured in kilobytes (not unlike megabytes or gigabytes, discussed earlier). A modem with less than 56 kbps is too slow.

6. *Do you have Ethernet?* **Translation:** Ethernet allows you to have a high-speed connection to the Internet.

7. If you are looking at used printers, have the seller print a page from the printer for you. *Do you like the quality of the print? How long did it take to print a page? If it's a black-and-white printer, was your heart set on getting one that can print in color?* If you decide to go ahead, make sure the seller includes all the cables and software for the printer (ideally the manual too). There should be a cord that goes from the printer to the computer and one that goes from the printer to the electrical outlet. Remember your workspace—does the printer fit where you want to put it?

8. *How much does it cost?* As a general rule of thumb, any used computer that costs $300 or more is likely too much. You can buy a new desktop that fits the criteria just described starting at about $500. And a new computer will come with some type of warranty and technical support. A used computer bought for the same price without that support would be a foolish purchase. Any used printer for $30 or more is too much. You can buy a new color ink-jet printer starting at around $60.

9. *Can it be upgraded?* Ask about the maximum CPU, hard drive, and RAM capacities. If the previous owner has upgraded the computer to

> "I figured I had nothing to lose if I bought a cheap used computer. I wasn't even sure I was going to like it. I did the math and decided it was worth it, even if I replaced it a year later with something better."
> —*Harvey*

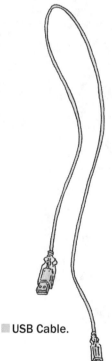

■ **USB Cable.**

"The thought of buying a used computer and having something go wrong with it made me too nervous. I chose to buy a new computer instead."
—*Charlotte*

its highest capacity—brought the CPU, hard drive, and RAM to the maximum—you might outgrow the machine, and you won't have the option to beef it up.

10. Trust your instincts. If something smells fishy with the used machine, say, "Thanks, but no thanks," and walk away. No obligation. If it smells sweet, buy it and enjoy.

Upgrading . . . Infuriating

It all sounds fine and dandy that an older computer can be upgraded, but it isn't that simple. Once someone opens up the machine to make an adjustment, you run the risk of something being damaged. The inside of a computer is very fragile, and the components there have a relationship to one another that should be left alone if at all possible. On more than one occasion I've had students whose upgrades turned into low-grade headaches. Tread carefully if someone says that the machine just needs an upgrade to meet your specifications. Upgrading the computer will also entail your taking the machine to a store for the work to be done.

Something else to keep in mind: When you upgrade a laptop, it can cost more than upgrading a desktop computer. Some manufacturers don't design their laptops to be compatible with other manufacturers' hardware. For example, if you want to increase the RAM in your laptop, you might only be able to buy your laptop manufacturer's upgrade at their price. It's the old monopoly game. This policy is less common with desktop models.

If New Is the Only Thing for You

I just gave you the minimums that you should accept for a used computer. If you're buying a new computer, use the following criteria as your minimums, but feel free to surpass them. (Once your computer purchase is made, you won't have to think about all this technical mumbo jumbo.)

➤ **Hard Drive**—40 GB to 160 GB

➤ **RAM**—512 MB to 2 GB

➤ **Modem**—Ethernet

➤ **CD-RW Drive**

➤ **DVD-RW Drive**

➤ **PC Operating System**—Windows XP

➤ **Mac Operating System**—Xv10.5

One of the great advantages when you buy a new computer is the warranty and technical service offered. Most new machines have a limited warranty of 30, 60, or 90 days offered by the manufacturer.

Are Extended Warranties Warranted?

An extended warranty will probably be from the store where you made your purchase, not the manufacturer. Double-check with your salesperson whether a warranty is from the store or from the manufacturer. Regardless of who offers the warranty, make sure you understand the terms. There is no advantage to the warranty being from either the store or the manufacturer. You just want to be sure that whoever offers the warranty is going to stay in business for the time that you have the computer.

Ask questions: How long has the store been in existence? Is it part of a chain? What is their reputation? When I bought my television, I purchased an extended warranty. In less than six months, the store I bought it from went out of business. At this point the manufacturer had the option of honoring my warranty. They chose not to. Surprise, surprise. Lucky for me, I've never had any problems with the set.

Once you've determined that the store is reputable, be sure to ask your salesperson what the extended warranty covers and what it costs. If it sounds good, I advise you to buy it. When things go wrong with a computer, it can be mighty expensive to repair. The episode I mentioned in Chapter 5, where I spilled

IF YOU NEED A TECHNICIAN
Ask friends and family if they know of a computer whiz who makes house calls. My mother was given a great recommendation through the computer class at her local senior center. She got the job done at home and paid a lot less than she would have at a technical service department.

milk on my laptop, could have set me back several hundred dollars, but thankfully, I was still under warranty. (By the way, you don't always need to let the technical support person know something like you were foolish enough to eat or drink by your computer. Your confession may affect whether your warranty is honored. In describing how the injury to your computer occurred, less is more.)

Some extended warranties are based on the price range of your total purchase. Others are based on the price of individual items. For example, one store may offer a certain priced extended warranty for purchases, say, from $1,500 to $2,000 (combining the cost of your computer and printer). Another store may require that you purchase separate warranties for each item. You will save money by purchasing a single extended warranty based on the total cost of your computer and printer or any other peripherals if the store allows that. Some salespeople may not tell you this is their store policy and will instead offer you two separate warranties. Be sure to investigate.

Also ask if the preinstalled application software (probably something like Microsoft Word and Quicken) is covered under the extended warranty. Remember when I warned you about having software bundled at the time of purchase on page 67 in Chapter 8? Some stores offer to give you support for the bundled software under their warranty. If this is the case, you can ignore the warnings I gave earlier.

THE REBATE DEBATE

Know thyself . . . A rebate is only a savings if you're really going to follow up and submit the necessary paperwork. If you know that you'll never get around to mailing the rebate in, do *not* take the rebate into cost consideration. If you are going to send in the rebate, don't throw away any of the computer or printer boxes, because usually the bar code printed directly on the box is necessary. Also, make copies of everything you send in to follow up in case you don't hear back.

The last thing you need to check out is where any repair work will be done. Can they come to your house? What is the charge for an on-site visit? An on-site visit is obviously the most convenient choice, but it may also be the most expensive. If it's too expensive, do you have to bring the machine to the location where you bought it? Does it need to be mailed somewhere else to be repaired? Mail-in repair may not suit you. It probably means that you need to keep the original boxes for packing so you can schlep it from your house to the post office—and you'll be without the machine longer because of mailing time. I think it is a huge inconvenience, but I live in Manhattan and would have to battle my way on the subway from my house to a post office lugging the monstrosity. Ugh.

Mail Order

Now that you've gone for a test-drive and have a feel for several different computers, you can think about the pros and cons of buying your machine by mail order. As with purchasing a computer in a store, buying mail order without test-driving is definitely not recommended.

Mail order is not limited to finding what you need in a catalog, picking up a phone, and placing your order. If someone you know is already on the Internet, have him or her help you visit the manufacturer's website so you can view the computers, configure your ideal machine, and order it on the spot. Delivery is usually a week to ten days.

Mail order can be a very convenient way to shop, but there is a downside. Most of the mail-order computer manufacturers do not offer on-site repair unless you buy one of their more expensive machines or pay extra for the service. If you don't want to make that kind of investment, your options are to hire someone to come to your home or to try to correct the problem yourself over the phone with a support technician. If you can't fix it with one of those options, you'll have to send the machine to the manufacturer . . . and you know what that entails. For me, that's a real turnoff.

Buyer's Remorse

Hold off on registering your computer until you're sure it's working properly. Once a computer is registered, the manufacturer may not be willing to replace it but instead will offer to repair it if there is a problem. Contact the store you bought it from. The store should be willing to exchange the computer, if you haven't registered it with the manufacturer. Ask your salesperson for the store's return policy before you seal the deal. If the computer has any bugs, you will find them out immediately. That's why it is so important to use the machine right away.

WHAT ARE FRIENDS FOR?
Shopping, of course! You may not be shopping on the Internet *yet,* but I bet you know someone who is. Invite yourself over for a computer-shopping "excursion." Don't forget flowers for your host or your credit card. (See Chapter 22 for more information about making online purchases.)

Additional Accessories

There are a few small items that you should purchase when you buy a used or new computer. All are relatively inexpensive, and it will be easier to get them at the same time you make your "big" purchase.

Surge Protector

The electrical cords for your computer and any peripherals should be plugged into a surge protector. It maintains a constant flow of power to whatever is plugged into it, thereby protecting your equipment from irregular power surges. A change in the flow of electrical power can cause damage to your computer.

Buy a surge protector that has a cord long enough to reach an outlet. If your outlet is only a two-hole outlet, you can purchase an adapter for the surge protector at any hardware store for about a dollar. The important thing to remember with a three-prong adapter is that it needs to be properly grounded. This isn't hard to do—someone at the hardware store can talk you through it.

■ If you are using a laptop and the computer is plugged into a surge protector, the surge protector needs to remain on for the battery to be able to charge.

Wrist Rest

A wrist rest allows your wrist to maintain an unbroken line from your elbow to fingertips when working on the keyboard. This keeps you from straining your wrist and can help prevent discomfort and, more specifically, carpal tunnel syndrome, a wrist injury that results from inflammation of the tendons. Carpal tunnel syndrome is common among tennis players, pianists, and computer users.

A wrist rest

Mouse Pad

A mouse pad helps you have better control of the mouse. It's a smooth pad similar in dimension to a face cloth and about a quarter-inch thick. You manipulate the mouse by sliding it on top of the mouse pad. It can be difficult to control a mouse without a pad.

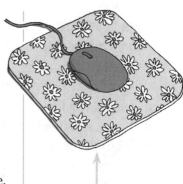

A mouse pad

Now What?

Well, it's finally time to go back to the store for your purchase, get on the phone, or have someone access a website where you can buy a computer. For this shopping trip you need many of the same things that you used for the test-drive:

- A blank piece of paper and something to write with.
- The measurements of your workspace.
- A list of what your computer must have to suit your needs.
- Your filled-in Test-Drive Form and your marked magazine articles. *(If you have already decided on the computer you want to buy, you may not need to bring these with you.)*
- A blank Test-Drive Form. *Have your salesperson fill this in with the details of your new computer. If you are ordering over the phone, you can still go over the form with your salesperson. If you are ordering over the Internet, the website should provide you with all the necessary information to fill out the form.*
- Means to pay for your purchase. *Preferably a credit card and proper photo identification.*
- If you are buying your computer at a store, bring a friend. *If for no better reason than to help you carry things to the car.*
- Butterflies in your stomach. *It's only natural when you're about to embark on a new adventure.*

RUBBER NO MORE
Used to be that mouse pads were about as fun as a flat tire and didn't look much better. Now you can get them with your favorite photo imprinted or made of paper that you can actually write on.

Get the Most Out of Your Salesperson

Never let a salesperson smooth-talk you into something you feel is excessive or that you're not comfortable with. You always have the prerogative to go home and think it over or say "no" on the spot.

> "I went back to the computer store with more questions and a friend. We gave the salesman a run for his money. . . . I don't think he expected us to know as much as we did. It all ended happily—we went home with computers and he made two big sales."
> —*Phyllis*

There is no need to be impulsive. Take all the time you need to make your decision, and ask all the questions you need answered to be well informed. The person selling you the computer needs you more than you need him or her.

Here are some suggestions on how to take control of your shopping experience and have the salesperson do the best for you.

Set the scene. Give salespeople as much information as you can. If they start to lead you around the store before you've explained exactly what you want, halt the process. Just stop in your tracks and say, "Let's first talk about what I know I want and some questions I have." In the middle of a crazy day, people can run on automatic—bring them back to a human level. I've seen salespeople relax when given a chance to deviate from their "routine speech." Look them in the eye and let them see you as an individual who needs their expert guidance.

Be honest. Let them know that you've done research. You can even show them your notes. If you're uneasy with something, tell them. Perhaps you're concerned about how to connect the cords to the ports at the back of the computer when you get home. Upon hearing this, your sympathetic salesperson might offer to send someone over to help you. Or might not. Instead, the salesperson may give you an in-store demonstration. Feel free to ask for such a demonstration. A refusal would be the worst that can happen, and it may be an indication you should take your business elsewhere.

TAKE YOUR TIME
These suggestions for getting the most out of your salesperson hold true if you're purchasing by telephone as well. Let the salesperson know you have all the time in the world to make the right decision.

Slow the process down. Computer salespeople often miss the mark because they assume we're all comfortable with computers and understand the jargon that goes along with them. I've been working with computers for over ten years and still find myself asking salespeople to slow down and explain themselves in plain English.

If, as you tell your salesperson what you need, he or she looks ready to start a 20-yard dash, state that you're not in any rush. "If you can't give me the time I need, I'd be happy to speak with someone else." I know it sounds a bit harsh, but the salesperson is probably used to people who want to come in, make their purchase, and get out. Asking the salesperson to slow down will come as a surprise, but it may be a welcome one—it gives him or her a chance to relax and not "work" so hard.

If You Still Aren't Sure

If after all your research you still haven't decided which computer you want, ask the salesperson to show you the top two computers that interest you. Then ask to see the models just higher and lower in price to give you a better feel for what's right for you. Don't deviate from your budget, but do make sure you're buying a computer that meets all your needs.

Review What You're Interested in Buying

Before you set foot into your local computer store to buy a machine, decide on the following:

- Laptop vs. desktop (Review Chapter 4)
- Mac vs. PC (Review Chapter 6)

Here are a few other things that you should have done by now:

- Checked out computers of friends and family
- Researched computer magazines for their recommendations
- Gone for a test-drive
- Reviewed your filled-in Test-Drive Form

Return Policy

What is the store's return policy? There may be a certain number of days that you can return your computer for no better reason than you've changed your mind or you don't like the color. However, if you want to take advantage of this, you'd better get the new machine up and running in that amount of time. No procrastinating on this or you will be in the soup! Be delicate with the packaging. Some stores won't accept returns if the package is damaged.

Keeping Track of Things

Be sure to ask your salesperson for a couple of business cards. If you have any questions down the road, his or her telephone number will be at your fingertips. Also ask the salesperson to fill in the blank Test-Drive Form. This will prove a helpful record of the computer and peripherals you have bought.

At this point, the success of your shopping trip is not based on luck. You have all the information that you need to make a wise computer purchase. I wasn't as well informed when I bought my first computer, and it served me well for seven years. Go to your computer store confident that you know more about computers than the average customer. When you get home with your new machine and you want to set it up, I will be waiting for you in Chapter 10.

Q: **How long should I wait to buy a new computer when I hear something new is coming?**

A: It is hard to know. I don't like to jump on the new technology right after it's been released. I want someone else to figure out the flaws and have the manufacturer update it accordingly, and then I start shopping around.

Q: **How do I find out what used computers are worth?**

A: Someone with more computer experience should test-drive the machine for you. A used computer can prove a very nice startup machine for someone, but you may outgrow it sooner than you think. There is a reason it's being sold, and my guess is that the computer is slow. Is it worth the hassles of uncertainty when you can buy a new computer for close to $500?

Q: **What criteria do you use to choose a salesperson?**

A: I want a salesperson who can explain things clearly and who I get an instinctively good feeling about. If there isn't anyone around that fits that description, it may not be the store where I want to shop.

BABY'S FIRST DAY HOME

CHAPTER 10

Counting Fingers and Toes

Taking your new computer out of the box and connecting all the parts

You are now in all likelihood the proud owner of a computer. Congratulations on the new addition to your home! Give yourself a pat on the back (or a pink cigar) from me. Not unlike the arrival of a newborn, you might be feeling a little nervous about whether you'll have what it takes to be a good computer parent. Don't give it another thought. You're a natural . . . you just don't know it yet.

From this point forward, we'll be doing hands-on work with your computer. Don't worry, I know you'll do great. You can read through the chapter if you want, but then come back to the beginning and follow the instructions step by step. Illustrated setup instructions will also be included with your new computer. (Be forewarned—these may be harder to follow than your tax return.) The instructions here will help simplify the process. Read them along with the instructions that come with your computer.

> "Some people may feel comfortable setting up their own computer, but I would rather spend the money to have someone come and do it for me."
> —*Kathy*

Set the Scene

There are three things that you must do before you even open your computer boxes.

1. Find a large (at least 8" × 12") mailing envelope or a gallon self-sealing plastic bag that can be closed securely. Label it "Computer Information." Put all your sales receipts and any other paperwork from the computer store into the envelope or bag. If your salesperson filled out the Test-Drive Form when you made your purchase, you can skip the next steps. If you don't have a filled-out computer Test-Drive Form, take a clean piece of paper and write down the following information on it:

• The date of purchase. (If you do have a Test-Drive Form, write the date of purchase at the top.)

• The store where you made your purchase, as well as the phone number and name of your salesperson (or staple the salesperson's card to the piece of paper).

• The length of the warranty and extended warranty, if you purchased one.

• Look on the outside of your computer's packing box. It will probably have a description of your computer. If it does, copy down the brand name of your computer and any numbers or letters that follow—this indicates the model. Most likely the speed of your CPU, size of your hard drive, and speed of your RAM will also appear on the outside of the box. Note these as well. Next, write down the speed of your modem. Last but not least, write down any peripherals you bought—printer, scanner, or modem (include brand and model). If this information isn't on the packing boxes, you can get the details when you set up the computer.

Put all this documentation inside your "Computer Information" packet.

2. The next thing you have to do is make space. Don't try to set up the computer in an area where there's a lot of clutter. A clean workspace not only makes for a pleasant work environment when there is plenty of space, but the computer also needs proper ventilation. Look at the workspace that you want to use for the computer, and move everything that's in your way to the other end of the room. You can move things back eventually, but it's much easier to keep track of what you're doing (and much less frustrating) if you have plenty of room to work in. If you are unsure of your workspace, go back to Chapter 5 for a quick review of some factors to consider in choosing one.

3. Finally, have a pair of scissors, box of rubber bands, wastebasket, roll of masking tape, and small box or an available section of a bookshelf at the ready.

Before you connect all the parts, feel free to ask a computer-owning friend or family member to help you. This is not a test of your ability to last four days in the forest alone. If someone in the know is willing to set up your computer, it's perfectly fine to let them do it. Maybe you've even convinced someone from the computer store—or a high school student—to help. Just be sure that you pay attention to what's done. Take notes if you want to. There may come a time when you'll move the computer, and it will be helpful to understand how it's all connected.

The Moment We've Been Waiting For

If you've bought a laptop computer, the unpacking stage is quite simple. There will only be your computer, an electrical cord, and a few incidental items to unpack. However, if you've bought a desktop, there will be several large items—a monitor, the computer case, the keyboard, and several cords to connect everything.

1. Use scissors to cut open the box. *Be gentle.* Not only is your investment inside, but if you do have buyer's remorse, you'll have to return the computer in its original package. Try not to destroy the box or the big pieces of packing materials. My sister saves all her equipment boxes. She has moved several times, and it gives her great comfort to have her computer happily secure in its original boxes— safe from the dangers of careless movers.

2. If you've bought a desktop, be aware that the computer case and the monitor can be quite heavy and unwieldy. It is a good idea to set the

> "I wanted to put it together myself. I figured it was the best way to get to know the machine. I did it very slowly."
> —*Ralph*

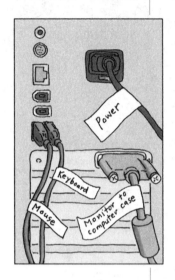

■ Labeling the cords that connect the parts of the computer proves helpful if you ever have to move the computer.

■ The main components of your desktop computer are the computer case, monitor, keyboard, and mouse.

box gently on its side and drag the piece of equipment out of the box along the floor. If you think it's too heavy for you, do *not* try to take it out of the box yourself. You don't want to hurt yourself or damage the computer. If it all seems manageable, gently remove the computer parts from their boxes and set them carefully on the floor.

3. Each packing box will also contain the proper cords. As an extra precaution, you can stop now and label each cord with masking tape. For example, mark "Monitor to outlet" on the cord that plugs into the wall and "Monitor to computer case" on the other cord. "Keyboard to computer case," and so on. That way, if you move the computer, there'll be no confusion about which cord goes to which part.

4. Until all the parts are situated, it's safest to have them where they can't be knocked over. The instructional books, warranties, installation disks, and small parts included with your computer should be placed by the parts they came with and kept together with a rubber band. It's very important that you don't misplace any of the CDs or DVDs that came with your equipment. These are the installation disks for the operating software and are used as backup if your computer breaks down. It is unusual, but there is always the chance that your computer might have a major failure and lose everything stored in its memory. If for some reason the software (either operating or application) is affected, you will use these disks to reinstall. Eventually all these things will be stored in the box that you set aside or on the available space on your bookshelf. If there is anything really tiny that might get lost, put it in your "Computer Information" envelope.

5. On each piece of equipment (whether it is a laptop or a desktop) there is a serial number (usually on the back or bottom). Take the piece of paper with all your computer information on it and jot down these serial numbers. Be clear about which serial number goes with which item. It's much easier to record these numbers now than after the computer has been set up. This is also the time to record the brand and model if it wasn't on the box.

Once all the parts of your computer are out of the box, sit down. Take a few minutes and just look at everything. Admire your purchase. Soon you'll be working with it.

Also set aside any registration cards that came with your equipment. They should be filled out and sent in after you're sure everything is in working order. The piece of paper where you recorded all the serial numbers will be your resource to complete the registration cards.

Take time to look over the written material that came with your computer, including the illustrated brochure on how to set everything up. No matter how tempting it is to forge ahead and hook everything up, don't. It is very important that you follow the instructions that the manufacturer has given, along with the steps here. Once a mistake has been made and something is hooked up improperly, it is a bear to backtrack and make a correction.

COMPATIBILITY

It is very important that whatever extras you buy for your computer are compatible with your system. If you get home and discover the salesclerk was wrong, the parts are not compatible, take them back to the store!

Examine the Ports

Before you plug anything in, get acquainted with the ports at the back of your computer. Notice that the cords and ports are designed as pairs; the number of holes in one port corresponds to the number of prongs on one of the cords. If, when you begin plugging things in, you feel any resistance, remove the cord and confirm that it matches the port.

Be aware that the prongs on the cords are very delicate. If you bend one of the prongs, gently, very gently, urge it back to its original position.

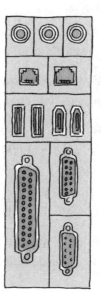

■ The ports at the back of the computer case are where the cords plug in.

Putting It All Together

If you have chosen a laptop computer, setup is very simple: Set the computer on your desk and plug the electrical cord into the back of the computer. *Do not* plug it into the wall yet.

If you have a desktop, the procedure for attaching all the parts of the computer is the same, whether you have purchased a Mac or a PC. Before you follow these directions, read the manufacturer's instructions.

HANDLE YOUR LAPTOP WITH CARE!

The screen of a laptop is very fragile, and some of them are not covered under the warranty. If by chance you damage the screen, that may be the end of the computer. Repairing a screen can cost almost as much as it would to replace the entire computer. Be careful!

1. Gently and carefully pick up the **computer case** and place it where you want it. (Remember: Don't place the computer case directly on carpeting because it may generate static electricity that can harm the unit.) Don't forget you're going to want the computer case where you can easily reach it. Position it so that the ports at the back are still within reach. You will swing it into its final position once everything is plugged in. Attach the electrical cord to the back of the computer case, but *do not* plug it into the wall outlet yet.

2. The **monitor** should be placed either on top of your desk or on top of the computer case on your desk. The monitor is very fragile. If you can't manage it, leave it where it is and ask someone to help you. Attach the cord that connects the monitor to the computer case. Then take the electrical cord for the monitor and plug it into the back of the monitor. *Do not* plug it into the outlet yet.

3. The **keyboard** should be placed on your desk or pull-out shelf and plugged into the appropriate port on the computer case.

4. Set the **mouse** to the right of the keyboard and plug it in. Usually the mouse plugs into the computer case. If it doesn't, it will plug into the keyboard or sometimes even the monitor. Refer to the setup page in the instruction book that came with your computer to be sure. If you have a mouse pad, place it under the mouse.

5. If the **modem** is not built into your machine or you are using a high-speed modem, connect the modem according to its instruction

ATTENTION, SOUTHPAWS

The mouse can also be positioned to the left of your keyboard. However, if you bought a PC, the function of the mouse buttons will be reversed. We're going to rectify that in Chapter 12. You might want to leave the mouse on the right side of the computer until then. If you bought a Mac, you can set the mouse on either side of the keyboard. I have several students who write with their left hand but manipulate the mouse with their right. Try it both ways to see which you prefer.

■ The mouse is positioned with the "tail" pointing away from you.

sheet. If you are using a dial-up connection to the Internet, the computer should have come with a phone cord for your internal modem. Plug this phone cord into the hole that looks like a phone jack on the modem. Plug the other end of the phone cord into the phone jack on your wall. If the phone cord isn't long enough to reach the jack, you may have to buy a longer one.

6. If you have bought a **printer,** a **scanner,** or any other peripheral, place it where you want it to be. Follow the manufacturer's instructions for proper installation. It is important that you plug in the cords to the computer only when instructed.

Before you plug anything into the electrical outlet, let's review what we have done so far.

• The monitor and keyboard are plugged into the back of your computer case.

• The mouse is plugged into either the computer case, monitor, or keyboard.

• The monitor and computer case also have cords that will eventually plug into an electrical source.

Sit back and view your creation. Take a break now and do something else, or if you're up to it, you can take the next big step of plugging it in, as described in the next section.

OOPS—SOMETHING'S MISSING

Are you missing a cord? Before you call the store, make sure that you've looked in all your boxes and on the floor where you unpacked everything. It is unusual for a cord not to be packed with the equipment, but it isn't impossible. Once you're sure the cord isn't hiding somewhere, inform your salesperson that you are missing a cord. It's a drag, but you will probably have to go back to the store to pick it up.

Plug It In, Plug It In

Okay, are you ready to take the final steps before turning the computer on? Here goes.

• Take the surge protector and position it near all the power cords. Do not plug it into the wall yet.

• Plug the monitor, computer case, printer, and any other peripherals into the surge protector.

• Finally—*plug the surge protector into the wall outlet!* There may be an indicator light on the surge protector to let you know that it is connected. If that light is not lit, there should be an on/off switch on the surge protector; flip the switch and the light should go on.

At this point all the parts of the computer are attached and they are plugged into a power source. In the next chapter you will turn the computer on and begin to learn what an incredible resource it really is. Congratulations!

Sit Safely

In the next chapter, we're going to begin working on the computer. For your well-being and good health, keep the following ergonomic guidelines in mind:

1. Your knees, hips, and elbows should be at 90-degree angles.

2. There should be an unbroken line from your elbows to your fingertips—no breaking at the wrists.

3. Your hand should be relaxed when using the keyboard and the mouse—no claws or strain.

4. Be very aware of your posture—it is easy to "sink into" the machine over time.

5. The monitor should be an arm's length away. This may require a special prescription if you wear glasses.

6. *Take a break!* Do not sit at the computer for more than 45 minutes without taking a break to stretch and rest your eyes.

Q: **I didn't save the original boxes, and unfortunately I want to return the computer. What can I do?**

A: Each store has a different policy, but if you are within the window of time for returning a purchase, the boxes (or lack thereof) shouldn't be a deal breaker.

Q: **My computer came with a phone cord. Why?**

A: Computer manufacturers still include phone cords in case you are going to use a dial-up connection to the Internet. If that is the case, you will need a phone cord.

Q: **Help! I can't find the cable to connect the printer to the computer.**

A: That's because neither the printer nor the computer comes with that cable. You need to buy it separately. Return to the store where you bought the printer, with receipt in hand, to be sure they sell you the correct cable. Make a point, before going to the store, of measuring how long the cable needs to be.

STEER CLEAR OF . . .

For your computer's health and well-being keep it away from:

1. Extreme heat or cold

2. Liquids of any kind

3. Dirt, dust, and animal hair

4. Magnets

5. High-pile carpeting

CHAPTER 11

Shaking Hands

Meet your computer and mouse

The time has come to turn on your new arrival. It may seem unnecessary to have part of a chapter devoted to turning on the computer, but it is a bit involved and can be a little confusing. You're about to embark on a wonderful new adventure, and I will be by your side through the whole process. However, feel free to have a friend or family member also join you during any part of this journey.

The Ground Rules

My experience with students is that most people ask too much of themselves during the learning process. If I'm teaching you how to use the computer, here are my rules for you to follow.

• Do *not* try to memorize what we do. Eventually it will become second nature. Just follow the instructions—time and repetition will take care of the rest.

• Do *not* get hung up on understanding everything. I don't understand exactly how the computer works, but I follow the formula of how to make it work.

• Trying can be trying. If you've hit your saturation point or you're frustrated, simply stop. Put down the book. Leave the computer as it is and go do something else. If you don't return to the computer for an hour or a few days, it doesn't matter. The computer isn't going anywhere. Eventually your computer is where you'll go for fun, but at the beginning it can seem more like work.

Turning It On

There is no hard-and-fast rule about which parts of the computer should be turned on in what order, but I always turn on the monitor, then any peripherals, and finally the computer case. Refer to the instructions included with your computer to confirm the precise procedure for your machine.

Instructional manuals may have been provided to you by the computer manufacturer and enclosed with your new purchase, but more likely you'll have nothing more than a diagram of how to connect the parts. Feel free to sit back and read whatever was provided to you at this time. Don't be surprised if you find the information confusing—most people do. You might want to read what you've been given in tandem with my instructions that follow.

"For three months I was afraid to turn my computer on. I would sit facing the ominous black screen and feel increasingly defeated. How times have changed —I just set up a friend's computer without a glitch!"
—*Mark*

CLICK AND GO

1. Turn on monitor.

2. Turn on printer.

3. Turn on computer case.

1. If the monitor is not on, turn it on. A monitor's "on" switch is usually, but not always, located in its lower front right corner. A light should indicate it's on, but nothing will show on the monitor until the brain of the computer in the computer case is up and running. So sit

"I knew I had time for the computer, but I was terrified of the technology. We don't even have an answering machine. But now, I've been scanning family photos to design a website. My grandchildren love it when I e-mail them pictures of when their dad was their age . . . and so skinny!"
—*Margaret*

tight and eventually something will appear. If you've bought a laptop or notebook computer there will be one "on" switch that turns on the computer as well as the monitor. If you can't find the "on" switches, refer to the instruction information that came with your machine.

2. If you bought yourself a printer, turn it on. The "on" switch can be located at the front, back, top, or side. Again, refer to the machine's literature if necessary.

3. Find the "on" switch for your computer case. The "on" switch can usually be found on the front of the computer case under the CD-ROM (D:) drives. This switch will activate the operating system, keyboard, and mouse. Press it, slide it, toggle it—whatever is the proper way to activate the switch. An indicator light, usually located on the front of the computer case, will light up when the unit is on (the keyboard may also have an indicator light, but the mouse may not). Give each computer component time to warm up—they don't always come to life immediately. Repeatedly pressing the "on" switch will only cause you and the computer to lose track of whether it's supposed to be on or off.

You may hear a sort of whirring or soft grinding sound as the hard drive in the computer case warms up. This can also be true throughout the time that you use the computer—the hard drive will periodically make a noise as it works. It's less disconcerting than it sounds and indicates that the computer is hard at work, which is a good thing.

IF IT ISN'T WORKING . . .

One of the most common problems with computers is also the easiest to fix…believe it or not. If the screen is blank or the mouse or keyboard isn't working, check to make sure they are properly plugged into the computer case and wall outlet. Sounds too easy, but it works nine times out of ten.

If the computer still doesn't come on, leave the computer as it is and find help. Remember, if you've purchased a new machine, you're entitled to call for technical service under the warranty.

Staying Turned On

If at any time you need to step away from the computer to answer the phone or run an errand, you can leave everything on without harming the machine. Some people never turn their computer off. Computers do, however, generate a certain amount of heat, and leaving them on unnecessarily is a waste of energy. If you plan to leave your machine on most of the time, make sure the area around the computer has good ventilation.

With a laptop, that means making sure there is circulation under the machine. If there are retractable legs on the bottom of the computer, use them to raise the computer. If not, use a small paperback or something similar under the back of the laptop to allow air circulation. This also angles the keyboard in a way that may be slightly more comfortable for you. Try it and see. However, I don't suggest leaving a laptop turned on indefinitely, as you might a desktop. A laptop just doesn't get the same circulation as a desktop.

Note: The screen may appear different after you let it sit for a while. It may even seem that the computer has shut off. Computer screens go into a standby, or "sleep" mode, or a screen saver may appear. (We'll talk more about screen savers in Chapter 12.) Simply move the mouse or hit any keyboard key to bring the screen back to life.

As I explained in Chapter 6, Macs and PCs have different operating systems (the mastermind that organizes everything in your computer), but all computers can do the same things—create documents, connect to the Internet, send e-mail, and so on. However, there are different computer instructions for PCs and Macs. If you've bought a Mac, turn to page 115, and I'll join you there. If you've bought a PC, stay right where you are and keep reading. We'll all meet again on page 128.

Welcome, PC Users

As your computer starts up, the background of your screen may remain dark as a series of startup messages appears. They might appear and disappear so quickly that you can't read what they say. That's okay. If by chance you can read what they say, they won't make any sense anyway. This is a process the computer goes through to make sure everything is in working order.

THE COMPUTER WILL NOT EXPLODE

With earlier computers there was a lot of talk about them crashing and dying, which simply means the computer shuts off for no apparent reason and, in the worst case scenario, can't be turned on again.

Those earlier machines were much less durable than the ones today. It just isn't that easy to hurt your computer. If you treat it gently and be sure to read what's on the screen before you take an action, you'll do no damage.

"Crashing" and "dying" are unfortunate descriptives because they cause unnecessary anxiety. Chalk it up to dramatic excess and don't lose sleep over it.

The First Step

If you're turning on a new PC for the very first time, there are some one-time-only setup procedures that you must go through.

Consult the *Getting Started* guide if one came with your PC for what to do at this point. Read it along with these simplified instructions. You will most likely be instructed to type in the "Product ID" or "Product Key" number located on your Microsoft "Certificate of Authenticity" on the cover of the Microsoft book enclosed with your computer. Don't confuse the "Product ID" with the "Product Key." These are two different numbers. This information has to be *exactly* correct, so take your time as you type it in.

The appearance of an hourglass ⌛ or a spinning circle ◯ in place of or along with the mouse's indicator arrow tells you that the computer is working on something and it is best not to use the keyboard or mouse until the hourglass goes away. For example, if you have just typed in your Product ID or Product Key number, the computer may take a moment to process that information—hence the hourglass or circle, indicating that time is needed.

Identify Yourself

If you have Windows Vista or XP, the next thing to appear on your screen may ask you to accept the license terms and then choose a time zone and confirm the date and time. The computer may ask you to choose a user or computer name. The machine will lead you through the process—follow the instructions step by step. Once you've completed a step, you move on to the next, clicking on either an arrow, the word Next, or the word Continue in the bottom right hand corner of the screen. If any of this becomes too much for you, call a friend to walk you through the steps, but I suspect you'll do just fine. For example:

Type whatever name you want to give the computer. If you want to have the first letters of the name capitalized, you need to use the **Shift** key, as you would on a typewriter. (There are two **Shift** keys—one near the bottom left of your

GET THEE TO A COMPUTER

If you haven't purchased a computer yet but want to continue reading—*beware*. Much of the book from this point forward is based on information that will appear on a computer screen. You will become *very* confused if you do not have a computer as a point of reference. Get yourself to someone's computer so you can follow along.

keyboard, next to the **Z** key, and one on the right, next to the **? /** key. It doesn't matter which one you use.) Depress **Shift** and hold it down as you type the letter that you want capitalized. If you make a mistake, use **BkSp** or the **Backspace** key. Remember to use the space bar to add a space between words.

If you are asked to enter a password, you don't have to. The password feature is really designed for computers that are part of a network or if you're going to have confidential information on your computer that you don't want anyone else to access. For the average at-home user, using a password means having to remember it and type it in every time you turn on the computer, which is unnecessary. So instead of typing anything in the box, click on **Skip**. This will instruct the computer to accept that there is not a password. If you choose to have a password, please be sure to write it down and include it in the packet where you plan to store all your computer information. No one will be able to help you recover your password if you forget it.

Wait patiently while this setup process takes place. There may be times that several minutes will go by while the computer is working. You may be asked to register your computer or to set up your Internet connection; skip both of these steps for now.

> **A GENTLE TOUCH**
>
> If you hold down a key on the keyboard, it will keep tttttttttttyping. Use a quick depress and release to hit the key you want without having it rrrrrrepeat.

Classic View

If you are used to Windows 2000 or XP but have a newer operating system and your computer offers you the option to choose "Classic View," take it. That will make the screen look similar to what you've seen in the past. If you are new to the computer entirely, leave everything as it is and you'll get accustomed to your operating system.

Welcome to Windows

As your computer starts up you may hear a sort of ping. That's the computer's way of saying "hello." Several different screens may appear briefly before the computer comes to a rest at the Desktop screen.

Oops—I Made a Mistake

If you make a mistake, you can erase your typing (from right to left) by using the **BkSp** or **Backspace** key. (It can usually be found on the upper right section of your keyboard next to the + = key.) Depress it once for each letter that you want to erase. You'll see that it moves from right to left, deleting whatever precedes it on the screen. If you hold your finger down on the key, it will continue to move and delete to the left until you lift your finger. You definitely have more control when you depress and release the key with each character than when you hold the key down. If you want to delete from left to right, use the **Delete** or **Del** key on the keyboard.

Manipulating the Mouse

Learning how to use the mouse is not unlike learning how to drive a standard-shift automobile. Do you remember how awkward it was trying to figure out when the clutch was in the right position to give the car gas or hit the brake? And do you remember how many times the car stalled before you got the clutch timing right? Well, welcome to the mouse. As you eventually conquered the clutch, you will eventually conquer the mouse. I promise.

Here we go:

• If you bought a desktop computer, gently rest your hand on the mouse with your index finger positioned over the button on the upper left side of the mouse. If you bought a laptop with a touch pad, trackball, or touch point, place your index or middle finger on the pad, ball, or point.

• *Slowly* move the mouse around on the mouse pad or your finger on the laptop mouse, and you'll notice that the arrow on the screen moves according to your manipulation of the mouse. If you have a desktop computer, lift the mouse off the mouse pad and move it around. You'll notice that when the ball or light on the bottom of the mouse doesn't have contact with a surface, there's no movement of the arrow on the screen. Place the mouse back on the mouse pad. If you find yourself without enough surface space on the mouse pad, simply lift the mouse

AN INDICATOR ARROW BY ANY OTHER NAME ...

There are many names for what appears on your screen and moves according to how you manipulate the mouse. I tend to call it the mouse arrow, the arrow, or the mouse (e.g., move the mouse arrow to the happy face). You may find it called the pointer, indicator, or cursor elsewhere. Whatever it's called, it gets the job done.

off the pad (your arrow will stay in place on the screen) and reposition it on the center of the pad.

• Do *not* press any of the buttons on the mouse yet, and be careful not to accidentally put pressure on the mouse buttons while you move it around or you may click on and activate something unintentionally. If the mouse seems out of control, use very small hand or finger movements to make it move *much* slower. Over time you can go faster, but for now we are striving for optimum control of movement.

• *Slowly* move the mouse arrow to the upper left corner of your screen. Now move it to the upper right, lower left, and lower right corners. Did the arrow ever disappear off the edge of the screen? Sometimes that happens when you get close to the edge of the screen. No harm done—gently move the mouse around a bit and the arrow will reappear on the screen. Don't ask me where it goes when this happens—it is the computer's version of hide-and-seek.

TENSION IS YOUR ENEMY

There's no reason for you to feel any tension or strain in your hand. Manipulating the mouse is a task that requires accuracy, not strength. If you feel strain, your hand is not relaxed, and it should be. You're probably concentrating too hard or your hand is in an awkward position. Periodically stop what you're doing and focus on your hand. If you feel any strain, relax your hand and try a slightly different position.

• Now *slowly* move the mouse arrow onto the little picture (which is called an icon) above the words **Recycle Bin**. The tip of the mouse arrow needs to be right on the icon, not on the edge of the icon or the words below. If you're using a desktop or an external mouse, push on the button under your index finger and release. This is clicking the mouse. There may also be a

■ Whatever type of mouse you use, try to keep your hand relaxed and tension-free. It takes very little physical effort to move the mouse.

CLICK AND GO

1. Move mouse to upper right corner.
2. Move mouse to lower left corner.
3. Move mouse to lower right corner.
4. Click on Recycle Bin icon.

button on the upper middle and right. I want you to depress only the button on the upper left. If you're using a touch pad or trackball mouse, use your thumb to depress the button to the left of the pad or ball (above or below it) and release. If you're using a touch point, use your thumb to depress the left of the two buttons at the base of your computer. There is no need for the mouse to move when you depress the button. Keep your eye on the screen and your hand steady so the arrow won't move from its position. If you're having trouble hitting your mark, take your hand off the mouse. Give your hand a rest; maybe shake it a bit. For some people manipulating the mouse is easy, and for others it takes a few tries. When you're ready, try again.

• Keep your eye on the mouse arrow on the screen and do not move the arrow when you depress the left button of the mouse. It's very common to move the mouse as you depress the button. That will unfortunately make the mouse click off-target. Keep trying—you'll get it eventually. Remember, it is like driving a car—keep your eye on the road (the screen), not the steering wheel (the mouse).

What About the Other Buttons on the Mouse?

For now I want you to depress only the upper left button of the mouse. The other buttons perform advanced actions that we aren't ready for. Be very careful not to let your fingers depress the buttons in the center or right by accident. Nothing bad will happen, but unfamiliar things will appear on your screen.

If something appears on your screen that you didn't intend to have there, either click on the ⊠ **Close Box** or, if there is no Close Box, move the mouse to a blank space on the screen and click once with the left mouse button. That should get rid of whatever happened when you hit the wrong button.

The Windows Desktop

A non-laptop computer is called a "desktop" computer. The main screen display of your computer (whether it is on a desktop or laptop) is also called the "desktop." Isn't the English language a beautiful thing?

Your screen is now displaying the Desktop. Think of it as the top of your desk in a virtual office. From this screen you can access everything that your computer has to offer, just as you can access what you need on your office desk. The Desktop is your home base.

First, find the brightness control on your monitor. It is most likely a dial or button somewhere on the bottom or side edge of the monitor. (Refer to your computer manual to locate it if you can't find it. It may be that you use the computer to adjust the monitor.) Fiddle with the control until the brightness of the screen is right for you. On a laptop the brightness control may be indicated on the keys of your keyboard. Look for a small image on a key that resembles a sun.

Your Desktop screen may not exactly match the screen in the illustration on the next page. Each manufacturer configures how the Desktop looks, so yours may have some of the same components, but they may appear slightly different.

The small pictures on your Desktop are referred to as icons. These icons offer access to different programs and parts of your computer. They are like doors but instead of knock, knocking to open the doors, you click, click, or "double-click" on them. You will get to

"In the beginning all sorts of things would appear on the screen and I couldn't figure out how they got there. As I calmed down and got more proficient with the mouse I realized I had been clicking on things without knowing it."
—*Fred*

Internet — Explorer

Recycle — Bin

Start —

Time

■ Your Desktop screen may appear slightly different from this one, but it will offer the same basic features.

know each of these icons and their capabilities in due time. But for now let's learn more about how to move about the computer.

EEK! It's a Mouse!

The mouse has a variety of functions. All of the tasks that the mouse performs are accomplished by moving the mouse to the designated area and depressing and releasing the button on the mouse.

In some ways it is more chameleon than mouse. You won't see its many mutations until later, but in the box on the right are the different faces and what they mean.

To Click or to Double-Click, That Is the Question

As I've said, to click the mouse means to depress and release one of its buttons. Clicking the mouse instructs the computer to perform a task (such as to open a document). You can click either the left button

What It Means

 This is the most common look for the mouse arrow. In this form it tells the computer where to take an action. When you move the mouse arrow, you need to be sure that the point of the arrow is on whatever you want to click on.

 When you move the mouse arrow into a text area, it changes into an I-beam. This shape can be positioned easily between letters or numbers to mark where you want to make editing changes. This shape can be referred to as the cursor.

 The hourglass or circle indicates that the computer is busy performing a task. You shouldn't use the keyboard or the mouse until the hourglass or circle changes back to an arrow.

 The combination of an hourglass and an arrow indicates that the computer is "multitasking," but you can still use the mouse. However, whatever you do may be slower than usual.

 An up-and-down arrow appears when the mouse is at the top or bottom edge of a window. This will allow you to click and drag to increase or decrease the height of the window (for more on this, see page 140).

 An arrow going right and left appears when the mouse is at the left or right edge of a window. This will allow you to click and drag to increase or decrease the width of the window.

 A two-ended arrow at an angle appears when the mouse is at the corner of a window. This will allow you to click and drag so you can change the window's height and width.

 A hand with the index finger pointing indicates that if you press the mouse button, more information will become available. It is the *finger* of the hand that must be on the item desired—just as it is the point of the arrow.

 A "don't" icon indicates that you're not allowed to take any action at this time. You're either in an area where you're prohibited from taking an action, or the computer is busy and will let you know when you can resume.

I THINK I CAN, I THINK I CAN, BUT MAYBE I CAN'T DOUBLE-CLICK

It may be that double-clicking is giving you some trouble. You have a second option. When you're required to double-click to open an icon, you can single-click (to highlight the icon) and then depress and release the **Enter** key on your keyboard.

or the right button on the mouse, but you will never click them simultaneously. For now, however, unless I instruct you otherwise, you will use only the left button.

With the left button you can either single-click or double-click. A single click is accomplished by depressing and quickly releasing the button. To double-click, you depress, release, depress, release in quick succession. (The right button will only require a single click.)

There's no clear way to explain when to single- or double-click. Generally, you double-click on an icon to open it, allowing you to access an application software program. Remember, think of it as a knock, knock to allow entry to the program. Usually when you're in a program (typing a letter or playing a game), you single-click on something to perform a task. You'll get the feel for what's best to do when. If you single-click when a double click is necessary, you'll know because you won't accomplish your desired task. If you double-click when a single click is called for, nine times out of ten nothing is affected. On occasion the double click opens another window unexpectedly, but you can press **Esc** (Escape key—upper left on the keyboard) to correct things or click on the ☒ **Close Box** or a blank area on the screen to get rid of the unwanted window.

Let's Experiment

It's time to experiment with the mouse arrow on your Desktop screen and become familiar with its movement.

1. Place your hand on the mouse (with the tail or cord of the mouse pointing away from you), and move the mouse arrow to a blank space on the Desktop screen. (Don't click on an icon yet.)

2. Click the left mouse button by depressing and releasing it with your finger.

3. Now depress and release the left button two times. Do it again as fast as you can. Continue double-clicking until you're comfortable with the action. For some people, double-clicking can be tricky.

4. Once you've had enough of that, click once on the *right* button just for fun. The little gray box that appeared on the screen has advanced options that we don't want to get into yet. To get rid of the box, move the mouse arrow anywhere on a blank area of your Desktop screen and click once with the *left* button.

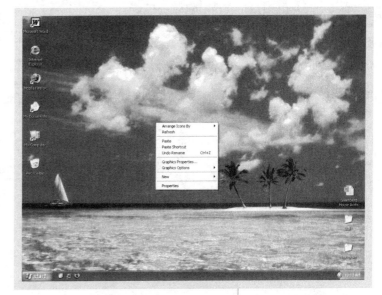

If you get lost along the way or make an error, go back to step 1 and try again. You can also "click and drag" with the mouse. I don't want you to try this yet, but when it's time, we'll move the mouse arrow onto an item and "drag" the item to a new position on the screen. We'll practice this movement when we play Solitaire. But first we need to learn how to open the Solitaire window.

▦ If you right-click by accident, a box will open. To get rid of the box, move the mouse arrow anywhere on a blank area of your Desktop screen and click once with the left button.

Place Your Bets

We're now going to open your Solitaire program, which is included in many Microsoft PC operating systems. The **Start** button (at the bottom left of your screen) **start** or ⊞ offers you access to everything on your computer, including any of your application software programs. It is also where you go to shut down the computer. Yes, you go to Start to stop the computer… don't ask me why.

Follow these steps to access Solitaire:

• Move the mouse arrow to the **Start** button or ⊞, located at the bottom left corner of your screen, and click once. *Remember, unless I instruct you otherwise, always click with the left button on your*

THE START BUTTON HAS DISAPPEARED
If the **Start** button disappears, hold down the **Ctrl** key (bottom left on the keyboard) and the **Esc** key (upper left on the keyboard) at the same time and release. The **Start** button should reappear on your screen.

CLICK AND GO

1. Click Start or ⊛.

2. Click All Programs.

3. Click Games.

4. Click Solitaire.

■ To access Solitaire, you open a series of menu boxes. What appears on your screen may be slightly different from what you see here.

mouse. What has now appeared on the screen is called the **Start Menu**. The Start Menu lists what is available on the computer.

• *Slowly* move the mouse arrow up to the words **All Programs**. You'll notice that if the mouse arrow lingers as it passes over a word, that word becomes highlighted in blue, and if there is an arrow to the right of the word, a small menu box appears. Don't let this confuse you—keep moving the arrow up to the word **Programs**. Stop when the arrow gets to the word **Programs**. (You don't need to click the mouse. The blue highlighting shows the computer where you want to take an action.) In this case, we're going to open **Programs**.

• When a menu box appears next to the word **Programs**, slowly move the mouse arrow across the word **Programs** until it's in the menu box.

• Move the arrow to the word **Games**. Don't click the mouse yet. You'll notice that if you move too far up or down you lose the desired menu box. Simply move the mouse back onto the area where you were and the box will reappear.

• When the mouse arrow is on the word **Games**, *slowly* move it across and into the menu box that contains the names of the games on your computer. Move to the word **Solitaire** and click the left button on the mouse once. At this point the Solitaire window should open.

If at any point you goof up and your mouse careens around the screen, don't worry. Just relax and try again. Move the mouse arrow to a blank spot on your desktop and click the left button once. That will make everything you opened from the **Start** button disappear. Return to step 1 on page 111 and begin again. If you opened another program by accident, move the mouse arrow to the ⊠ **Close Box** and click once to get rid of it.

If that was rough going, don't despair. This is your first time playing with the mouse and accessing a program. It's all about practice, practice, practice. Keep repeating the steps just listed until you have opened the Solitaire window.

Learning the Parts of a Window

Look at the Solitaire window. The top blue bar, or the **Title Bar,** contains the name of the program you are now in. In this case it indicates that we are in the Solitaire window. The words in gray below the Title Bar are contained in the **Menu Bar**.

At the far right corner of the Title Bar are three small boxes. You remember that the ⊠ to the far right is the **Close Box**. The box in the middle ▣ is the **Maximize Box**. And the box to the left ▣ is the **Minimize Box**.

These same features will appear on nearly every window that you open on your computer. There will be a Title Bar at the top that tells you which window you are viewing. There will be a Menu Bar, and a Close, a Maximize, and a Minimize Box. Once you learn how to use these features within the Solitaire window, you will be able to use them on any window you open.

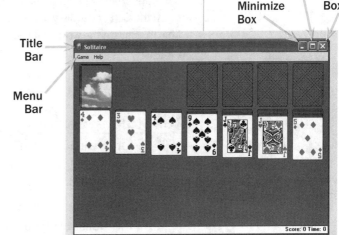

Maximize Box

Close Box

Minimize Box

Title Bar

Menu Bar

Maximize Box ▣

To maximize a window is to make the size of the window as large as possible. The advantage of this is that you will see more of what is contained in that window.

■ Most PC windows have a Title Bar, Menu Bar, Minimize Box, Maximize Box, and Close Box.

"I thought I would never be able to control the mouse. It took me a long time to feel comfortable with the clicking and the movement. I made a lot of mistakes along the way, but eventually it got easier. Sometimes I don't even think about it now— I just do it."

—Eileen

Move the mouse arrow into the ▣ **Maximize Box** and click once. It's a little tricky to position the arrow exactly inside the box. If the Solitaire window disappears, you probably clicked the ☒ Close Box by accident. No harm done. Just go back to step 1 (page 111) and follow the instructions until you've reopened the Solitaire window. That's what we were going to do soon anyway—you get a little extra practice.

If you have clicked successfully on the ▣ **Maximize Box**, the Solitaire window will now take up the whole screen. It is maximized! Now look at the ▣ **Maximize Box**. It has changed to look like this: ▣ . It has now become the **Restore Box**.

Why Are Some Letters Underlined?

Select letters within a word may be underlined on the screen (e.g., File). This underlining allows you to take the action associated with that word (i.e., opening a program or performing a task within a program) by using the keyboard rather than the mouse. You can do this by either depressing the letter on the keyboard that is underlined on the screen or by holding down the **Ctrl** key while you depress the letter on the keyboard. It varies how to activate the word, but you won't hurt anything by trying both methods.

Restore Box ▣

To restore a window is to bring it back to its original size, which is smaller than when it is maximized. This allows you to view other items on the screen at the same time that you view part of what is contained in the restored window.

Move the mouse arrow onto the ▣ **Restore Box**, and click once to restore the Solitaire window to the size it was before you maximized it. Did the Solitaire window return to the size it was when you started? If the window disappeared, you might have clicked on one of the other boxes on the Title Bar instead. To catch up to where we are, go back to step 1 (page 111) and follow the instructions to reopen the Solitaire window. If it didn't disappear, you did it right.

Minimize Box 🔳

To minimize a window is to shrink the window to its smallest form and store it in the **Task Bar** at the bottom of your screen. The advantage of this is that you can access the window quickly, but it isn't taking up space on your screen.

Let's see the Minimize Box in action. Move the mouse arrow onto the 🔳 and click once. If you click on the correct button, the box seems to disappear, but it doesn't really. You'll find a small gray box in the Task Bar at the bottom of your screen that contains the word **Solitaire**. This is the Solitaire window minimized.

`start    Solitaire                                      10:21 AM`

The advantage of minimizing a window is that you can, in one click, get the window off the screen so you can view other items, then just click on it in the Task Bar to open it again. Return the window to its original size by moving the mouse arrow onto the word **Solitaire** and clicking once. The Solitaire window is back on your screen.

Now, we're going to use the Close Box. Move the mouse arrow to the ❌ **Close Box** and click once. Good-bye, Solitaire window. Now go back to step 1 on page 111 and bring the Solitaire window back up on your screen, then meet me on page 128. It is the repetition and practice that will make you master of your computer.

▓ The Solitaire game is now minimized onto the Task Bar.

Welcome, Mac Users

As your computer starts up, you will hear a "ding," perhaps more of a "bing"—you get the idea. That's the Mac's way of saying "hello." The first thing to appear on your screen will probably be the Mac logo with a spinning circle below it.

The First Step

If you're turning on a new Mac for the very first time, there are some one-time-only setup procedures that you must go through.

As the Mac starts up, the screen looks something like this.

If an Everything Mac guide came with your Mac, consult it. Read it along with these simplified instructions. The appearance of a round spinning ball in place of the mouse's indicator arrow tells you that the computer is working on something and it is best not to use the keyboard or mouse until the spinning ball goes away.

Identify Yourself

The next thing to appear on your screen may ask you to accept the license terms, then choose the location of the computer (i.e., U.S.). The computer may ask you to choose an Apple ID. Follow the instructions step by step. Once you've completed a step, move to the next by clicking on an arrow, the word **Next**, or the word **Continue** found on the bottom right of the screen. If any of this becomes too much for you, call a friend over to walk you through the steps, but I suspect you'll do just fine. For example:

Type whatever ID you want to have on the computer. (You can name it after yourself or your cat—anything you want.) If you want to have the first letters of the name capitalized, you need to use the **Shift** key, as you would on a typewriter. (There are two **Shift** keys—one near the bottom left of your keyboard, next to the **Z** key, and one on the right, next to the **?/** key. It doesn't matter which one you use.) Depress **Shift** and hold it down as you type the letter that you want capitalized. If you make a mistake, use the **Delete** key.

If you are asked to enter a password, you don't have to. The password feature is really designed for computers that are part of a network or if you're going to have confidential information on your computer that you don't want anyone else to access.

GET THEE TO A COMPUTER

If you haven't purchased a computer yet but want to continue reading—beware. Much of the book from this point forward is based on information that will appear on a computer screen. You will become very confused if you do not have a computer as a point of reference. Get yourself to someone's computer so you can follow along.

For the average at-home user, having a password means having to remember it and type it in every time you turn on the computer, which is unnecessary. You can instruct the computer to accept that there is not a password. If you choose to have a password, please be sure to write it down and include it in the packet where you will be storing all your computer information. No one will be able to help you rediscover your password if you forget it.

Wait patiently while this setup process takes place. There may be times that several minutes will go by while the computer is working. You may be asked to register your computer or to set up your Internet connection. Skip both of those steps for now.

The Mac Desktop

A non-laptop computer is called a "desktop" computer. The main screen display of your computer is also called the "desktop" (whether it is on a desktop or laptop). Isn't the English language a beautiful thing?

Your screen is now displaying the desktop. Think of it as the top of your desk in a virtual office. From this screen you can access everything that your computer has to offer, just as you can access what you need on your office desk. The desktop is your home base.

While you are here, find the brightness control on your monitor. It is most likely a dial somewhere on the bottom or side edge of the monitor. (Refer to your computer manual to locate it if you can't find it.) Fiddle around with the control until the brightness of the screen is right for you. There is no standard about what is the appropriate brightness—it's what you find comfortable. On a laptop the brightness control may be located on the keys of your keyboard. Look for a small image on a key (usually found above the row of number keys) that resembles a sun.

What you see in this illustration may not exactly match your screen. The small icons offer access to different programs and parts of your computer. They are like doors but instead of knock, knocking to open the doors, you click, click, or "double-click" on them. You will

> **A GENTLE TOUCH**
>
> If you hold down a key on the keyboard, it will keep tttttttttttyping. Use a quick depress and release to hit the key you want without having it rrrrrrepeat.

Time

Apple

Safari

Trash

Finder File Edit View Go Window Help

Macintosh HD

Documents

Mon 1:21 PM

Your Desktop may appear slightly different from this one, but it will offer the same basic features.

get to know each of these icons and their capabilities in due time. But for now let's learn more about how to move about the computer.

Oops—I Made a Mistake

If you make a mistake, you can erase your typing (from right to left) by using the **Delete** key. (It can usually be found on the upper right section of your keyboard next to the **+ =** key.) Depress it once for each letter that you want to erase. You'll see that it moves from right to left, deleting whatever precedes it on the screen. If you hold your finger down on the key, it will continue to move and delete to the left until you lift your finger. You definitely have more control when you depress and release the key with each character than when you hold the key down.

Manipulating the Mouse

Learning how to use the mouse is not unlike learning how to drive a standard-shift automobile. Do you remember how awkward it was trying to figure out when the clutch was in the right position to give the car gas or hit the brake? And do you remember how many times the car stalled before you got the clutch timing right? Well, welcome to the mouse. As you eventually conquered the clutch, you will eventually conquer the mouse. I promise. Let's try.

• If you bought a desktop computer, gently rest your hand on the mouse with your index finger positioned on the upper portion of the mouse. If you bought a laptop with a touch pad, place your index or middle finger on the pad.

• *Slowly* move the mouse or your finger around, and you'll notice that the arrow on the screen moves according to your manipulation of the mouse. If you have a desktop computer, lift the mouse off the mouse pad and move it around. You'll notice that when the bottom of the mouse doesn't have contact with a surface, there's no movement of the arrow on the screen. Place the mouse back on the mouse pad. If you find you don't have enough surface space on the mouse pad, simply lift the mouse off the pad (your arrow will stay in place on the screen) and reposition the mouse on the center of the pad.

• Do **not** press down on the mouse yet, and be careful not to put pressure accidentally on the mouse while you move it around. If the mouse seems out of control, use very small hand or finger movements to make it move *much* slower. Over time you can go faster, but for now we are striving for optimum control of movement.

TENSION IS YOUR ENEMY

There's no reason for you to feel any tension or strain in your hand. Manipulating the mouse is a task that requires accuracy, not strength. If you feel strain, your hand is not relaxed, and it should be. You're probably concentrating too hard or your hand is in an awkward position. Periodically stop what you're doing and focus on your hand. If you feel any strain, relax your hand and try a slightly different position.

■ Whatever type of mouse you use, try to keep your hand relaxed and tension-free. It takes very little physical effort to move the mouse.

CLICK AND GO

1. **Move mouse to upper right corner.**

2. **Move mouse to lower left corner.**

3. **Move mouse to lower right corner.**

4. **Click on File.**

5. **Click on New Folder.**

• Slowly move the mouse arrow to the upper left corner of your screen. Now move it to the upper right, lower left, and lower right corners. Did the arrow ever disappear off the edge of the screen? Sometimes that happens when you get close to the edge of the screen. No harm done—gently move the mouse around a bit and the arrow will reappear on the screen. Don't ask me where it goes when this happens—it's the computer's version of hide-and-seek.

• Now slowly move the mouse arrow to the word **File** at the top left of your screen. *If you're using a desktop computer or an external mouse,* depress and release the button under your index finger. *If you're using a touch pad,* use your thumb to depress the button below the pad and release. There is no need for the mouse to move when you depress the button. *Keep your eye on the screen and your hand steady.*

• Now move the mouse arrow onto the words **New Folder**, and then release the button. Keep your hand very steady so the arrow won't move from its position. If you're having trouble hitting your mark, take your hand off the mouse. Give your hand a rest; maybe

shake it a bit. For some people this is easy, and for others it takes a few tries. When you're ready, try again.

• When you release the mouse button, a new icon looking like a file folder with the words **Untitled Folder** enclosed in a box below should appear on the screen. We need to open this folder to produce a window. Move the mouse arrow onto the folder itself (not the words below) and depress the mouse button and release. The folder should now be highlighted.

• Move the mouse arrow back up to the word **File** (at the top left of the screen). Depress and release the mouse button. Now move the mouse arrow down to the word **Open** and depress and the mouse button. You have just opened a window on your computer screen!

• Now we're going to close the window. Find the ⊗ red circle box in the upper left corner of the window. This is

CLICK AND GO

6. Click on Untitled Folder.

7. Click on File.

8. Click on Open.

9. Click on Close.

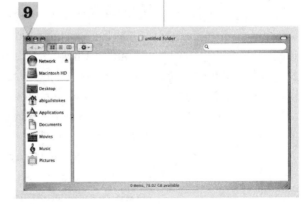

AN INDICATOR ARROW BY ANY OTHER NAME . . .

There are many names for what appears on your screen and moves according to how you manipulate the mouse. I tend to call it the mouse arrow, the arrow, or the mouse (e.g., move the mouse arrow to the happy face). You may find it called the pointer, indicator, or cursor elsewhere. Whatever it's called, it gets the job done.

"I thought I would never be able to control the mouse. It took me a long time to feel comfortable with the clicking and the movement. I made a lot of mistakes along the way, but eventually it got easier. Sometimes I don't even think about it now—I just do it."
—*Eileen*

the **Close Box.** Move the mouse arrow *inside* the ⊗ **Close Box**. An X appears in the circle. It is important that the tip of the arrow is inside the Close Box, not on the edge of the box. Keep your hand steady so the mouse won't move from its position. Depress and release your mouse button. The **Untitled Folder** window has now disappeared. Well done.

If the box hasn't disappeared, there is nothing wrong with you or the computer; you simply didn't click the mouse correctly inside the ⊗ Close Box. Keep your eye on the mouse arrow on the screen and do not move the arrow when you depress the left button of the mouse. It's very common to move the mouse as you depress the button. That will unfortunately make the mouse click off-target. Keep trying—you'll get it eventually. Remember it is like driving a car—keep your eye on the road (the screen), not the steering wheel (the mouse).

EEK! It's a Mouse!

The mouse has a variety of functions. All of the tasks that the mouse performs are accomplished by moving the mouse to the designated area and depressing the button.

In some ways it is more chameleon than mouse. You won't see its many mutations until later, but the chart on the next page shows the different faces and what they mean.

To Click or to Double-Click, That Is the Question

As I've said before, to click the mouse means to depress and release the button. Clicking the mouse instructs the computer to perform a task (such as open a document). This can take a single or a double click. A single click is accomplished by depressing and then quickly releasing the button. To double-click, you depress, release, depress, release in quick succession.

There is no clear way to explain when to single- or double-click. Generally, you double-click on an icon to open it, allowing you to access an application software program. Remember, think of it as a

What It Means

▲	This is the most common look for the mouse arrow. In this form it tells the computer where to take an action. When you move the mouse arrow, you need to be sure that the point of the arrow is on whatever you want to click on.
I	When you move the mouse arrow into a text area, it changes into an I-beam. This shape can be positioned easily between letters or numbers to mark where you want to make editing changes. This shape can be referred to as the cursor.
⊛	This round spinning ball indicates that the computer is busy performing a task. You shouldn't use the keyboard or the mouse until the clock changes back to an arrow.
👆	A hand with the index finger pointing indicates that if you press the mouse button, more information will become available. This configuration is seen often when you're on the Internet. It is the finger of the hand that must be on the item desired—just as it is with the point of the arrow.

knock, knock to allow entry to the program. Usually when you're in a program (typing a letter or playing a game), you single-click on something to perform a task. You'll get the feel for what's best to do when. If you single-click when a double-click is necessary, you'll know because you won't accomplish your desired task. If you double-click when a single click is called for, nine times out of ten nothing is affected. On occasion the double click opens another window unexpectedly, but you can press **Esc** (Escape key—upper left on the keyboard) to correct things or click on the ⊗ **Close Box** or a blank area on the screen to get rid of the unwanted window.

Let's Experiment

It's time to experiment with the mouse arrow on your desktop screen to become familiar with its movement.

I THINK I CAN, I THINK I CAN, BUT MAYBE I CAN'T DOUBLE-CLICK

It may be that double-clicking is giving you some trouble. You have a second option. When you're required to double-click to open an icon, you can single-click (to highlight the icon) and then depress and release the **Return** key on your keyboard.

1. Place your hand on the mouse (with the tail or cord of the mouse pointing away from you) and move the mouse arrow to a blank space on the desktop screen. (Don't click on an icon yet.)

2. Click the mouse button by depressing and releasing it with your finger.

3. Now depress and release the mouse button two times. Try it again and do it as fast as you can. Continue double-clicking until you're comfortable with the action. For some people, double-clicking can be kind of tricky.

Learning the Parts of a Window

Reopen the Untitled Folder that you created on page 121 by moving the mouse onto the folder (not the words below) and double-clicking. If you are having trouble with the double click, you can single-click on the folder to highlight it, then click on the word File at the top left and single-click on the word Open. Your Untitled Folder window should now be open.

Look at the window. The words at the top of the screen are contained in the Title Bar. In the far left corner of the **Title Bar** is the ⊗ Close Box. In the left corner of the Title Bar are two more circles. The green circle on the right is the ⊕ **Zoom Box,** and the yellow circle in the middle is the ⊖ **Collapse Box**. There is also the ⁄ **Size Box** (sometimes called the **Grow Box**) in the bottom right corner. (We'll go over this later.)

These same features will appear on most windows that you open on your computer. There will always be a Title Bar at the top that tells you which window

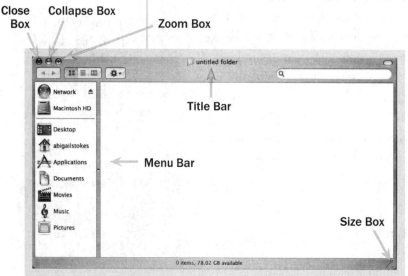

Close Box   Collapse Box

Zoom Box

Title Bar

Menu Bar

Size Box

you are viewing. There will always be a Menu Bar, a Close Box, Zoom Box, and Collapse Box. Once you learn to use these features in this window, you will be able to use them on any window.

Zoom Box ⊕

When you use the Zoom Box, it makes the size of the window as large as possible. The advantage of this is that you will see more of what is contained in that window.

Move the mouse arrow to the ⊕ **Zoom Box** and click once. It's a little tricky to position the arrow exactly inside the box. If you've clicked successfully on the Zoom Box, you'll see that the **Untitled Folder** window now takes up more of the screen. Note: Sometimes the window thinks it's maximized, but it isn't taking up the entire screen. In that case the window can be maximized by using the ⟋ **Size Box**. We'll play with the Size Box later.

To restore the **Untitled Folder** window to the size it was when you started, move the arrow back onto the ⊕ Zoom Box and click once. If the window is now the original size, you did it right.

Collapse Box ⊖

When you use the Collapse Box, it shrinks the window to its smallest form on the Dock at the bottom or left of your screen next to the Trash. The advantage of this is that you can access the window quickly but it isn't taking up space on your screen.

Let's see the Collapse Box in action. Move the mouse arrow onto the ⊖ Collapse Box and click once. If it seems as though the box has disappeared, leaving behind only the Title Bar, you have successfully collapsed the window. To restore the window to its original size, move the mouse arrow onto the Dock and click on the **Untitled Folder** once. The **Untitled Folder** window is back on your screen.

Close Box ⊗

To close the window completely, move the mouse arrow into the ⊗ **Close Box** and click once. Good-bye, **Untitled Folder** window. If that was rough going, don't worry. This is your first time playing with the mouse. It's all about practice, practice, practice.

Mouse Play

Unlike a PC with a Microsoft operating system, a Mac doesn't come with Solitaire preinstalled on the hard drive. If you purchased Solitaire software when you bought your computer, you can either follow the steps below or skip this section and go directly to "Place Your Bets" (page 127) to play Solitaire.

It isn't my intention for you to become a game nut. What I really want you to do is master the mouse. Your homework is either to play solitaire or follow the steps here as often as you can. Once the mouse is your slave, go on to the next chapter. Remember, it is practice and only practice that will allow you to conquer the mouse or any other aspect of the computer.

To access a new folder:

• Move the mouse arrow up to the top of the screen.

• Click on the word **File** at the top of the screen.

• A menu will have opened. Move the mouse down into the menu and click on the words **New Folder**.

• Take a look at the desktop and you will notice that there is now a folder there with the name **Untitled Folder**.

My goal here is to have you learn to click and drag the mouse. It is a mouse tool that you will use later when you are on the Internet.

Here's what I would like you to do:

• Double-click (as you did on page 124) on the **Untitled Folder**.

• The folder has now opened to a window. Move your mouse onto the title bar where it says **Untitled Folder**.

• Depress the mouse button and keep it depressed while you move the **Untitled Folder** to the left, then to the right.

• Release the mouse. You'll notice the folder remains where you moved it.

Good! Before you know it you will have mastered the mouse. Remember, it is practice that allows you to conquer the mouse or any other aspect of the computer. Repeat this exercise every time you visit your computer.

Place Your Bets

If you aren't going to play Solitaire, skip to **Ready to Call it a Day?** on page 132.

CLICK AND GO

1. Double-click on Untitled Folder.

2. Move mouse onto title bar.

3. Click and drag untitled folder window.

TRIVIA

There are many versions of Solitaire and many names for each game. The familiar version is often called Klondike. It most likely dates back to the Klondike gold rush in the late 19th century.

**MAC USERS: A VERSION
TO DIFFERENT VERSIONS**

Your version of Solitaire
may differ slightly from
what we have described
here. This is true of any
software package. Follow
my instructions as best
you can, but when in
doubt refer to your
software manual.

You can try to install the Solitaire software following the
instructions that came with it. But if it seems too hard, don't
hesitate to call and ask someone who has a computer to help you.

Once the software is installed, open your Solitaire program
using the following steps:

1. If there is a **Solitaire** icon on your desktop screen, move the
mouse arrow onto the icon and double-click. It is important
that the arrow be on the icon and not on the words below.

2. If there isn't an icon, move the mouse arrow to your
Hard Disk icon and double-click.

3. Find the **Application** folder. Move the mouse arrow onto
that folder and double-click.

4. Now find the **Solitaire** folder. Move the mouse arrow onto that
folder and double-click. The Solitaire window is now opened.

PC and Mac Card Sharks, Unite!

S o here we are with the **Solitaire** window opened. Let's review
the rules of Solitaire, and then we can play a hand. If you already

A PC Solitaire
window.

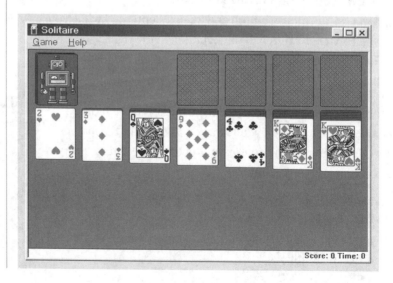

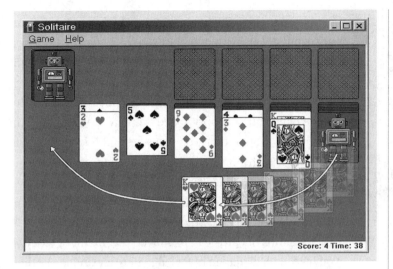

A king is the only card that can be moved to an empty space.

know how to play Solitaire, skip this section and we'll catch up with you at "How Do the Cards Get Moved?" (page 130).

• The ultimate goal of Solitaire is to have all the cards in four piles in the empty spots of the Solitaire window. Each stack must be of a single suit and in ascending order, with the ace on the bottom and the king on top (ace, 2, 3 . . . jack, queen, king).

• Along the way, your challenge is to build on the cards that are face-up in the seven piles. You add cards to these piles moving down in value (10, 9, 8 . . .), but you must alternate in color (black, red, black, red).

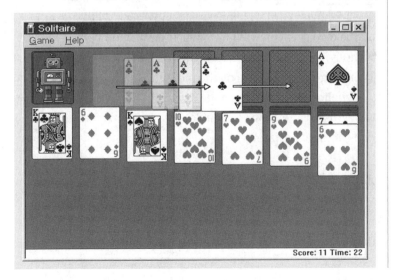

Aces are moved to the spaces at the top right of the window.

HUH? WHAT HAPPENED?
You'll discover that the computer will not allow you to make a mistake or cheat! If you choose a card and try to play it on another card incorrectly, the computer will send your choice flying back to its original spot as soon as you release the mouse button.

• You can play the top card in any of the seven piles or play the card that is faceup in the draw pile. When you take a card from the draw pile, the card below will be revealed and may then be played.

• As you use a card from the seven piles, the card below it can be played. If an empty space is created, only a king can be moved to that spot; then you can start building on the king in the same way the other piles are built (king, queen, jack . . . alternating red and black).

• If you come upon an ace, move it to one of the open four spots and build up your stacks by suit (ace, 2, 3 . . .).

• A series of cards can be moved together. For example, if you have a black queen revealed in one pile and in another stack you have built a series with a red jack, black 10, and red 9, you can move the series, starting with the red jack, onto the black queen.

• Keep in mind, the strategy in Solitaire is to try to expose as many facedown cards as possible.

Don't get frustrated if you don't often win. If you win one out of five games you're doing quite well. Remember: It isn't whether you win or lose, it's how you control the mouse.

How Do the Cards Get Moved?

To move a card, you must click and drag it. Place the mouse arrow on the card that you want to move. Press the mouse button, and, without lifting your finger, drag the card to where you want it to be. Then let go of the button on the mouse.

To flip over a card from the draw pile, move the mouse arrow onto the card and click once. If you double-click here you will turn over two cards, so be careful.

Let the Games Begin

Look at the cards that are faceup in your seven piles.

If there is an ace, move the mouse arrow onto the ace. Press down the mouse button. With the mouse button held down, move the card

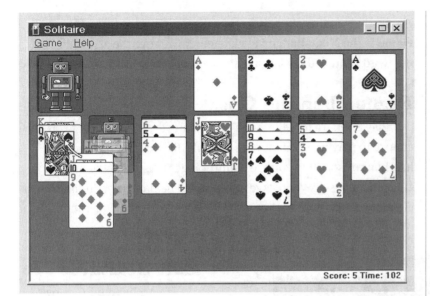

A series of cards can be moved together by clicking on the highest card of the series and dragging it to the appropriate spot. All the cards in the series will move together.

onto one of the four designated blank spots. Take your finger off the mouse button. If this didn't work, give it another try.

Look for a card one less in number than any of the cards faceup in the seven piles. Is the color different? (The cards must alternate black and red or vice versa.)

• If you have a card to move, move the mouse arrow to that card and click and drag the card to its new position.

• If you don't have a card to move, can you play the faceup card in the draw pile?

• If you can't play that card, click once on the face-down pile. Can you use that card? Keep flipping cards until there's a card to play. If the draw pile is depleted, click once on the empty area so you can go through the pile again.

The game continues like this until you can't play any of the cards available to you. Unfortunately, that means you've lost. But if you manage to complete the four piles by suit from ace to king, that means you've won.

CLICK AND DRAG ... IS IT A DRAG?

Are you having some trouble with the click-and-drag maneuver? Let's review:

• Place the mouse arrow on the object you want to move and depress the mouse button.

• Keep the mouse button depressed while you drag the object by moving the mouse to where you desire.

• Take your finger off the mouse and the object will remain where it has been moved.

My advice is, keep playing Solitaire! It may seem silly (or drive you nuts), but it is the best way to master the mouse.

If you want to play again, move the mouse arrow onto the word **Game** in the Menu Bar and click once. Now move the arrow down to the word **Deal** and click again.

Remember the Goal

Play Solitaire for at least half an hour every day for a week. If you choose to play more, make sure you take five-minute breaks every half hour or so. What you are really doing is mastering the mouse. Once the mouse is your slave, go on to the next chapter. Remember, it is practice and only practice that will allow you to conquer the mouse or any other aspect of the computer.

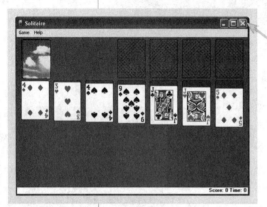

Close Box

Exit Solitaire

If you have a PC, move your mouse arrow to the ⊠ Close Box of the Solitaire window and click once.

If you have a Mac, move your mouse arrow to the ⊗ Close Box of the Solitaire window and click once.

Ready to Call It a Day?

Get into the habit of shutting down your computer properly. You must try to avoid simply turning the power off instead of going through the shut-down process. If you do not go through the proper shut-down procedures, you can damage the computer. It is best to close all the windows that are open and quit any programs that you are in. If you forget to do this, the computer will remind you.

Putting the Computer to Bed

If you have a PC:

1. Move your mouse arrow to the **Start** button in the bottom left corner of your screen and click once.

2. Move your mouse arrow up to the words **Shut Down** or **Turn Off**, and click once. A window will appear. Click on **Turn Off** or make sure that the circle next to the words **Shut Down** is filled in. If not, move the mouse to the words **Shut Down** and click once.

3. Now you may have a choice. You can either hit the **Enter** key or move the mouse arrow to the word **OK** or **Yes** and click once. Both will instruct the computer to shut down.

4. If your screen says "It is now safe to turn off your computer," wait a moment to see if it shuts off automatically; if not, you can turn the power source off. Many computers shut off automatically after the "Please wait while your computer shuts down" screen turns black.

5. Turn off any peripheral that may still be on—your monitor, the printer, and so on.

If you have a Mac:

1. Move your mouse arrow to the 🍎 in the top left corner and click once, then to the words **Shut Down** and click once.

2. Click on **Shut Down** in the little window that has opened. This will instruct the computer to shut down.

3. Turn off any peripheral that may still be on—your monitor, the printer, and so on.

CLICK AND GO

1. Click Start.

2. Click Turn Off.

DON'T DESPAIR

If you purchased a laptop computer and you continue to have trouble manipulating the pad, ball, or point mouse, you have the option of purchasing an external mouse. Make sure that your new mouse is compatible with either your PC or Mac.

CLICK AND GO

1. Click on Apple logo.

2. Click Shut Down.

3. Click Shut Down.

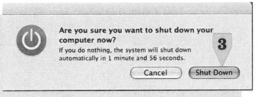

If You Have a Laptop:

Be sure to close the cover after completing the preceding steps.

Let's Review

Here is a quick guide to get you up and running with Solitaire (or opening a new folder for Mac users).

If you are using a PC

TO ACCESS SOLITAIRE:
- Turn on the computer and wait for it to warm up.
- Move the mouse arrow to the **Start** button and click.
- Move the mouse arrow up to **Programs** and across to **Games.**
- Move the mouse arrow across **Games** and onto **Solitaire;**
  then click once. Have fun!

TO SHUT DOWN:
- Close the **Solitaire** window and any other windows that are open.
- Move the mouse arrow to the **Start** button and click.
- Move the mouse arrow up to the words **Turn Off** or
  Shut Down and click.
- You may need to move the mouse to **OK** or **Yes** and click once..

If you are using a Mac

TO OPEN A FOLDER:
- Turn on computer and wait for it to warm up.
- Click on **File** in the Menu Bar.
- Click on **New Folder.**
- Double-click on the new **Untitled Folder.**

TO CLICK AND DRAG:
- Move mouse onto the words **Untitled Folder.**
- Depress the mouse and keep it depressed as you move (or drag) the window around the screen.

TO SHUT DOWN:
- Close the **Untitled Folder** and any other windows that are open.
- Move your mouse arrow to the in the top left corner and click once.
- Move the mouse arrow to the words **Shut Down** and click once.
- Move the mouse to **Shut Down** in the small window and click once.

Hurrah!

That was a huge amount to accomplish! If you are bleary-eyed, you are not alone. We covered a lot of material for your initiation, but initiated you are!

When you want to come back to the computer, you can repeat any or all of this chapter. What you *must* do is open the Solitaire window (or **Untitled Folder** for Mac users) and practice for at least half an hour every day for a week. I want you to be skilled with the mouse and have an understanding of your options within a window. At the end of that time, you'll never have to do it again unless you want to.

Q: Why does it take my computer so long to shut down?

A: Computers can take a bit of time to start up and shut down because they need to check that everything is working properly and to put data in its proper place. If this start up and shut down time has lengthened dramatically, you made need to have someone do some housecleaning on your computer. (See Chapters 20 and 25.)

Q: Do I need to turn off my monitor, speakers, and/or printer when I turn off the computer?

A: You don't *need* to turn them off, but to leave the monitor, speakers, and printer on is an unnecessary waste of energy.

Q: I seem not to have enough space on my desk for the mouse. Do I need a bigger desk?

A: You definitely do not need a bigger desk. You need to harness your use of the mouse. Instead of sweeping all over your desk, lift the mouse up to reposition it on your desk. You'll notice that when the mouse does not make contact with the desk's surface, the arrow on the screen will stay in place.

CHAPTER 12

Getting to Know You

Experimenting with what you can do on the computer

In the last chapter you were introduced to the mouse. This chapter will introduce you to the Mac and PC operating systems, as well as to some other features that your computer has to offer. Mac users, turn to page 153. PC users, continue reading. And remember: Don't sit at the computer too long without taking a break. Also check the position of your back, arms, and legs in relation to the computer and review the ergonomic safety tips on page 96.

Welcome, PC Users

Turn on your computer. Let's open some of the icons on the desktop screen and see specifically what they have to offer. If you don't have the icons I refer to on your desktop screen, click on **Start** 🏁 **start** or 🪟 (bottom left of your screen) and find them in the Start menu that opens.

My Computer

First we'll open the icon labeled **My Computer**. The **My Computer** window allows access to both the software and hardware on your computer. From here you can get to all the information stored on your hard drive, as well as the drives that hold your CD and DVD disks.

Move the mouse arrow onto the ▨ **My Computer** icon and double-click. If the icon is highlighted in blue but the window didn't open, your double click wasn't successful. Place the mouse arrow on the icon again and depress, release, depress, release the mouse button in as rapid succession as you can. Think knock, knock. Keep trying, and eventually you will get the timing.

As I describe each icon contained in the **My Computer** window, feel free to double-click on the icon to open it and see what's inside. To get back to the **My Computer** window, move the mouse arrow to the word **Back** or to a left-facing arrow on the upper left side of the **Menu Bar** and click once. If you have somehow closed the window, simply find the **My Computer** icon on the desktop screen and double-click on it to reopen it.

The **(C:)** icon allows access to anything on your computer's C: drive. Because the C: drive is the storage space for everything on your computer, you can find anything you need through this icon.

Find a folder titled **Documents** in the C: drive. (In Windows Vista you may find the Documents folder in the sidebar of the Computer window.) That folder will store whatever writing you eventually do on the computer. You may not be able to see all that is contained in the C: drive, but if you

PLACEMENT COUNTS
To open an icon or folder, it's important to place the arrow on the icon and not on the text description or name below the icon.

▨ The "Computer" window. Notice that it has a Title Bar, and Minimize, Maximize, and Close Boxes. Most PC windows have these features.

Title Bar

Menu Bar   Minimize Box

Maximize Box

Close Box

WHEN ALL ELSE FAILS

If you absolutely cannot double-click, there is a solution. Single-click on the icon. Now that the icon is highlighted you can depress and release the **Enter** key on your keyboard to open the icon.

click on the **Maximize Box**, you will be able to see more of what's in the window. Later I will explain how to view the entire contents of a window utilizing the Scroll Bar (page 142).

The (**D:**) icon (also referred to as **E:**) allows you to hear and/or see a compact disc (CD) or DVD on your computer. When a music CD is in the D: drive, this icon will offer you choices about which track you may want to listen to and the volume you prefer. We will experiment with this later in the chapter.

To navigate between these windows you can close each window when you are done and start from scratch. You may also notice an arrow in the top left of the window. That arrow, when clicked on, will also send you back to the previous window viewed.

The Control Panel

Now let's visit the **Control Panel** and see what it has to offer. If there isn't an icon on the Desktop for the Control Panel, click on **start** or 🪟 and then click on **Control Panel**. Once the Control Panel has opened, click on "Classic View" in the sidebar on the left, if it is available.

The **Control Panel** is where you get to customize certain aspects of your computer. I'm only going talk about the features that you'll use most in the Control Panel window.

Printers

The **Printers** icon allows you access to both the printer you're already using and a new printer that you might add at any time. This is also the place to go if you change your mind once you start printing a document and want to stop the printer (or "purge print documents" in computer-speak).

The **Network and Sharing Center** icon is something you will probably never use. This is where you set up your access to the Internet. If at some point you decided to reconfigure your Internet connection, you would double-click on this icon to access the area where you would make those changes.

The **Date and Time** icon allows you to adjust the date and time. We're going to do that together in a bit, but first I want you to experiment with the parts of this window now that it is open.

What's in the Window?

The size of the window dictates how much of the information it contains is visible to you. This is where the **Scroll Bar** comes in handy. The Scroll Bar allows you to move the information in the window up and down for full viewing.

You will notice that this window has the same features as the Solitaire window. It has a **Title Bar**, ▣ **Minimize Box**, ▣ **Maximize Box**, and ☒ **Close Box**. What we haven't discussed yet is the Scroll Bar on the bottom and right side of the window.

If you see a Scroll Bar on the right edge or bottom of a window, it tells you that there is more in the window than you can see. (If there is no Scroll Bar on the window of your screen, don't worry. On page 142 there are instructions on how to make a Scroll Bar appear.) You can increase the size of the window or scroll the window to see what else it contains. Students often call me in distress because they can't find an item that they know is supposed to be in a certain window. Usually it is right where it should be, but they didn't see all the contents of the window. The Scroll Bar is your clue that there is more to be unveiled.

■ You can customize certain parts of your computer using the Control Panel.

Scroll Arrow

Scroll Box

Scroll Bar

Scroll Arrow

Enlarging the Window The most efficient way to see all the contents of a window is to increase its size. You can do that in a number of ways. For the sake of experimentation, try each option. Once you have seen how each choice works, follow the instructions in italics to restore the window and go on to the next option. We will experiment with scrolling after you have tried the following options.

Option 1. There is a box in the **Title Bar** that will increase the size of the window. As you may remember, it's the 🔲 **Maximize Box**. Move the mouse arrow into the 🔲 and click once. To restore it back to its original form, move the mouse arrow to the 🔲 Restore Box and click once.

Option 2. Move your mouse arrow to the bottom right corner of the Control Panel window. Your arrow will become a two-ended arrow at an angle ↖. (If the double arrow eludes you it is because you are moving the mouse too quickly. Slow down.) As you did with the Solitaire cards, click and drag the arrow to the bottom right of your screen, then release the mouse button. To restore, place the mouse arrow in the bottom right corner of the window to activate the two-ended arrow. Now click and drag the corner to the left and up until the window is the size it was when you first opened it.

Option 3. Move the mouse arrow to the right side of the Control Panel window. The arrow now becomes an arrow going right and left ↔. Click and drag the arrow to the far right edge of the screen and then release the mouse button. This increases the width. (The same can be done with the left side of the window.) To increase the height, move

1. Click on the Maximize Box.

2. Click on the Restore Box.

Restore Box

PRACTICE MAKES PERFECT
It is a delicate business to get the mouse arrow exactly on the edge of the window to activate the arrows that will allow you to stretch or shrink it. Move the mouse *very* slowly and you'll get the hang of it. Be patient and don't give up.

CLICK AND GO

1. Click and drag the corner of the window to enlarge.

2. Click and drag the corner of the window to restore to previous size and shape.

the right-left arrow to the bottom of the window. Now the mouse arrow becomes an up-and-down arrow ↕. Click and drag the arrow to the far bottom edge of the screen and then release the mouse. (The same can be done with the top of the window.) *To restore, place the mouse arrow on the right of the screen to activate the arrow going right and left. Now click and drag the edge to the left until the window is about the width it was when you first opened it. Do the same with the bottom edge of the window.*

Click and Drag . . . Is It a Drag?

Are you having some trouble with the click-and-drag maneuver? Let's review:

- Place the mouse arrow on the object you want to move and depress the mouse button.
- Keep the mouse button depressed while you drag the object (by moving the mouse) to where you desire.
- Take your finger off the mouse and the object will remain where it has been moved.

My advice is, *if you have Solitaire, keep playing.* It may seem silly (or drive you nuts), but it is the best way to master the mouse. If you haven't been faithfully doing your homework, start today!

CLICK AND GO

1. Increase the width by clicking and dragging right edge out.

2. Click and drag back to restore to previous size/shape.

3. Click and drag bottom edge to increase window height.

4. Click and drag back to restore previous size/shape.

Scrolling Along

Sometimes there can be more icons contained in a window than you can see, no matter how large you make the window. In this case, you will have to use the Scroll Bar to see all that is available. The Scroll Bar is similar to an elevator: A button is pressed to activate it, it moves up and down, and you can get off anyplace you want.

Does your window look something like the window seen here? Make sure a Scroll Bar is on the right side of the window. If there isn't a Scroll Bar, move the mouse arrow onto the lower right corner of the window. It will now be the two-sided arrow at an angle ⬊. Click and drag the corner up and left to create a Scroll Bar on the right side and bottom of the window.

There should be a set of arrows at the top and bottom of the Scroll Bar positioned on the right edge of the window. If there is a Scroll Bar at the bottom of the window, it will also have a set of arrows positioned at the right and left. Now let's take a scroll . . .

• Place the mouse arrow on the bottom ▾ scroll arrow on the right edge of the window and click a few times. With each click the image on the screen moves down. Be careful that the mouse arrow stays within the box that contains the scroll arrow. If your mouse wanders, you will not be able to activate the Scroll Bar, or the window may scroll in increments larger than you desire.

- The contents within the window will move up if you place the mouse arrow on the top ▲ scroll arrow and click.

- The window will scroll left or right with the bottom ◄ left and ► right scroll arrows.

- If you hold down the mouse button rather than depressing and releasing it, the window will scroll very quickly. This technique is more difficult to control but faster than individual clicks.

- You can also reveal what's inside the window by placing the mouse arrow on the **Scroll Box** within the Scroll Bar and clicking and dragging the Scroll Box up or down. This is faster than using the scroll arrows and is most convenient if you're in a very large document wanting to get from, for example, page 1 to page 40.

Scroll Bar

■ If you see a Scroll Bar, it indicates that there's more to see in the window.

CLICK AND GO

1. Click on bottom arrow repeatedly.

2. Click on top arrow and hold mouse down until scroll box is at the top of the scroll bar.

3. Click and drag the scroll box within the scroll bar to reveal the contents of the window again.

"For the longest time I couldn't use the Scroll Bar. I kept moving the mouse off the arrow or clicking too fast. Eventually it became easier. You really can't take advantage of websites without it."
—Dan

Scroll Bars play a big role in viewing websites on the Internet. I strongly recommend that you spend time maneuvering a Scroll Bar every time you play on the computer until you have the technique down.

Does Anybody Really Know What Time It Is?

Maximize the Control Panel window if you can't see all the icons contained in it. (Remember, you do that by clicking on 🔲.) We're going to be sure that the date and time are set properly on your computer. Once set, the computer, even when it is shut off, will keep perfect time and the current date. Open the Date and Time window by double-clicking on the 🕑 **Date and Time** icon.

At the bottom of the Date and Time window there are three buttons: **OK**, **Cancel**, and **Apply**. These are your action choices. Sometimes a window will offer you **Help**, **Yes**, or **No** as choices. When you click on any of these buttons, you're instructing the computer to take that action. You must be **very sure** of the action you want to take—sometimes it is irreversible.

Notice that the box containing **OK** has a slightly darker outline. In this case the computer assumes **OK** to be the choice you'll most likely make and has preselected it for you. (You can always choose a different option—it's just trying to make life easier for you.) Be forewarned: If you depress the **Enter** key on your keyboard, whatever action the computer has preselected will be taken. *That is why it is so important not to depress the* **Enter** *key arbitrarily; you may unwittingly take an action that cannot be reversed.* (Note: It may not be **OK** that the computer preselects for you. It could be any action button that the computer

■ This window allows you to set the date and time.

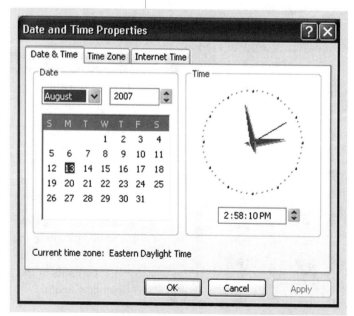

deems will be your likely choice.) In the case of what we are playing with here, not to worry—nothing is irreversible.

Setting the Date and Time Follow these steps to adjust the date and time on your computer:

- Click once on the **Change Time Zone** button.
- There is a box with a down  arrow to the right. Is the time zone that is visible your time zone? If not, click on the arrow. Find your time zone (you may have to use the Scroll Bar), point on it with the mouse arrow, and click once.
- Does **Automatically adjust clock for daylight saving changes** have a check ☑ in the box to the left? If not, move the mouse arrow to the box and click once. Yes, like magic your computer will make the adjustment for daylight savings time from now on! Adjust your screen brightness if you have difficulty seeing the map.
- At this point click once on the word **Apply.** This instructs the computer to accept your changes without closing the window.
- Now click on the **Change date and time**.
- Is the month correct? If not, click on the ⌄ arrow to the right of the month until you are in the correct month.
- Is the date correct? If not, click on the correct date.
- Is the hour correct? If not, move the mouse arrow onto the hour display, then click and drag over the hour to select it. It should be highlighted in blue. You can either type the correct hour using the number keys on your keyboard or use the ⌄ arrows to the right of the time to increase or decrease the hour.

PATIENCE, PLEASE
Remember that if there is a spinning circle ○ or an hourglass ⧗, sit back and let the computer finish what it's doing before you use the mouse or keyboard.

CLICK AND GO

1. Click on down scroll arrow.
2. Click on your time zone (you may have to use the Scroll Bar).
3. Click OK.

Date and Time Properties

Date & Time | Time Zone | Internet Time

(GMT-05:00) Eastern Time (US & Canada)

(GMT-05:00) Eastern Time (US & Canada)
(GMT-05:00) Indiana (East)
(GMT-04:00) Atlantic Time (Canada)
(GMT-04:00) Caracas, La Paz
(GMT-04:00) Manaus
(GMT-04:00) Santiago
(GMT-03:30) Newfoundland
(GMT-03:00) Brasilia
(GMT-03:00) Buenos Aires, Georgetown
(GMT-03:00) Greenland
(GMT-03:00) Montevideo
(GMT-02:00) Mid-Atlantic
(GMT-01:00) Azores
(GMT-01:00) Cape Verde Is.
(GMT) Casablanca, Monrovia, Reykjavik
(GMT) Greenwich Mean Time : Dublin, Edinburgh, Lisbon, London
(GMT+01:00) Amsterdam, Berlin, Bern, Rome, Stockholm, Vienna
(GMT+01:00) Belgrade, Bratislava, Budapest, Ljubljana, Prague
(GMT+01:00) Brussels, Copenhagen, Madrid, Paris
(GMT+01:00) Sarajevo, Skopje, Warsaw, Zagreb
(GMT+01:00) West Central Africa
(GMT+02:00) Amman
(GMT+02:00) Athens, Bucharest, Istanbul
(GMT+02:00) Beirut
(GMT+02:00) Cairo
(GMT+02:00) Harare, Pretoria
(GMT+02:00) Helsinki, Kyiv, Riga, Sofia, Tallinn, Vilnius
(GMT+02:00) Jerusalem
(GMT+02:00) Minsk
(GMT+02:00) Windhoek

1. If month is not correct, click on the month and select the correct month.

2. If date should be changed, click on correct date.

3. If the hour or minutes are not correct, click on each and use the arrows to adjust.

4. Click OK to keep changes.

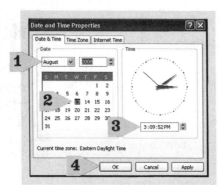

• Do the same for the minutes and seconds—highlight them and make the necessary changes.

• Once the correct hour, minute, and second are visible on the screen, click on **OK**. The window should close, accepting your changes and putting you back in the Control Panel window.

Mouse Traps

Now we'll customize the mouse to suit you. If you prefer to have the mouse to your left, you can also reverse the functions of the mouse buttons here (see "Attention Again, Southpaws" box). Let's adjust the double-click speed.

• Double-click on the **Mouse** icon in the Control Panel box. You may click on all the file tabs and read what each contains, but the one we'll focus on is **Buttons.**

• Click on the **Buttons** tab to adjust the double-click timing.

• Look at the pointer that indicates how slow or fast the clicking is set. If you found you need some extra time to double-click, then click and drag the pointer toward "Slow." If you naturally double-click faster than where it's set at present, click and drag the pointer toward "Fast."

ATTENTION AGAIN, SOUTHPAWS

If you're a lefty, this is your chance to have the mouse cater to your needs. Some of my students who are left-handed are quite content to place the mouse to the right of their keyboard, but you can also swap it to the other side. It depends on what works better for you.

As the mouse is now configured, the left button is set up for **Click/Select** and the right button for **Context Menu/Alternate Select**. If you have an external mouse and want to position it to the left of the keyboard, these buttons are in the reverse position of how they might work best for you. See "Reversing the Buttons" on the next page.

• When you have found the right timing, move the mouse arrow to **Apply** and click once. (Remember, this means that your change has been accepted and the window will remain open.)

• Now let's click on the **Pointer Options** tab.

• Here we're interested in the **Motion**. There is a pointer that indicates the speed with which the mouse arrow will move across the screen (the computer may refer to the mouse arrow as a cursor here). Move the mouse arrow onto that pointer. Click and drag the pointer to the speed where you think it should be based on how quickly or slowly the mouse arrow currently moves across your screen. Mine is set on the slowest speed, which is easiest for me, but only you can judge what's best for you. You can always come back to this window and readjust it at a later date.

• Once you've selected your preferred speed, click on **OK**. Your changes will be made and the window will close.

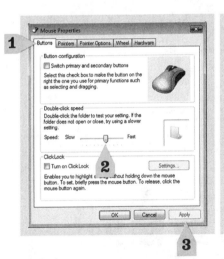

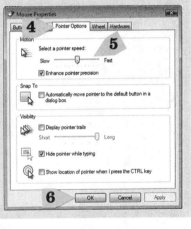

Right-Clicks

The right button on the mouse opens an advanced menu that offers different actions depending on what you *right*-click on. For now we won't use the right side of the mouse, but later in the book (see page 261) we'll practice using it together. In the meantime, if you accidentally hit the right side of the mouse, you can get rid of the menu that you opened by clicking anywhere off that menu.

REVERSING THE BUTTONS

To reverse the functions of your mouse's two buttons:
• Click in the box below **Button Configuration** to switch primary and secondary buttons.
• A check will appear in the box.
• Now click **Apply**.

▦ This window allows you to adjust your mouse settings.

CLICK AND GO

1. Click on Buttons tab.

2. Click and drag "double-click speed" pointer to what best suits you.

3. Click on Apply to keep your setting.

4. Click on Pointer Options tab.

5. Click and drag the "pointer speed" to what best suits you.

6. Click on OK to keep the changes.

Hanging Wallpaper

The background on your desktop screen is also referred to as wallpaper. Your operating software comes with several different styles of wallpaper, and you can personalize your desktop by selecting one that appeals to you.

• Double-click on the **Personalization**  window in your Control Panel. (If you are using Windows XP, double-click on **Display** and follow along. Things may appear differently on your computer screen, but if you use your intuition you'll likely be able to follow along.) Here we can choose your wallpaper, change the look of the screen, and create a screen saver.

• Click on **Desktop Background**. This is where you decide the background for the desktop screen. Click on the wallpaper choices and select one that appeals to you. Then at the bottom of the window, click

CLICK AND GO

1. Click on Desktop Background.

2. Click on wallpaper that appeals to you.

3. Click to select how you want the wallpaper positioned.

4. Click OK to accept your choices.

5. Minimize the window to see your handiwork.

6. Click on Desktop Background to restore window to previous size.

to position that wallpaper (either as full screen, tile, or stretch) by clicking in the little circle to the left of your preference. Feel free to click on **OK**, and then minimize the **Personalization** window. This allows the wallpaper to be viewed in its actual size.

• Personalization is now minimized on the Task Bar at the bottom of the screen. Click on the **Personalization** box in the Task Bar to restore it to full size on the screen. Move the mouse arrow to **Desktop Background** and click to reopen it. You can now try selecting a different wallpaper. Keep repeating this process until you find the wallpaper that suits you. And remember, you can select different wallpaper whenever you please.

> **PERSONALIZE IT!**
> In addition to the wallpapers offered by the computer, you can create a desktop background from photos or images that you have brought onto your computer. Chapter 18 will guide you through how to get images onto your computer.

Choosing a Screen Saver

Now, let's select a screen saver. A screen saver is an image that appears on the screen when the computer is on and has sat unused for a period of time. This choice allows you to decide what the screen saver will look like and when it will appear.

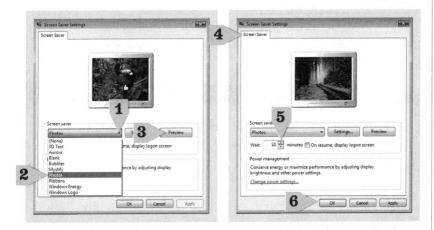

> **CLICK AND GO**
>
> **1.** Click on arrow.
> **2.** Click on your choice of screen saver.
> **3.** Click on Preview to see screen saver in action.
> **4.** Click to get back to settings window.
> **5.** Adjust timing by using up and down arrows.
> **6.** Click OK to accept your changes.

• Click on the **Screen Saver** tab. Under the words **Screen Saver** is a box with an ▾ arrow to the right. Click on the arrow to expose the screen saver options. You may have to use the Scroll Bar to see everything that is available. Click on the screen saver you want to see displayed and then click on **OK**.

• Click on **Settings** to see the options available to customize your choice. Some screen savers offer a choice of colors or images.

• Click on **Preview** to see your screen saver choice displayed in its actual size without having to close the window. Click the mouse button to get back to the **Screen Saver** window.

• The last decision that you need to make is how much time should elapse before the screen saver is activated. Do this by changing the number next to the word **Wait**. Click on the up and down arrows to the right of the number. Once you have decided on the length of time (I have mine set at ten minutes), click on **OK**. Your changes have been made and the window will be closed.

• Close the **Personalization** window. Now you're back at the Desktop screen.

This might be a fine time to take a break. Just leave your computer as it is and come back when you're ready. When you return, we'll go over some more features.

The Task Bar

The **Task Bar** is the gray or blue bar at the bottom of your screen. It offers an alternative way to access application software and other areas of the computer.

The Task Bar.

The computer usually offers more than one way to skin a cat. By that I mean that there is usually more than one way to accomplish a task or complete an action on the computer.

For instance, move the mouse arrow onto the time in the right-hand corner of the Task Bar and click the *right* mouse button. Now move the arrow to **Adjust Date/Time** and click once with the *left* mouse button. You've just opened the same **Date/Time Properties** window that we accessed from the Control Panel. All the date and time changes that we made before can also be done by opening the window this way.

Close the **Date/Time** window. (Remember, use the ⊠ **Close Box**.) Now with the mouse arrow on a blank spot on the desktop screen, click once with the *right* mouse button. Move the arrow to the word **Personalize** (in Windows XP, click on **Properties**) and click once with the *left* mouse button. Ta-da! It's the **Personalize** window that we used to pick your wallpaper and screen saver. Click on the ▣ **Minimize** box. It appears that the **Personalization** window has closed, but in fact it is waiting for you in the Task bar. Click on **Personalization** in the Task Bar and voilà! the window is back on the screen.

Experiment with what happens when you click the left or right mouse button on an item. You can open all the icons on the desktop screen and see what they contain. For that matter, you can click on anything on the computer screen as long as you don't press the **Enter** key, which instructs the computer to take an action, or you don't click on an action key (**OK, Yes, Apply** . . .). If you open a window and are concerned that you're heading into unknown territory, simply close it by using the ☒ **Close Box** or click on the word **Cancel**, **Finish**, or **Exit**, or click on a blank area of the screen.

Getting in the Swing

It's a lovely thing to listen to music while working (or playing) at the computer. Grab a CD that you enjoy, and let's learn how to play music.

• Open the D: drive on your computer case by pressing the button near the drive.

• Place the CD, label side up, into the CD tray and press the button again to close the tray. *You don't ever want to force the tray closed by pushing the tray in—it is a very delicate component of the computer.*

• An AutoPlay window will appear with options for how to open the CD to play it. Click on **Play Audio CD**.

• A window will appear on the screen with options for the track you want to play and what volume you prefer. Here you will use the mouse to choose your options. For example, move the mouse onto the volume arrow. Click and drag the arrow either up or down to increase or decrease the volume.

• After you've set your preferences, click on the ▣ **Minimize Box**. To maximize the window, click once on the box that contains the minimized window in the **Task Bar**.

LEARNING THE ABC'S

Each computer can vary slightly. In my experience some computers refer to the drive for the CD-ROM as the E: drive instead of the D: drive. The literature that came with your machine will clarify if your CD-ROM drive is referred to as D: or E:.

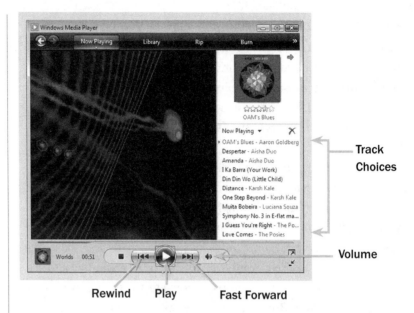

Track Choices

Volume

Rewind   Play   Fast Forward

You can also access the D: drive through the **Computer** icon. Double-click on **Computer**. The D: drive is accessed by double-clicking on the **D:** icon.

There are a couple of other options for controlling the volume. If your computer came with speakers, they may have controls, or your monitor may have a volume control. Fiddle around until you find a comfortable volume. The other place where the volume can be adjusted is the little horn 🔊 on the right side of the Task Bar near where the actual time is displayed. Left-click on the symbol and a box will appear where you can control the CD's volume.

When the CD has stopped (either by your choice or because it came to an end), simply press the button near the D: drive on your computer case to "eject" the CD. Remove the CD and press the button again to close the now-empty drive.

Job Well Done

If you've been using this book sequentially, at this point you should see a light at the end of the tunnel. The computer is more and more under your control. Stick with the book, and by the end you'll be in total control. You can repeat any part of this chapter and the previous one until you are ready to go on the Internet in Chapter 13.

Welcome, Mac Users

Turn on your computer. In this chapter we will customize some features on your computer and investigate a few others. Feel free to move at your own pace. You can stop and start wherever and whenever you want.

Let's investigate what the desktop screen has to offer. First, move the mouse arrow onto the 🖥 **Hard Drive** icon (probably in the top right of the screen). Double-click on the icon. If you have trouble with the double click, you can single-click on the icon to highlight it, then click on the word **File** at the top left of the screen and single-click on the word **Open**, or you can single-click on it and then hold down the ⌘ Command key and the letter O simultaneously. Your **Hard Drive** window should now be open.

PLACEMENT COUNTS
When you open an icon or folder, it's important that the arrow is placed on the icon and not on the text description or name below the icon.

What's in the Window?

Notice that the **Hard Drive** window has the same features as the **untitled folder** window. It has a **Title Bar**, ⊗ **Close Box**, ⊕ **Zoom Box**, ⊖ **Collapse Box**, and a 🔲 **Size Box**. Almost every window you open will contain these elements. Remember, if you get overwhelmed and want to start from scratch, close any open windows by moving the mouse arrow into the **Close Box** and clicking once. What we haven't discussed yet on this window is the **Scroll Bar** on the bottom and the right side of the window.

Collapse Box   Title Bar

se Box   Zoom Box

■ You can access different parts of your computer using the hard drive.

Size Box

The size of the window dictates how much of the information in the window you will be able to see. This is when the Scroll Bar comes in handy. The Scroll Bar allows you to move the information in the window up and down for full viewing.

A Scroll Bar indicates that the window has more to offer than what's on your screen. You can increase the size of the window or scroll the window to see what else it contains. Students often call me because they can't find an item that they know is in a certain window. Usually it is right where it should be, but they didn't see all the contents of the window. An active Scroll Bar is your clue that there is more to be unveiled. Be sure to use a Scroll Bar whenever you see one or you may miss all that the window has to offer. We'll experiment with this shortly.

Enlarging the Window The most efficient way to see all the contents of a window is to increase its size. You can do that in two ways. Once you have seen how each choice works, follow the instructions in italics to restore the window to its original form and go to the next option. We will experiment with scrolling after you have tried the following options.

Option 1. There is a box in the Title Bar that will increase the size of the window. As you may remember, it's the ⊕ **Zoom Box**. If you don't see a plus symbol in any of the three circles in the top left corner of the window, move your mouse arrow closer to the circles. Voilà! The symbols appear. Now move the mouse arrow into the ⊕ **Zoom Box** and click once. (As I said in Chapter 11, sometimes the window

CLICK AND GO

1. Click on Zoom Box once to change size of window.

2. Click on Zoom Box again to restore the previous size.

Click and Drag . . . Is It a Drag?

Are you having some trouble with the click and drag maneuver? Let's review:

- Place the mouse arrow on the object you want to move and depress the mouse button.
- Keep the mouse button depressed while you drag the object (by moving the mouse) to where you desire.
- Take your finger off the mouse and the object will remain where it has been moved.

My advice is, *if you have Solitaire, keep playing*. It may seem silly (or drive you nuts), but it is the best way to master the mouse. If you haven't been faithfully doing your homework, start today!

thinks it is maximized, but it isn't taking up the entire screen. In that case the window can be maximized by using the **Size Box** as described in Option 2.) To restore, place the mouse arrow on the Zoom Box and click.

Option 2. Move the mouse arrow to the **Size Box** at the bottom right corner of the Macintosh HD window. As you did with the untitled folder window, click and drag the corner down and to the right, so it fills the entire screen. The Size Box allows you to click and drag the window to the exact size you desire. To restore, place the mouse arrow in the bottom right corner of the window. Click and drag the corner to the left and up until the window is the size it was when you first opened it.

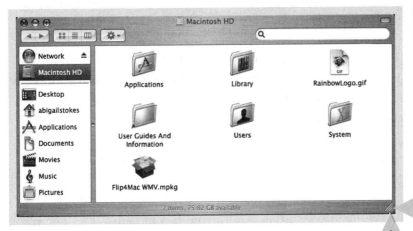

CLICK AND GO

1. Increase the size by clicking and dragging bottom right edge out.

2. Click and drag back to restore to previous size.

Scrolling Along

Sometimes there can be more icons contained in a window than you can see no matter how large you make the window. In this case, you will have to use the Scroll Bar to see all that is available. The Scroll Bar is similar to an elevator: A button is pressed to activate it, it moves up and down, and you can get off anyplace you want.

Does your window look like the window in the illustration below? Make sure that the Scroll Bar on the right side of the window is active. If the Scroll Bar isn't active, double-click on **Applications** and a window should open in place of the Hard Drive that will have a Scroll Bar on the right (and even maybe on the bottom). If a window opens up that is too big to reveal the Scroll Bar, click and drag the bottom right corner until a Scroll Bar appears.

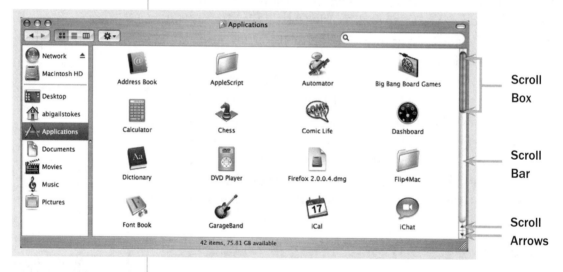

The appearance of a Scroll Bar indicates there's more to see in the window. Mastering the Scroll Bar is critical when you're on the Internet.

There should be a set of arrows at the bottom of the Scroll Bar positioned on the right edge of the window. If there is also a horizontal Scroll Bar there will be a set of arrows on the bottom of the window positioned at the right. Let's take a scroll . . .

• Place the mouse arrow on the bottom scroll arrows on the right edge of the window and click the bottom of the two arrows (the one pointing down) a few times. With each click the screen moves down. Be careful that the mouse arrow stays within the box that contains the bottom scroll arrow. If your mouse wanders, you

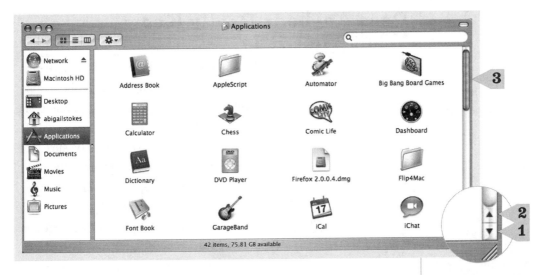

will not be able to activate the Scroll Bar, or the window may scroll in increments larger than you desire.

• The image within the window will move up if you place the mouse arrow on the top ⬍ scroll arrow and click.

• The window will scroll left or right with the bottom left and right ◀▶ scroll arrows.

• If you hold down the mouse button rather than depressing and releasing it, the window will scroll very quickly. This technique is more difficult to control but faster than individual clicks.

• You can also move what's in the window by placing the mouse arrow on the **Scroll Box** within the Scroll Bar and clicking and dragging the Scroll Box up or down. This is faster than using the scroll arrows and is most convenient if you're in a very large document wanting to get from page 1 to page 40, for example. Be sure to keep your mouse arrow on target when you scroll. It is easy to lose aim when you are looking at the contents of the window, especially when the contents are moving. Try to hold your hand as steady as you can.

• Close the Applications window by clicking in the ⊗ **Close Box**.

Scroll Bars play a big role in viewing websites on the Internet. I strongly recommend that you spend time maneuvering a Scroll Bar every time you play on the computer until you have the technique down.

CLICK AND GO

1. Click on bottom arrow repeatedly.

2. Click on top arrow and hold mouse down until scroll box is at the top of the scroll bar.

3. Click and drag the scroll box with the scroll bar to also reveal the contents of the window.

Does Anybody Really Know What Time It Is?

Move the mouse onto the in the top left corner of the screen and click once. A box with a lot of options will open. Move the mouse arrow down onto the words **System Preferences** and click once. The System Preferences window will open.

This window allows you to set the date and time.

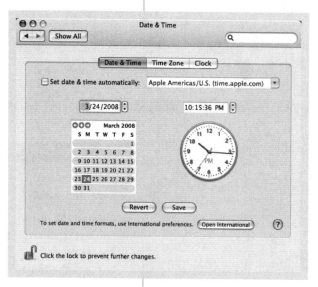

We're going to check to be sure that the date and time are set properly on your computer. Open the **Date & Time** window by single-clicking on the icon found in the **System Preferences** window.

Is there a check in the box to the left of "Set time & date automatically"? If so, click in the box to remove the check. At the bottom of the window are two buttons: **Revert** and **Save**. These are your action choices. Sometimes a window will offer you **Help**, **Yes**, or **No** as choices. When you click on any of these buttons, you're instructing the computer to take that action. You must be *very sure* of the action you want to take—sometimes it is irreversible.

You might notice that the **Save** button has a slightly darker outline. In this case, the computer assumes **Save** to be the choice you'll most likely make and has preselected it for you (you can always choose a different option—it's just trying to make life easier for you). Be forewarned: If you depress the **Return** key on your keyboard, whatever action the computer has preselected will be taken. *This is why it is so important not to depress the **Return** key arbitrarily; you may unwittingly take an action that cannot be reversed.* (Note: It may not be **Save** that the computer preselects for you. It will be any action button that the computer deems will be your likely choice.) In the case of what we are playing with here, not to worry— nothing is irreversible.

PATIENCE, PLEASE!

Remember that if there is a spinning round ball (jokingly referred to by a friend as the "spinning beach ball of death"), sit back and let the computer finish what it's doing before you use the mouse or keyboard.

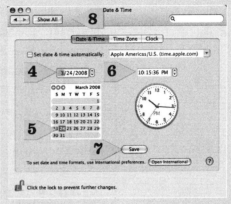

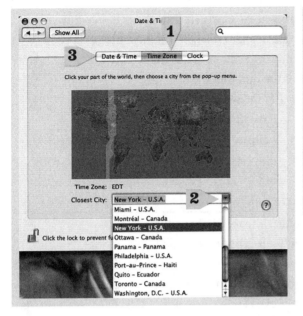

Follow the steps below to adjust the **Time Zone**:

• Click on the **Time Zone** tab.

• Click on the down arrow to the right of the city listed.

• Scroll to the city nearest where you live and click once on that city's name.

Follow the steps below to adjust the **Current Date**:

• Click on the **Date & Time** tab.

• If the month is not correct, move the mouse arrow onto the arrows to the left of the month and click until the present month is displayed.

• If the date is not correct, click on the correct date.

Experiment

As I describe some of the many icons contained in the System Preferences window, feel free to double-click on the icon to open it and see what's inside. To get back to the System Preferences window, simply close the window you've opened. (Remember the ⊗ Close Box?) If somehow you have closed the System Preferences window, move the mouse onto the and down to the words System Preferences and click once.

CLICK AND GO

1. Click on the Time Zone tab.

2. Click on down arrow and select a city in your time zone.

3. Click Date & Time tab.

4. If month is not correct, click on arrows to choose correct month.

5. If date should be changed, click on correct date.

6. If the hour or minutes are not correct, click on each and use the arrows to adjust.

7. Click Save to keep changes.

8. Click Show All to return to System Preferences.

• Is the hour correct in the **Current Time** box? If not, move the mouse onto the hour and click to select it. Hit the number on your keyboard to type in the correct hour or use the ⬆⬇ arrows.

• Do the same for the minutes and seconds.

• Click on **AM** or **PM** to switch between the two.

• Click on **Save** to have the clock display the current time.

• Move the arrow to **Show All** and click to get back to the System Preferences window.

Mouse Traps

Now we'll customize the mouse to suit you.

• Single-click on the **Keyboard & Mouse** icon.

• Click on **Mouse** (**Trackpad**, if you have a laptop) in the tabs.

• **Tracking Speed** has an arrow indicating the speed with which the mouse arrow will move across the screen. Click and drag the arrow to the speed you think it should be. Mine is set on the slowest speed, which is easiest for me; only you be the judge can what's best for you. You can always come back to this window and readjust it at a later date.

• You can also adjust the double-click timing. Click and drag the arrow to whatever point on the continuum you think best represents how you double-click. This, too, can be changed easily if you find you need the timing adjusted.

• Once the **Mouse** window is closed, your changes will be made. You can always come back to this window and change these preferences whenever you wish.

This is a fine time to take a break. Just leave your computer as it is and come back when you're ready.

▣ **This window allows you to adjust your mouse settings.**

CLICK AND GO

1. Click and drag "tracking speed" pointer to what best suits you.

2. Click and drag the "double-click speed" to what best suits you.

3. Click ⊗ to close the window and save changes.

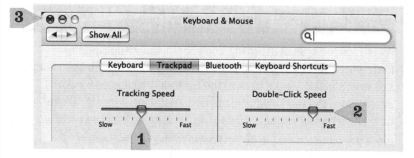

Selecting a Background

The background on your desktop screen is also referred to as wallpaper. Your operating system comes with several different styles of wallpaper, and you can personalize your desktop by selecting one that appeals to you.

• Is the **System Preferences** window still open on your screen? If not, go to the and access the **System Preferences** or you might only have to click on **Show All** to get there, if your **Keyboard & Mouse** window is still open (start on page 158 for how to open the **System Preferences**). Find the **Desktop & Screen Saver** icon. Single-click on the icon to see its contents.

• You will see a menu of image folders to the left. For this exercise, click on the **Nature** folder.

• If a Scroll Bar is available, scroll using the arrows at the bottom of the image to see what other images are available.

• When you find an image you like, click on it with the mouse.

• Bingo! There's your background.

Now, let's select a screen saver.

• Click on **Screen Saver** icon.

• Click on any of the screen savers in the left side of the window. You will see a sample appear in the right side of the window.

CLICK AND GO

1. Click on Nature folder.

2. Click on wallpaper that appeals to you.

3. Click on Screen Saver.

4. Click on screen saver of your choice. Or click on Options to see more choices.

5. Click and drag arrow to adjust when screen saver will appear.

6. Click Close Box to close window and save changes.

• Click on the **Options** button to view a list of **Display Options**. To activate one of the choices, click in the box to the left. A check will appear. To deactivate an option, click in the box to remove the check.

• There is an arrow you can click and drag to indicate how many minutes or hours should elapse before the screen saver is activated. (Mine is set for ten minutes.)

• If you click on **Test** the entire screen will show your choice of screen saver. You can simply move the mouse or click anywhere on the screen to return to the **Desktop & Screen Saver** window.

• Click on ⊗ to close the window and save changes.

WHAT AM I SAVING MY SCREEN FROM?

Screen savers were originally designed to protect the screen from "screen burn." Computer screens used to become damaged when the same screen image remained on the screen for too long. Improvements in the design of screens make this unlikely. Nowadays screen savers are more for visual entertainment.

You can open all the items in the **System Preferences** to see what they contain. For that matter, you can click on anything on the computer screen as long as you don't hit the **Return** key, which instructs the computer to take an action, or you don't click on an action key (**OK**, **Yes**, **Apply**). In fact, it is a good idea to return to the **System Preferences** window and make changes to the mouse and the background whenever you feel inspired. It is only through practice that you will really become comfortable with your computer. Play around here as often as you would like. If you open a window and are concerned that you're heading into unknown territory, simply close it by using the ⊗ **Close Box** or clicking on the word **Cancel**, **Finish**, or **Exit**.

Getting in the Swing

It's a lovely thing to listen to music while working (or playing) at the computer. Grab a CD that you enjoy, and let's learn how to play music.

• Place the CD, label side up, into the CD slot and give it a gentle push. The computer will pull the CD into the slot.

• Wait a moment and an image of a CD will appear on the Desktop.

• Next, a window containing the software iTunes should open automatically.

• Click on the ▶ arrow to play the CD.

• The songs (or "tracks") on the CD are listed in the largest pane of the iTunes window. To play a specific track, move your mouse over the one you want to play and double-click it.

• There is an arrow at the top of the iTunes window that you can click and drag to increase or reduce volume.

There are a couple of other options for controlling the volume. Your speakers or monitor may have a volume control. Fiddle with them to set a comfortable volume for you.

• When you want to remove the CD, close iTunes by clicking in the ⊗ **Close Box**. Then simply click and drag the CD icon into the 🗑 **Trash** on the desktop, which now that you're dragging the CD may look like ⏏ for **Eject**. If that doesn't expel the CD, you might have to depress and release the ⏏ button on the top right of the keyboard.

■ When you insert an audio CD, a window may appear that looks something like this. It allows you to choose a CD track and adjust the volume.

Job Well Done

If you've been using the book sequentially, at this point you should see a light at the end of the tunnel. The computer is more and more under your control. Stick with the book, and by the end you'll be in total control. Repeat any part of this chapter and the previous one until you are ready to go on the Internet in Chapter 13.

Q: **The Task Bar at the bottom of my computer screen has moved from the bottom of the screen to the side. It works where it is now, but how did it get there and can I move it back?**

A: Click and drag is the answer for both how it moved and for how you can move it back to its original position. Believe it or not, at some point you accidentally clicked and dragged the Task Bar (some call it a System Tray) to the side of the screen. Place your mouse anywhere on the Task Bar and now click and drag to the bottom of your screen. Release the mouse. The task bar should be back where you like it.

Q: **Is there a way to open an icon without double-clicking?**

A: Yes. If double-clicking is really a struggle for you, you can single-click on the icon and then depress and release the **Enter/Return** key.

Q: **Is there a way to scroll without using the mouse?**

A: Yes, you can also move up and down a page using the arrow keys located on the bottom right of your keyboard. Sometimes it helps to click on the web page first, then use the arrow keys. But I would like you to practice with the mouse because the other option does not work on all websites.

Q: **What does PBKC stand for?**

A: PBKC is a charming acronym to tease computer users. You ask a technician, "What's wrong with my computer?" He responds, "It's a PBKC (pronounced *pebkack*)." It stands for "problem between keyboard and chair"!

THE NEWLYWED
GAME

CHAPTER 13

Spanning the Globe

"Surfing the net"—traveling around the World Wide Web

The Internet looms in front of us as the Wild West did for the early settlers. As we hear more about the Internet and its limitless possibilities, none of us wants to be left behind. It is the land of opportunity, yet it is full of unknowns and it may seem like a long, hard journey to get there. Take heart, we will access the Internet and learn about websites together, and in no time at all you'll be zipping around the Web with ease.

If you are chomping at the bit to get to e-mail, you can move on to the next chapter and come back to this one later. However, I strongly suggest that you go through this chapter first because it has information that will enhance your e-mail experience.

A Quick Overview

As you likely know, the Internet is a huge system that connects computers all over the world. The World Wide Web is today's modernization of the old government-issue Internet, which consisted of convoluted codes on a black screen. The World Wide Web (www) was designed to make the Internet accessible, with colorful graphics, sound, and a user-friendly environment.

"I was skeptical that the Internet could follow the progress of the companies I helped develop before my retirement, as all the younger folks at the company kept saying it could. They were right. I monitor the companies' status daily and feel very much in the loop. I've never been better informed."

—Joshua

Surfing the net (net = Internet) isn't very different from channel hopping on your television set. Sometimes something will really hold your interest; other times it's fun to change from one channel to the next; and then there are times when you can't find anything that suits your needs. The Internet, like TV, can be seductive, a great way to escape, and an opportunity to learn something new. All you need to connect to the Internet is a computer, a modem, and an Internet Service Provider (ISP).

Finding Your Internet Service Provider (ISP)

The process of choosing an online service is another one of those cases where you might want to call in the cavalry. Ask a friend or relative for their advice on which company to choose and even have them come over and help you get started. Start by contacting your local phone company (Verizon, AT&T, SBC, etc.) or your cable television company (Time Warner, Comcast, etc.) to see what sort of a package they offer in combination with services they already provide you. When you buy your computer, one or several online services (for example AOL or EarthLink), may have arranged to have their software preinstalled on the hard drive. If the service you choose is among them, you can click on the icon on the desktop and follow their step-by-step instructions to get started.

When you've registered with an ISP, you have the benefit of the online services that it has put together for you. Your service may have chosen from the Web certain periodicals, travel resources, shopping areas, and so on, and will have direct links to them for your convenience. Each online service varies with what it offers. All of them provide access to the Internet and e-mail.

I highly recommend that you choose a high-speed connection. As I mentioned earlier in Chapter 8, dial-up connections to the Internet are slow and no longer competitively priced. You can get a high-speed connection for almost the same price and zoom around the Internet with greater speed and less chance of being cut off.

Getting Connected

Depending on which Internet Service Provider you choose, you may have to set up the connection or they may send a technician to your home to do it for you. If you're setting it up, you will have received a box containing the modem and some cables. The modem is the device that will ultimately connect your computer to the Internet. If you're uncomfortable or timid about installing the modem or the software on your own, either call the company's 800 number and have one of their technicians on the phone while you go through the installation steps or ask a friend or family member to help you. It may even be worth it to pay someone to help you. You can often find an industrious high school or college student who would be happy to offer assistance for a lot less money than you would pay a professional computer technician. Whoever is helping you, don't let him or her leave you until you've turned the computer off after installation, turned it back on, and are sure it is all working properly.

At some point during the installation you may be asked to type in your name, address, telephone number, and credit card information so that your online service can bill you monthly. A form may actually

CUSTOMER SERVICE

As you register with your ISP, pay very careful attention: if a customer service telephone number crosses your path at any time, be sure to write it down. After you've completed the registration process, that number can be rather elusive. This may be your only opportunity to note it. Grab it while you can.

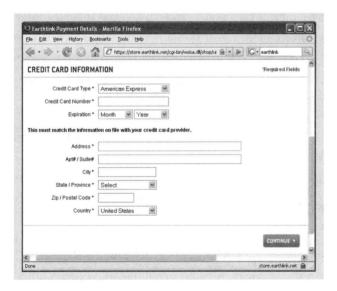

A page of the registration process for EarthLink.

DON'T FORGET TO CLICK IN THE BOX!

This is a crucial thing to remember. It is the most common thing that people forget. You must click inside the text box to activate it so it will accept your typing instructions.

appear on your computer screen asking for this information. Generally, you can move from one text box to another by hitting the **Tab** key (located to the left of Q on the keyboard). If you want to access a text box out of sequence, you can move the mouse arrow anywhere inside the white part of the text box and click to activate the text box. You'll see a flashing vertical line (referred to as the cursor or blinking cursor) in the far left of the box. That indicates that you can start typing at that location. (Refer to Chapter 12 if you need a refresher on how to use the Scroll Bar.)

A Reminder to Keep Track of Your Trial Subscription

Many online services offer a free trial period. But you must remember to cancel your trial subscription if you no longer want the service. Even though you won't be billed for the trial period, the online service provider will have asked for your credit card information to start your account. If you forget to cancel the account, it will start billing your credit card when the trial period is over and continue to do so until you cancel the subscription. Mark your calendar—there will be no reminder from the online service provider.

Choosing a User Name and Password

A user name is the name you use when you're on the Internet or sending e-mail. The next chapter goes into more detail about e-mail, but you may need to decide what your user name will be now, in order to connect to the Internet. Here's an example: If I was an America Online customer, and my user name was Peach,

my e-mail address would be peach@aol.com

Now that I've mentioned it, let's identify all the parts of my fictitious e-mail address.

peach@aol.com is the e-mail address.

peach is the user name.

@ means "at."

aol.com is the "domain name," or mailing address.

"Case sensitivity" means that it matters whether the letters are in upper- or lowercase. At this time, most online services

KEY TO PASSWORDS

Most passwords need to be at least six characters long. It's a good idea to make your password a combination of letters and numbers—that makes it harder to guess.

are *not* case sensitive when dealing with user names. Having said that, I still try to type my user name in the same case that I originally chose. Because passwords can be case sensitive, be sure to type your password in the same case as you originally chose. For this reason it is easier to choose a password that is all in lowercase.

Caps Lock

Shift Key

When deciding on your user name, keep in mind that people will need to know your e-mail address so that they can send you e-mail. It seems silly to point that out, but I've had clients pick rather embarrassing user names and regret it when they had to tell people, "My e-mail address is iamanidiot@aol.com."

Be prepared not to get the user name that you hoped for. With millions of people on the Internet, it's probable that someone may already have your first choice of user name. Have several options ready.

The e-mail service will also ask for a password. A password verifies who you are each time you sign on to the service. Choose a password that comes easily to you. There isn't a whole lot of espionage with home computers, so you needn't come up with something really far out. But please don't use the same password that you use for your bank account or ATM card.

Make sure you write down your e-mail address and password. For safekeeping, why not stash it in your "Computer Instructions" envelope?

Once you've successfully registered, I want you to sign off and sign on from scratch. Practice, practice, practice.

EVERYTHING IS IN CAPS. WHY?

Beware. Above the **Shift** key is the **Caps Lock** key. If your finger accidentally depresses **Caps Lock,** you will need to depress it again to deactivate it. *Example:* I HIT THE CAPS LOCK KEY AND EVERYTHING IS IN UPPERCASE. i just hit it again and everything is in lowercase.

Signing Off and Signing On

S ome online services require you to sign on to access the Internet. Others allow you to connect to the Internet just by double-clicking on an icon on the Desktop. Some remember your user name and password, and others ask that the information be typed in every time. If you need to type information into a text box, remember to click on the box with your mouse to activate the text box and use **Tab** to get from one text box to the next.

1. Click in text box to activate, then type username.

2. Click in text box to activate, then type password.

3. Click Sign On or hit Enter or Return key to sign on.

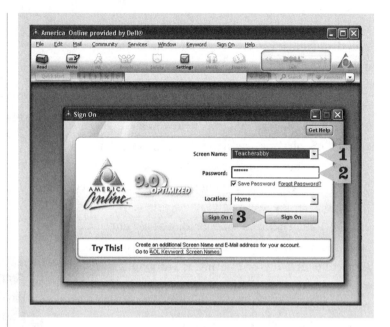

Each online service also has its own way of signing off. For some it is simply clicking on the **Close Box**. For others you need to maximize their box in the **Task Bar** and then click on **Disconnect**. There may be a tutorial or a tour offered that will help you discover the ins and outs of your particular service.

Errors, Messages, and Busy Signals

You may have heard people complain about how long it takes for them to sign on to their online service. This can happen with any dial-up service, and it often happens because of the number of people who are signed on. Dial-up services simply aren't always equipped to handle a high volume of their members signing on because the phone lines can't handle all the traffic. If you have trouble, try getting online at off hours. Before I got my high-speed connection I used the Internet very early in the morning and late at night and rarely had any problems signing on. Again, consider a high-speed connection to avoid traffic jams when you're on the Internet.

BROWSING WITH A BROWSER

Internet Explorer, Safari, and Firefox are browsers. Browsers allow you to interact with the Internet, but a browser is not the company you pay to connect to the Internet.

Action Buttons

When the computer asks you questions, such as "Do you want to save the changes to Document 1?", it offers you choices of actions to take (i.e., Yes, No, Cancel, OK, Save.) Usually one of the action buttons is either framed in a darker box or surrounded by dots. As discussed in Chapter 12, the computer is presuming that this is the action you will take. You can take this action by either hitting the **Enter** or **Return** key, or moving the mouse arrow on the action key you want and clicking once.

Occasionally, an error message may appear when you are trying to sign on. Read it carefully. It could be telling you something as simple as your phone line isn't plugged into your modem or that it got a busy signal. At any rate, don't hesitate to call for technical help. Technical support is offered by every online service, so take advantage of it. If you're using a dial-up connection and you have only one phone line, the technician will have to describe the solution. He or she won't be able to walk you through the problem while you're signed on because you'll be calling from the same phone line that your computer uses when you're connected to the Internet. In this case it is especially important to write down exactly what appeared on the screen so you can tell the technician.

There are times when an error message might appear and have nothing to do with anything you've done. Be patient and try what you were doing again. Even try signing off and on again. Sometimes the computer gets a false start and needs a second try.

THE SOUND OF DIAL-UP
What is that squeaking and squealing? If you are using a dial-up connection you may hear the sound of the modem calling the online service. Find the volume control and adjust it, but remember to turn the volume back up when you get online because some websites have sounds that you won't want to miss.

Your Home Page

The first page that appears when you connect to the Internet and open your browser is your Home Page. This is the website that the manufacturer of your computer chose to have come up first when you turn on the computer. (So, if I were a betting person, I would bet it is their website.) When you choose your ISP (Internet Service Provider) it may change your Home Page to its website. In Chapter 20 I show you how to choose whatever website you would like to be your Home Page.

A REAL PAGE-TURNER

Home Page = the first page of any website on the Internet. It also refers to the page that opens when you first connect to the Internet.

Web Page = any page that follows the home page of a website.

Slowly move the mouse arrow around the Home Page. Do you notice that when it is over certain words the arrow becomes a hand? Whenever the hand appears, you are being notified that there is an item you can click on that will link you to more information on that topic. Generally, a single click will open an item on the Internet.

Feel free to open *any* and *all* areas of the Home Page. You can't get into any trouble.

A hand indicates that if you click you will get more information on that topic.

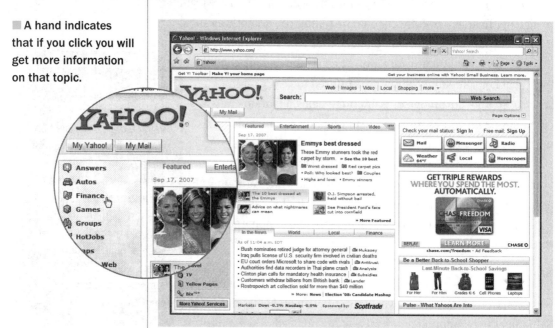

Advertisements

Most online services allow advertisements to pop up. Usually they appear when you first sign on. You do *not* want to approve any purchase by accident, but don't worry because this isn't an easy thing to do. I never even read these ads. I simply close the window or click on whatever action button indicates that I am not interested (**No**, **Exit**, **Close**, etc.). Don't click on any action button (**Yes**, **OK**, **Apply**, etc.) or hit the **Enter** or **Return** keys casually or unexpected things may happen.

Websites and Their Addresses

Y our online service connects you to the Web, and your browser (Explorer, Safari, Firefox are a few) allows you to navigate it. Before we venture out to cyberspace, let's review some basic elements of all websites. A website is much like a book. It's full of information and made up of pages. The pages of a website are called web pages.

There are several different parts to a web address. Each part gives the Internet information about how to locate the website you're seeking. Don't confuse a website address with an e-mail address. A website usually starts with www. and doesn't have the @ symbol. Here is what an e-mail address looks like:

peach@aol.com

Here is what the average web address looks like:

http://www.abbyandme.com

Now let's define the parts:

http:// is the hypertext transfer protocol. AAAAaaaarrrrgggghhh! The good thing is that you don't need to know what that means. You don't even have to type it when you're inputting a web address.

www. stands for World Wide Web. Notice there is a period after www. Some websites don't require that you type www., but I suggest that you do until none of the websites require it (so there is no confusion). You need to be very careful about typing the address exactly as it appears; a spelling or punctuation change can send you to a different website. It's just as if you dialed a wrong number on the phone. There will never be a space in a website address because that breaks the line of communication.

abbyandme. is the domain name, not unlike the user name in your e-mail address. If you wanted to create a website, you would start by purchasing a domain name.

.com is another part of the domain name. This extension gives you a clue to the type of website. In this case, "com" indicates that it is a commercial website. Note that it is

"One night I couldn't sign on to the Internet and none of the people I usually rely on for computer guidance were around. So I had no choice but to call for technical help. It wasn't fun and it took almost an hour. But we fixed the problem. I wouldn't ask for it to happen again, but if it does, I know I can handle it."
—*Evelyn*

MAXIMIZE
Remember to maximize your window whenever possible. It makes reading things on the Internet much easier and much more pleasant (refer to Chapter 11).

preceded *not* followed by a period or "dot." Here are the most common domain name extensions:

.com = commercial

.edu = educational

.gov = government

.org = nonprofit organization

.net = network business

So take a stab at what the website might be for 1600 Pennsylvania Avenue, Washington, D.C. You guessed it! *www.whitehouse.gov.*

SURFING THE NET VS. SURFING THE WEB

Essentially they are one and the same. And when you're doing either, you're on the information superhighway. (In fact, the World Wide Web is part of the Internet, but that is just a technicality.)

Look Out, Web, Here We Come

It's time to surf the net. At the top of the Home Page there is a long text box. It may or may not already have text in it. No matter. Move the mouse arrow anywhere inside the box and click once. If there was text in the box, it is now highlighted probably in blue or gray. This is where you will type in a web address. Remember, you don't need to type in http://

To access a website, you type the address in the website address box. On the next page are some examples of the website address boxes for Internet Explorer, Safari, and Firefox.

• Move the mouse arrow into the text box and click once. (If you are using a Mac, not a PC, you will need either to single-click on the small icon in the left of the address box or triple-click on the existing address.) When you start typing, the now-highlighted text will automatically be replaced with what you type.

• Type *www.cnn.com* and hit **Enter** or **Return** or move the mouse and click on **GO**.

Before your very eyes is the Home Page of the website for CNN. If it hasn't appeared yet, be patient.

A website with a lot of graphics (pictures) can take quite a while to appear on the screen. If it's taking so long that you want to throw in the towel, click on the **Stop** or **X** on the Toolbar (not to be mistaken for the Close Box in the Title Bar).

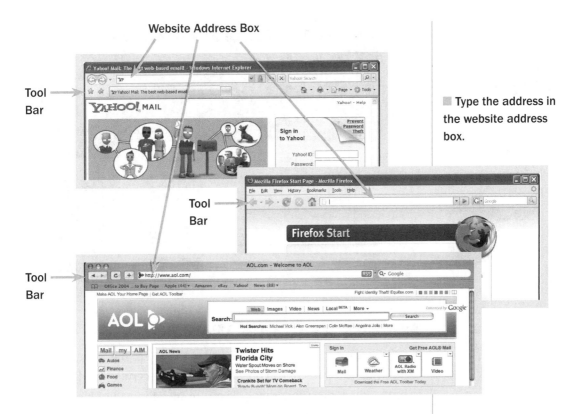

Website Address Box

Tool Bar

Tool Bar

Tool Bar

■ Type the address in the website address box.

Want to do something fun? Let's access my website.

• Move the mouse arrow into the text box and click once.

• Type: *www.abbyandme.com* and hit **Enter** or **Return** or click on **GO**.

Welcome to my website. Make yourself at home. Click on anything that tickles your fancy. I want you to feel that my website is a safe and comfortable place for you to return to whenever you feel like it. It may be the only website that you go to for a while. That is perfectly fine. Take your time to get acquainted with this site and all it has to offer. Before you know it, you'll be skillfully zooming around the Internet.

If you return over time you'll notice that the information in abbyandme.com changes and is updated. Websites need to be movable feasts; why else would you go back for a second visit?

There is a list of recommended websites on page 380. Check it out and visit any of the sites that interest you.

HOME PAGE

The term **Home Page** is used both for the first page of any website and the first page that opens for you when you connect to the Internet. Don't ask me why they didn't choose two different terms, but they didn't. I don't even know who "they" are, but sometimes I'd like to give "them" a piece of my mind!

■ The home page of my website.

CLICK AND GO

1. Click inside website address box.
2. Type *abbyandme.com.*
3. Hit Enter or Return key.

Moving Around a Website

Open up one of the websites listed at the end of the book. Look carefully at the website you opened. Notice that certain words may be in brighter colors or underlined. They are specifically designed that way to get your attention. Remember, when the mouse arrow becomes a hand, it indicates there is more to be found if you click on those words.

The words or images that you can click on are called links. They link you to more information or sometimes to another website on the same topic. On my website, you'll find that each page is designed to have links to specific categories of websites (travel, finance, etc.). Once you've clicked on one of these links, you will be taken to a different website. Those sites, in turn, may offer links to others. It just goes on and on and on. Play around with my website or others as much as you want, and then come back to the book.

Some websites have so much text it can be dizzying. Take your time. Don't feel obliged to read everything. Also don't feel obliged to stick to a website that doesn't appeal to you. That's what surfing the net is all about—riding the wave of your choice.

WANDERLUST

It may be your personality to meander along without a destination. This is usually not fulfilling on the Internet. Have a website you want to visit or a topic you want to research in mind. Otherwise, you may find yourself spending a lot of time going nowhere.

Come Back Again and Again

When you read a book and you want to return to a page to continue reading, you simply stick a bookmark in that page. The same is true on the Internet. If there's a website you'll want to visit often, you can bookmark it so you won't have to type in the web address every time you want to go there. Each online service or browser has a slightly different way to bookmark a website. Usually there is an icon in the tool bar or in a pull-down menu. (See below for examples.)

When you want to open a website that you have bookmarked, you simply click on your **Favorites** or **Bookmark** icon to reveal the websites you've stored. Then click on the website you want to access, and your online service will take you directly there.

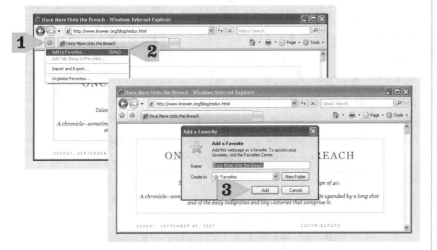

CLICK AND GO

1. Click Bookmarks/ Favorites.

2. Click Add Bookmarks/Add to Favorites.

3. Click Add or OK to accept Bookmark or Favorite.

■ Click on Favorites or Bookmarks to save website addresses for future visits.

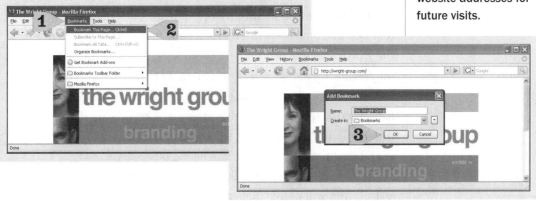

Huh? What Happened?

Strange things do happen. Sometimes after typing in a web address to access a web page, you might receive an error message. First, make sure you typed the web address correctly. If there is no mistake in the address, the error might have nothing to do with you. Perhaps the website is no longer active, or it's under construction or being updated, or the online service is experiencing difficulties. Give it another try or go somewhere else and come back and try later.

Search Engines: Seek and Ye Shall Find

A search engine is a website that finds information for you on the Internet. Think of search engines as competing libraries, each with slightly different archives and filing systems. When I found the Jack Russell terrier doormat and the theater tickets for Mom, I used a search engine. Many search engines are available. Your browser probably has a search engine box on one of its toolbars. Because each search engine has a different library, you may find different information on different search engines. See "Some Recommended Websites" at the back of the book for a list of different search engines.

To see a search engine in action, we're going to visit one of my favorites—Google.

• Move the mouse arrow inside the website address box at the top of the screen and click to activate the box.

• Type in *www.google.com* and hit **Enter** or **Return**, or click on **GO**.

• When the Google Home Page appears, click inside the search text box and type the word *recipes*. Now move the mouse arrow to the words "Google Search" and click. A page will appear with the first ten results of your search. Your search word or words, in this case "recipes," appears in bold in the link (the blue title of the result), the sample contents, and the web address. The results are in a particular order with the most popular sites at the top of the list.Whichever search engine you use, these will be the basic steps.

• Remember to use the Scroll Bar to view all of the results of your search. You will notice that each search result has a title in blue that is

CLICK AND GO

1. Click inside website address box.

2. Type *www.google.com*. Hit the Enter/Return key.

3. Click inside text box to activate. Type the word *recipes*.

4. Click Google Search.

■ When using the Google Search engine, you must click in the search text box before typing in your desired search. Now type the keywords for your search and click on Google Search below the text box.

underlined. Move the mouse onto the blue underlined title of any of the results that you want to see, and click. This will bring you to a website that pertains to your search. If it isn't what you want, use the back arrow (top left of the screen) to return to the original results of your search.

When you type in your search, be very specific. Search engines sort the results by the percentage of how it fulfills your search, but you may still find there's a lot to weed through. Sometimes it helps to

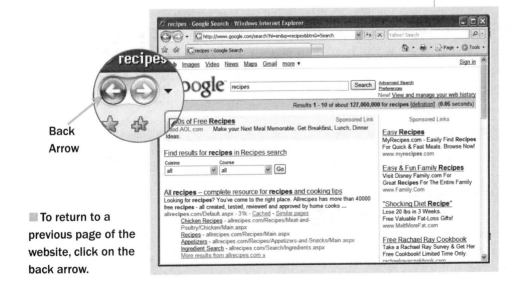

Back Arrow

■ To return to a previous page of the website, click on the back arrow.

put the request in quotes. This instructs the search engine to look for websites that contain all the words in the order you typed them, not any order. Each search engine also has categories listed on its Home Page. You might want to take a peek at these before you look further. We delve deeper into search engines in Chapter 21. You can either skip ahead or stick with me and we'll get there soon enough.

Print for Your Scrapbook

For those times when you want to have the information from a website to read later or perhaps to pass on to someone else, you can always use your printer to print what appears on your computer screen.

You can either click on the **Printer** icon at the top of your screen or click on the down arrow to the right of it, or you may have to click on the word **File** (it depends on which browser you are using) and then move the mouse arrow down to the word **Print** and click. When the Printer window opens, hit the **Enter** or **Return** key on the keyboard or click on **Print** or **OK**. It's as simple as that. But don't be

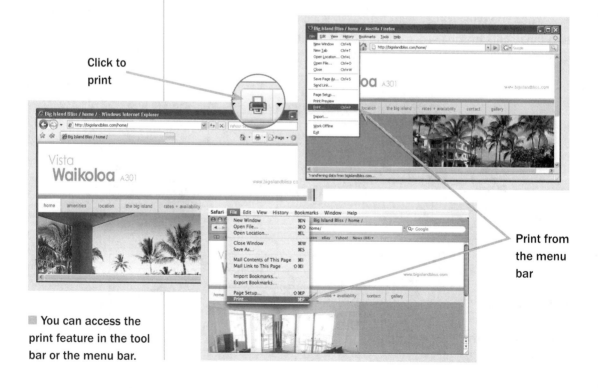

Click to print

Print from the menu bar

You can access the print feature in the tool bar or the menu bar.

surprised if certain parts of the screen do not print out properly. That happens on some websites and not on others.

If the page didn't print at all, check that the printer is turned on and plugged into the computer. You may have to click once on the web page that you want to print. Move the mouse arrow to a blank area on the web page and click. This signals the printer that this is the page you want to print. Then go back and try to print again.

Wi-Fi: Whys and Why Nots

Wireless technology allows your computer to communicate with the mouse, keyboard, printer, and even the Internet, wirelessly without cords and cables mucking up the room where you use the computer. A wireless setup in your home also allows you to have a network so other family members or houseguests can be online when you are with no interference between the computers. And, you can share a printer or scanner wirelessly.

Wireless technology isn't limited to your home. Do you remember when a hot spot was somewhere you wouldn't take a person under the age of eighteen? "Hot spots" are now also public areas where you connect your computer wirelessly to the Internet. With wi-fi technology you can bring your laptop to a coffee shop, the airport, or to the mall, and, if there's a signal, you can connect to the information superhighway.

It's all amazing technology, but unfortunately wireless connectivity increases your vulnerability to someone sneaking into

Some people would rather not see wires and cables on their desk. You can connect to your printer, mouse, and keyboard wirelessly.

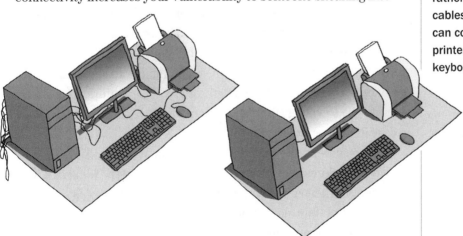

your computer. When you're on a cell phone instead of a land line, your conversation is sent through the air rather than traveling through phone cables. The uncomfortable truth is that someone with the smarts and inclination can easily intercept your cell phone conversation. The same is true when you are on your computer wirelessly. The data being transmitted to and from the Internet is vulnerable to being detected and intercepted.

I don't want to take all the fun out of wi-fi, but if you choose to partake in this incredible technology, I want you to be as safe as possible.

Be sure that during the setup of your wireless network that standard security precautions are taken. Ask whoever is helping you if WPA (wi-fi protected access) and WEP (wired equivalent privacy) are activated. Both of these aid in the prevention of uninvited people piggybacking on your wireless signal or viewing any of the contents of your computer.

On the Road

Here are some measures to help you safely enjoy wi-fi when you're traveling with your laptop.

• Check that your firewall is activated (page 217). A firewall protects you from an intruder viewing the contents of your computer. Keep in mind, however, that a firewall doesn't protect against someone seeing what you send to the Internet wirelessly.

• Delete any cookies (page 226) before you hit the road because they may contain password or credit card information that can be seen if someone gains access to your computer.

• Remove any documents from your computer that contain passwords, Social Security numbers, or credit card information. You shouldn't be traveling with that information on your computer anyway in case it's lost or stolen.

• If you access a website requiring a login or password, be sure the website address begins with **https** instead of **http**. Think of it as **s** for security. When you see https, it indicates the web page is encrypted for safer transmission.

• Avoid banking online when utilizing a wireless hot spot.

I apologize if that wi-fi jargon (WPA, WEP, firewall, cookie, etc.) was a bit overwhelming. My intention is to let you know the benefits of wi-fi, along with some cautionary advice. Chapter 16 will help your computer experience be as safe as it can be. When you feel like your head is swimming in unfamiliar terms, it's time to step back and take a break.

What Did You Do Before the Internet?

Surfing the net can get addictive. There's so much out there, and one site can lead to the next, but now and again you should sign off and do something else for a while. Seriously, a lot of time can pass while zooming around the Web. Keep track of how long you're on. I set my kitchen timer for 40 minutes to make me aware of how long I have been online. Then I take a break, reset the timer, and continue my surfing. The point of the Internet is not to put you into a trance but to give you access to things you would otherwise not have available. Enjoy it, but don't let it take over your life.

Q: How do I get back to my Home Page?

A: There's a shortcut on your browser that allows you to return quickly to your Home Page without having to go to your Favorites or type in the website address. In Explorer, Safari, and Firefox, you will see an icon in the Toolbar that resembles a house . Click on the house and your Home Page will appear.

Q: How can I stay online to go from one site to another and not close the Internet and sign on again?

A: I see people new to the Internet do what you describe all the time. You don't close the Internet or the window you are viewing to access another website. Instead, you just click in the website address box and type the address of the new website you want to visit. Hit the **Enter/Return** key on the keyboard to open that website.

Q: **Why does it take so long for the Internet to open when I double-click on Internet Explorer?**

A: First, think about whether it has always taken a long time or if this is a new issue. The answer may determine the cause. Without knowing your answer I would say, if you use a dial-up, connecting to the Internet can take a very long time. Alternatively, the Home Page you have chosen may always take a long time to open. Maybe you should change your Home Page. If none of that works—or if this is an issue that has come up suddenly—you might want to get someone in to look at your computer to see if it needs some fine tuning.

Q: **Where can I find information about children safely using the Internet?**

A: There is a lot of very justified concern about how to keep children safe when they access the Internet. If you're going to invite your children or grandchildren to use your computer, please sit them down and explain the dangers of meeting someone over the Internet. They should never give anyone their full name, home address, or phone number. You can also call the National Center for Missing and Exploited Children (1-800-843-5678) to receive the brochure "Child Safety on the Information Highway."

Homework Assignment

We will send e-mail in the next chapter, so ask your family and friends for their e-mail addresses.

CHAPTER 14

Shall We Dance?

Let's send e-mail

"Neither rain nor sleet nor gloom of night shall keep the carriers from their appointed rounds."

No matter how romantic that sounds, mail delivery via the postal service often lives up to its new name: "snail mail." Not only does e-mail (electronic mail) arrive anywhere in the world within the blink of an eye, but you can also send as many e-mails as you want, and it's included in the cost of your Internet connection. Pretty impressive.

An e-mail you write to your daughter goes on quite a journey before it arrives on her computer screen, and yet amazingly it all happens in seconds. Here's how it works:

You write the e-mail and send it to your daughter. Your e-mail service routes the e-mail to a central brain for the Internet. That brain reads the e-mail address and routes it to your daughter's e-mail service. Her e-mail service holds it until she signs on. When your daughter signs on, any e-mail sent to her (including yours) will arrive in her mailbox, referred to as the "Inbox." She then reads the e-mail, replies to you, and the cycle continues.

Again, recipients do not have to be home or have their computer on for you to send them e-mail. Their e-mail service keeps it until they sign on.

"Letter writing had become a lost art form. I missed it. Now with e-mail I am writing more and loving it!"
—Alida

If you've chosen to skip over Chapter 13 and come straight here to send an e-mail, please go back and read the previous chapter. It is full of helpful information for you to use while on the Internet.

If you didn't sign onto an e-mail account with your Internet Service Provider, you'll want to establish an e-mail account now. There are free web-based e-mail services. That means you can get on any computer in the world that is connected to the Internet and access e-mail from these sites. The three I would look into are yahoo.com, gmail.com, and hotmail.com. When you visit the website, click on the words "sign up" and fill out the necessary form to open an e-mail account. (Revisit page 170 for advice about how to choose a user name for your e-mail address.) Again, don't hesitate to ask a friend or relative to help you, if you want someone by your side through the process.

The E-mail Address

Your e-mail address is your user name (what you sign on with) plus the e-mail service address. For example, if Brendan is my user name and Yahoo is the e-mail service, then my e-mail address is Brendan@yahoo.com

Brendan is the user name.

@ means "at."

yahoo.com is the domain name or mailing address. It could have been aol.com, hotmail.com, gmail.com, or whatever entity handles my e-mail.

When people tell you their e-mail address, repeat it back to them. Better yet, get them to write it down. One error in letter, number, or punctuation and your e-mail could be sent to someone else. Be sure not to type in *Brendanatyahoo.com*. "At" is represented by holding down the **Shift** key and depressing the **2** key—**@** will then appear; "dot" is another way to say "period."

Time to Send a Missive

Sign on to your e-mail service. When you've connected to your e-mail provider, look around for what you click on to write an

e-mail. You should have options along the lines of **Compose**,
Create, **New**, or **Write**. Click on whichever you have. Each
service is different, but they all have someplace to click to
generate an e-mail template.

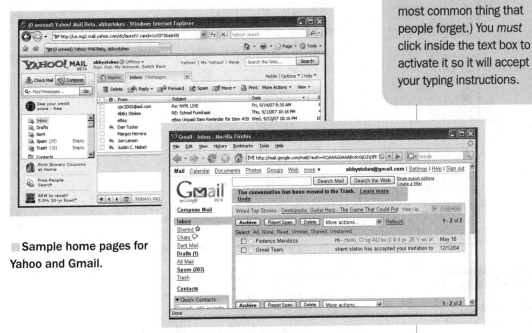

■ **Sample home pages for Yahoo and Gmail.**

An e-mail form is now on your screen, ready and waiting to be filled
in. It should look something like the template on the following page.

Compose Button

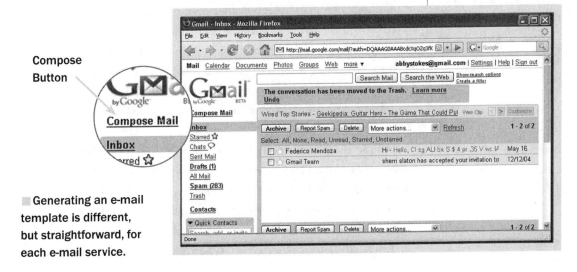

■ **Generating an e-mail template is different, but straightforward, for each e-mail service.**

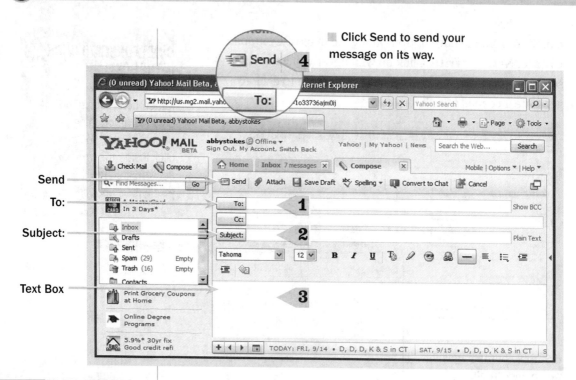

Click Send to send your message on its way.

Send

To:

Subject:

Text Box

A Yahoo e-mail template. The recipient's e-mail address is typed in the "To:" box and your message is typed in the large text box below it.

1. Click in To:, type recipient's e-mail address.

2. Click in Subject, type subject.

3. Click in Text Box, type missive.

4. Click on Send.

You're going to send your first e-mail to yourself. Again, each e-mail service is slightly different, but here are the basic steps:

• There should be a flashing vertical line (referred to as the cursor or blinking cursor) in the left corner of the **To:** text box. If there isn't, move the mouse arrow into that box and click once.

• Type the recipient's e-mail address in the **To:** box. (In this case, because you are sending it to yourself, type in your e-mail address.) Look at it and be sure there are no mistakes. Hit **Tab** to move to the cursor to the **Subject:** box or click in the Subject box with the mouse to activate it.

• Type something in the **Subject:** box, even if it is only "Hello." Some services won't let you send an e-mail without a subject. The purpose of the subject box is to give the recipient a sense of the contents so they can prioritize which e-mails to open first.

• Now either move the mouse into the large text area and click or hit **Tab** again. This is where you'll type your message.

Before we type a message, I'll explain a couple of things. One of the big differences when you're typing on a computer as opposed to on a typewriter is that you don't need to hit **Enter** or **Return** at the end of a line. The text automatically moves, or wraps around, to the next line.

You do, however, need to use the **Return** or **Enter** key to create a new paragraph or to insert a blank line between text. (The **Tab** key is still used to indent a paragraph.)

Now we get to type a message.

- Type in whatever you would like to say. For example,

> Mirror, mirror on the wall, who is playing with the computer and having a ball?

- When you're done, move the mouse arrow onto the word **Send** or **Send Now**, and click once.

- Some e-mail services ask that you acknowledge that the e-mail was sent. If this is the case, move the mouse arrow onto the word **OK** and click.

And away it goes!

You're e-mail provider keeps a copy of your sent mail for you. If you want to see the message you sent, look for a button with the word **Sent**, **Sent Mail**, or **Outbox**.

> **TO:, CC:, AND BCC:**
>
> **To:** is where the recipient's e-mail address is typed.
> **Cc:** stands for carbon copy. It means that this e-mail is also being sent to another recipient.
> **Bcc:** is a blind carbon copy. The primary recipient won't know that you sent the e-mail to anyone you put in the Bcc:.

Oops—I Made a Mistake

If you make a mistake, you can erase your typing (from right to left) by using the **BkSp** (Backspace) or **Delete** key. (Both can usually be found on the upper right section of your keyboard next to the **+ =** key.) Depress it once for each letter that you want to erase. If you hold your finger down on the key, it will continue to move and delete until you lift your finger up. You definitely have more control when you depress and release the key with each character than when you hold the key down.

You've Got Mail!

If the service is very busy, it might take a few minutes for the e-mail to arrive, but generally it should be in your **Inbox** or mailbox almost instantaneously. There are several ways to retrieve mail, depending on which e-mail service you use.

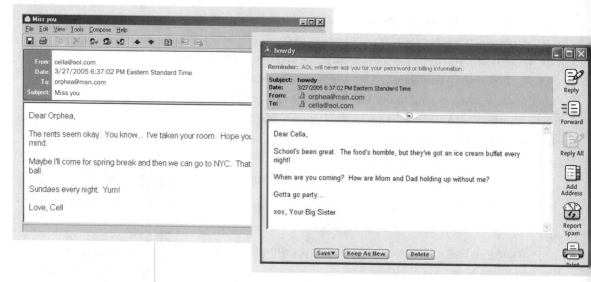

An example of e-mail correspondence.

Move the mouse arrow down to either **Read Mail**, **Get New Mail**, **Get Messages**, **Check Mail**, or **Mail**, and click. Your inbox or mailbox should appear on the screen.

Your new unread mail may be in bold or have some other indication that it hasn't been read. To open it, double-click on it or single-click on the mail to highlight it, and then click on **Read**, or single-click on either the sender's name or the subject of the e-mail received. Each e-mail service is different. Your mouse arrow changing to a hand will help lead you to where to click.

Voilà, the note you sent yourself!

Another Item for the Scrapbook

Let's print your new e-mail! Is the printer plugged in and turned on? Either click on the **Printer** icon in the Toolbar or move the mouse arrow to the word **File**, click, and then move the mouse arrow down to the word **Print** and click. When the Print window appears, hit **Enter**, **Return**, or click on **Print** or **OK**. Also be on the lookout for the words "Printer Friendly" above (or maybe to the right of) the e-mail. If you see "Printer Friendly," click there to print a copy of the e-mail. Mission accomplished!

Reply to Sender . . . Address Is Known

You cannot send an anonymous e-mail. The sender's address will always appear on the e-mail. As a matter of fact, with some services the whole routing path will appear. (That is the indecipherable code at the top or bottom of your e-mail.)

To reply to the sender (in this case, yourself), click once on **Reply**, **Reply to Sender** (this will send the return e-mail to the sender only), or **Reply to Everyone** (this will send the return e-mail to everyone who received the initial e-mail). Each service is a little different, but you'll find the reply button easily.

Reply vs. Reply All

If you got a group e-mail (i.e., you were one of multiple recipients), be extra cautious about whether you are replying exclusively to the sender or to everyone else who received the e-mail along with you. Some things are meant for only one set of eyes.

Look what happened when you hit the **Reply** button! How convenient—an e-mail is all set up with the sender's (soon to be recipient's) e-mail address in the **To:** box. Now you can take it from here. Perhaps you want to try sending another e-mail to yourself. Better yet, do you have someone else's e-mail address? If you don't have anyone's e-mail address on hand, it would be my pleasure to receive an e-mail from you. My e-mail address is abby@abbyandme.com.

Forward March

An e-mail you receive can be passed on to others. To do this, click on the button that is labeled **Forward** or **Forward Message** in the open e-mail that you received. The e-mail you got is now ready for you to forward. Click on the **To:** box and type in the e-mail address of the person you want to send it to. You can also type a message in the large text box if you want. Click on the text box and type away. When you're ready, simply click on the **Send** button to send both messages as one e-mail. But, what if you wanted to only

"I love that I can e-mail at any time. I am often awake in the middle of the night and I would never think to call my girls at that time. When it happens now, I just sit at the computer and write them an e-mail."
—*Ed*

BREAK THE CHAIN
Just as there are chain letters in snail mail, there are chain e-mails. I hate these! My retaliation for a chain e-mail that threatens bad luck unless it is sent to ten other people is to return it to the sender ten times.

send one part of the e-mail received and not the entire thing? You can. You and I will go over that and other more advanced e-mail activities in Chapter 17.

Your Little Black Book

Every e-mail service has an address book where you can store the e-mail addresses of people that you will correspond with frequently. As each e-mail service is different, I can't tell you exactly where to find your address book, but I can give you some clues . . . Does the word **Address** or **Contacts** appear in the window? If so, click on it. If not, go to the Menu Bar. Is the word **Mail** in the Menu Bar? If so, click on that and see if you might find the address book there. When the address book appears on the screen, be extremely accurate when entering e-mail addresses. The last thing you want is to store a wrong address.

Once you've put an e-mail address in the book, try sending an e-mail (you can start with mine, abby@abbyandme.com, if you don't have any others). You can either generate a new e-mail form when you have your address book open or you can open a new e-mail form and then access the address book from there. In either case, you must click on the address in the book and then click on either **To:** or **Send Mail**. Some services then ask you to click on **OK** to confirm your choice.

The real advantage of the address book is that you don't need to remember or keep typing e-mail addresses. This is handy because it's easy to make a mistake in even a short e-mail address, and just one wrong letter means your missive won't arrive.

Deleting Old Mail

Again, there are several ways to delete old mail, depending on which service you use. When e-mail is open or even just highlighted, there might be a button with an **X** on it (not to be mistaken for the Close Box) or the word **Delete**. Click on whatever your service offers as a way to throw away read mail. It is wise to delete mail you don't need, to keep things nice and tidy.

E-mail Etiquette

E-mail is generally more casual than letter writing, but for some, e-mail's code of conduct is right up there with the rules of how to behave at a wedding or which fork to use at dinner. Here are some guidelines on "netiquette." Take what you want and leave the rest behind.

1. Generally you should respond to most e-mails received, even if it's only to acknowledge that you got the message. *Unless, of course, it is an unwanted solicitation—I delete these immediately.*

2. Be selective about what you forward. Forwarding silly jokes you receive can be a bother for the recipient (ask if he or she wants them). Chances are, this isn't the first time these jokes have gone 'round the circuit.

3. DON'T SHOUT! When you type in all caps, it is the equivalent of shouting at someone.

4. Unless you use Bcc:, if you send an e-mail to multiple recipients, you're revealing the e-mail addresses of all the recipients. Some people prefer to keep their e-mail addresses under wraps. Ask before you release them into the world.

5. Be prepared to read e-mails without capital letters, a proper greeting, and creative grammar and punctuation. This is a very casual form of communication where you and others may take liberties with what Emily Post and your English teacher instructed.

6. Before you forward anything, try to clean it up by deleting all the gobbledegook that you may find at the beginning and end of the e-mail. Sometimes the list of who has seen the e-mail is longer than the message.

Again, when you join me in Chapter 17 we'll go into more detail about responsibly sending on part of an e-mail you've received.

Junk Mail

Eventually your e-mail address will get on someone's mailing list. Sad to say, even the Internet has junk mail. I delete junk mail right away. You can reply to the sender that you want to be taken off

"I love e-mail. The only thing I don't love is getting all of those silly jokes. I wish I could ask my friends to stop, but I don't want to be rude."
—*Virginia*

the mailing list, but I wouldn't hold my breath. We discuss how to manage junk mail (also called spam) in more detail in Chapter 16.

Be Adventurous

Click on and read all the different parts of your e-mail system. You know how to get yourself out of an area that doesn't appeal to you. (Hint: Close Box!)

I have complete faith in your ability to dig deep into what your e-mail service and the Internet have to offer you. You have all the tools at your disposal. Be brave and strike out on your own.

Q: Can I spell-check e-mail before sending?

A: Most e-mail services offer spell check. Look carefully at your e-mail template and see if you can't find **Check Spelling**, **Spell Check**, or ⚏ . Spell check may also appear in the Tools. Try clicking there as well.

Q: How do I cancel my Internet account?

A: The best way to cancel your account is to speak with someone on the phone. Search around your Internet provider's site for the words **Contact Us** or **Customer Service**. You should be able to find a phone number there.

Q: How can I correct an e-mail address after writing a long message?

A: Nothing you draft in an e-mail is set in stone, until you click **Send**. To correct an e-mail address, click on the existing address and make any changes you want.

Q: Once I have clicked Send can I get an e-mail I've sent back?

A: Unfortunately once you hit **Send** the e-mail is on its way to the recipient. That's why it's a good idea to move the mouse away from the word **Send** when typing an e-mail so you don't accidentally click on it.

Mind Your Ps & Qs

An introduction to word processing

M any of my students now have their lives stored on their computers. Some use word-processing software for correspondence, others are working on their memoirs, and others use it to keep track of dinner parties, birthdays, or travel plans. Even if you don't see yourself as a "writer," at some point it'll come in handy and you'll be glad to know how to use it.

Microsoft Word dominates the word-processing software market. It used to be computers came with Microsoft Word preinstalled. Now you must buy the software either through a trial version (which lasts 30 days before you are required to give it up or pay) or when you buy the computer. If you choose the latter, the store may be willing to install it before you bring the computer home. All computers come with either Note Pad, Word Pad, or Text Edit, which are pared-down versions of word processing software but will not ultimately serve your needs if you are doing anything more than simple note taking.

"Software suites" are integrated software programs that combine word processing, spreadsheets, a database, and graphics and/or communication options. Leading the market are Microsoft Office, Microsoft Works, and

PerfectWorks. If you think that you won't be doing a great deal more than word processing, there's no need to spend the extra money for a software suite. Stick with basic word-processing software.

Even if you're not planning on doing a lot of writing, some of the editing tips in the chapter will come in handy when you're writing an e-mail. So take frequent breaks, but do complete the chapter.

Meeting Your Word-Processing Program

Word-processing software is used to write letters, make lists, and do whatever else a typewriter was used for in the past. We're going to open your word-processing program, create a document, and then play around with the options available to you.

Owing to its ubiquitousness, I am talking about Microsoft Word here. Most other word-processing software is similar. Do your best to follow along.

Look at your desktop. Is there an icon for Microsoft Word? If so, double-click on the icon.

If not and you are using a PC, click on **Start** (bottom left) or , then up to **Programs**. A large menu opened for you. Move your mouse onto **Microsoft Office** or **Word** and click.

If there was no icon on the desktop and you are using a Mac, double-click on the **Hard Drive** (top right), then double-click on the **Applications** folder, then double-click on the **Microsoft Office** or **Word** folder. Once you see the **Microsoft Word** icon, double-click on that.

If you don't see an option for Microsoft Word (or perhaps WordPerfect), it may be that you don't have any word-processing software on your computer. That means you will need to purchase the software and install it. Don't hesitate to ask someone to help with this.

Starting from Scratch

Now we have a blank slate in front of us. Let's see what the Menu Bar and Toolbar have to offer, and then we'll work with an actual document.

USE THE TUTORIAL

A tutorial or tour will be included with your word-processing software. It may appear when you first open the software program or you can access it by clicking on the word Help. The tutorial will help you find your way around the program. Take the time to read the introduction it provides.

Make Word 2007 Look More Familiar

For those of you who already own a computer and have now purchased Microsoft Word 2007, the format of the program has changed from past versions. (Those of you who are new to Microsoft Word can skip this box entirely.) Take the following steps to customize it to be less confusing to view:

1. Click on the ⊟ **Customize Quick Access** Toolbar.
2. Click on **Minimize the Ribbon** (bottom of list).
3. Reclick on the ⊟ **Customize Quick Access** Toolbar.
4. Click on **New**; then repeat step 3.
5. Click on **Open**; then repeat step 3.
6. Click on **Quick Print**; then repeat step 3.
7. Click on **Print Preview**; then repeat step 3.
8. Click on **Spelling** and **Grammar**.

If you've ever used past versions of Microsoft Word, this will at least include some familiar and common items at the top of the window.

Also the symbol ⊟ brings you to most of the items found in **File** in your earlier version of Word. **Home** is where you will find most of your formatting. **Insert** remains very much the same as it was in Word 2003 and before. **Page Layout** includes some actions previously seen in **Format**. **Review** is where you will find most items that used to be in **Tools**. In other words, take a tour of the program and see where the common tasks you performed in previous versions of Word can be found.

Move the mouse arrow onto the word **File** on the Menu Bar and click. Read the commands available in this box. You may not know what each of these many instructions refer to, but it's valuable to be familiar with what's available. When the time comes that you need one of the tasks offered in the menu bar, a bell may ring in your head that you saw it listed when you first got to know the software. (I don't expect you to remember where you saw it, just that it exists.) Do the

A Microsoft Word window contains a Menu Bar and Toolbar. These will be used to edit, format, and print documents.

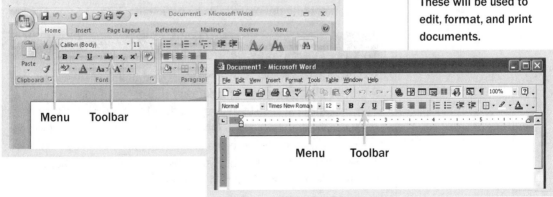

Menu   Toolbar

Menu   Toolbar

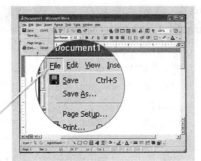

Click File to see what the File menu offers.

■ The File menu allows you to save your document, alter the page layout, and print, among other features. The icons in the Toolbar are shortcuts to items in the Menu Bar.

same for each word in the Menu Bar. Click on the word and read what is contained in the box below.

Now slowly move the mouse arrow over the icons in the Toolbar. As the mouse rests on each icon, a small box or bubble, as it can be referred to, may appear that describes the task associated with that icon. Almost every task in the Menu Bar can also be accomplished with an icon in the Toolbar. This allows you to take an action through a text format (the Menu Bar) or through a graphic format (the Toolbar). Go with whatever suits you. I switch between the Menu and Toolbar randomly.

Nice to Meet You

Let's try creating a new document:

• Move the mouse arrow onto the ☐ **New** (document) icon and click. Or you can move the arrow up to the word **File**, click, and move down to the word **New** or **New Blank Document** and click. A fresh clean page will now present itself. Type the word *Hi*.

• The next thing we're going to do is name the document. In the Title Bar the name of your software package appears, and next to it are the words Document 1 (or possibly Document 2). Keep your eye on the Title Bar. After we rename this document, the new name will appear there.

• Move the mouse arrow up to the word **File**, click, and move it down to the words **Save As** and click. A window will appear where you can rename the document. (Take notice of where the window

Oops—I Made a Mistake

If you make a mistake, you can erase your typing (from right to left) by using the **BkSp** (Backspace) or **Delete** key. (Either can usually be found on the upper right section of your keyboard next to the **+ =** key.) Depress it once for each letter that you want to erase. If you hold your finger down on the key, it will continue to move and delete until you lift your finger up. You definitely have more control when you depress and release the key with each character than when you hold the key down.

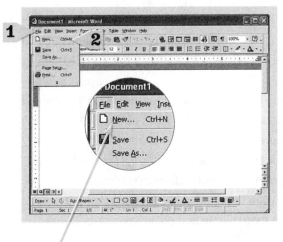

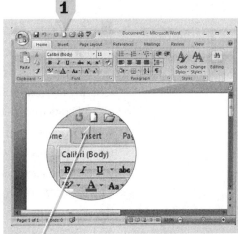

New   New Document icon

says it will save the document. My bet is it says "My Documents" to the right of Save. It's important to notice the location so we can go find your document at a later date.)

• Type the word *Smile*, and hit **Enter**, **Return**, or click on the **Save** button. The Title Bar has now changed to reflect the new name of the document. Nicely done.

It's always best to name the document right at the beginning. If you get distracted or exit the program quickly and forget to name the document, you'll be stuck sifting through a bunch of Documents 1, 2, 3, and so on. It's easier to sort through documents whose names give a clue as to what they contain rather than a generic name.

CLICK AND GO

1. Click on File in the menu bar.
2. Click on New.
   or
1. Click on New Document icon in the toolbar.

CLICK AND GO

1. Click File.
2. Click Save As.
3. Type *Smile*.
4. Click on Save.

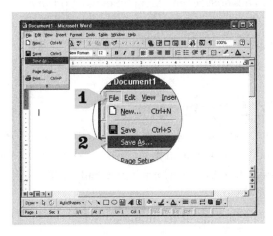

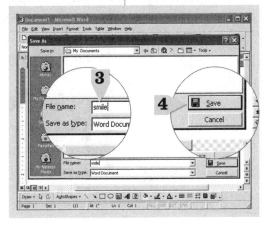

See You Soon

I want you now to close the document that you renamed "Smile." I'm having you do this so that you experience what it's like to open an existing document.

• Close the document by using the **Close Box** ⊠. On some word-processing programs there are two sets of Close Boxes. You'll have to be careful where you place the mouse arrow. The bottom ⊠ (in the Menu Bar) is for the document; the top ⊠ (in the Title Bar) is for the software program itself. Don't close the software, but do close the document. Or, you can move the mouse to the word **File**, click, and move down to the word **Close** and click. Poof! Your "Smile" document is stored.

Welcome Back

To open your "smile" document back up, do the following:

• Move the mouse arrow onto the 📂 **Open** icon and click. Or move the arrow to the word **File**, click and move it down to the word **Open** and click again.

• Now you need to double-click on the document titled "Smile." If the double-clicking still proves troublesome, you can single-click on "Smile" and then hit the **Enter** or **Return** key or click **Open**. Your "Smile" document should appear.

• Another way to open your document with some programs is to move the mouse arrow to the word **File**, click and move down to the bottom of the file box. The most recent documents that you've worked on may be listed here. Click once on "Smile," and it will open on the screen. If you want to try this technique, you can close the "Smile" document and reopen it this way.

Let's Get Typing

Open your "Smile" document if it isn't already on the screen. You will see a flashing vertical line in the left corner of the window. This is called the **cursor**. It indicates where typing will begin.

• Please type the following:

My summer vacation

Make sure that the M is in uppercase. To do this, use the **Shift** key.

• Notice that when the mouse arrow is in the text box, it changes to an I-beam (vertical cursor—see What It Means, page 109) instead of the arrow; this makes it easier to position between characters. Now insert the word "hot" before the word "summer" by moving the mouse just before the "s" of "summer" and clicking once. The cursor is now before the "s" of "summer." Another way to change the location of the cursor is to use the arrow keys beside the right **Shift** key.

• Once the cursor is properly positioned, type the word "hot." Did you notice that "summer" wasn't typed over but instead moved to the right to accommodate the new letters? (If this is not the case, depress and release the **Insert** key located on the top right of the keyboard.)

Now your screen should read:

My hot summer vacation

Save Me!

As I mentioned earlier in the book, it's very important that you regularly save the document you're working on. If the computer shuts off unexpectedly, the "Smile" document would exist, but the new text that we just typed would be lost.

• Move the mouse arrow onto the word **File**, click and move the arrow down to the word **Save** and click, or click on the **Save** icon ▣ in the Toolbar. Such an important task and such an easy thing to execute.

Now we're going to move on to some editing tools. This is where the computer proves much more efficient than a typewriter. If you made a mistake with a typewriter or changed your mind about how you wanted your document to look, you would have no choice but to retype it. Not with a computer; it allows you to edit within the document before you print it out.

EVERYTHING IS IN CAPS. WHY?

Beware. Above the Shift key is the **Caps Lock** key. If your finger accidentally depresses **Caps Lock**, you will need to depress it again to deactivate it. For example, I HIT THE CAPS LOCK KEY AND EVERYTHING IS IN UPPERCASE. i just hit it again and everything is in lowercase.

The word "hot" is now highlighted. This means the computer is waiting for your instructions for what to do with the word "hot."

What if you decided that you wanted to move the first paragraph of a letter to the end of the letter? This would be accomplished by "cutting" the text from where it is and "pasting" it to a different location. Follow along and you'll see what I mean.

• Move the cursor to the left of the word "hot." Do this with the mouse (remember to click) or with the arrow keys. Before the text can be altered, you must inform the computer of what text you want to change. This is accomplished by highlighting the text.

You can highlight the word "hot" several different ways:

Option 1. Click and drag the mouse arrow over the word "hot" and then release the mouse button. (This is tricky at first, but it becomes easier with practice.)

Option 2. Set the cursor at the start of the word "hot," depress the **Shift** key (on the left side of your keyboard), and hold it down. While the **Shift** is held down, use the **arrow keys** (on the right side of the keyboard) to move across the word.

Option 3. Move the mouse to the center of the word and double-click.

Using one of these methods, the word should now be highlighted. Of the three options, number 2 is the easiest to execute, but try them all and see which you prefer. You can highlight a single word, several words, or entire paragraphs and pages. Whatever you highlight will take on the changes that you instruct the computer to perform.

IF YOU GOOF

If you goofed when you tried to highlight, fear not. Simply move the mouse to a blank spot in the text box and click once—that will undo any highlighting. Go back and try again.

You Must Cut Before You Paste

Now that you have highlighted the word "hot," you are able to either cut and paste text or copy and paste text.

• Move the mouse arrow to the word **Edit** in the Menu Bar (if you have Word 2007, click on **Home**), click, and then move it down to the word **Cut** and click. Right now the word "hot" has disappeared because the computer is storing the word until you tell it where to paste it. Now comes the paste!

• Move the cursor one space after the "n" of "vacation" by clicking the mouse after the "n" and then using the space bar.

• Move the mouse arrow to the word **Edit** and click.

• Then move it down to the word **Paste** and click. The word "hot" will now reappear after the word "vacation."

Instead of using the Menu Bar, you could have accomplished all of that with the icons in the Toolbar. ✂ is the icon for **Cut** and ▣ is the icon for **Paste**. Try cutting and pasting again using the icons instead.

NOW SHE TELLS ME ...
There are a few shortcuts to highlighting:
• If you click once, this is where the cursor will be positioned in the text.
• If you click twice on a word, the word will become highlighted.
• If you click three times on a word, the line or paragraph that contains the word will be highlighted.

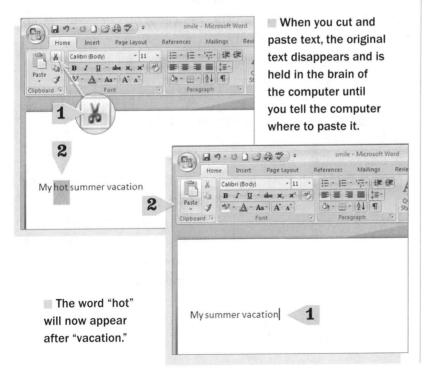

▣ When you cut and paste text, the original text disappears and is held in the brain of the computer until you tell the computer where to paste it.

▣ The word "hot" will now appear after "vacation."

CLICK AND GO

1. Click cut ✂.

2. The word "hot" has disappeared.

CLICK AND GO

1. Click after "n."

2. Click paste ▣.

Copy That

Instead of cutting the text and pasting it, you might want to repeat a section of your document in another location. This is accomplished by copying and pasting the selected text.

Let's try to copy and paste:

• Go back to highlighting Options 1 through 3, pick one of the techniques, and highlight the entire sentence. If you choose number 3 it takes a little practice, but place the cursor in the middle of the sentence and click the mouse three times in rapid succession. Double-click highlights a word—triple-click highlights the whole line.

• Move the mouse arrow to the word **Edit** in the **Menu Bar**, click, and then move it down to the word **Copy** and click. The sentence is still on the screen, but the computer has a copy of it stored until you tell it where you want it pasted.

• Place the cursor at the end of the sentence and hit **Enter** or **Return**.

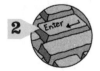

• Move the mouse to the word **Edit** and click.

• Then move down to the word **Paste** and click.

• Repeat the three preceding actions five times. You should have a total of seven sentences on your screen. We'll use them next to show how many ways you can change the look of your text.

Copying and pasting can also be done with the icons in the Toolbar. ▣ represents **Copy**. ▣ represents **Paste**. Give it a try.

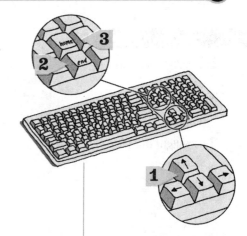

Finish Your Sentence

We're going to make this into a complete sentence.

• Place the cursor just to the left of the "h" of "hot" in the first sentence, click to activate, and type the word "was." Your screen should now read:

My hot summer vacation was hot.

• Put a period at the end of the sentence by placing the cursor after the last word and hitting the period key. Alternatively, you could get to the end of the sentence by holding down the arrow key or the **End** key on the keyboard, and then add the period.

Choices, Choices, Choices

There are so many different things that can be done to change the look of the text. All are done by highlighting text, which is a fundamental element with word processing. I'll run through a series of editing choices. Try each one now. Then come back later and repeat the process until it starts to jell.

• Using whichever option you prefer (page 204), highlight the word "My" in the first sentence. Move the mouse arrow up to the **B** **Bold** icon in the Menu Bar and click once (click on **Home** in Word 2007). The word **My** is now bold.

• Highlight the word "vacation" in the same sentence, move the mouse arrow to the *I* **Italics** icon in the Menu Bar, and click once. The word *vacation* is now in italics.

• Highlight the word "hot" in the same sentence and move the mouse arrow to the **U** **Underline** icon in the Menu Bar. The word hot is now underlined.

CLICK AND GO

1. Hit arrow keys to move the cursor.

2. Hit End to move to the end of a line.

3. Hit Home to move to the beginning of a line.

CLICK AND GO

1. Highlight "My."

2. Click on **B** for bold.

3. Highlight "vacation."

4. Click on *I* for italics.

5. Highlight "hot."

6. Click on U for underline.

1. Highlight second sentence.

2. Click on ☰ for Center.

3. Highlight third sentence.

4. Click on ☰ for Align Right.

■ Play around with your document to try out all of the many editing and formatting possibilities.

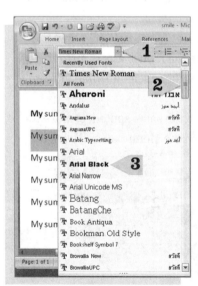

Note: You can change each word back to its original state by highlighting it and then reclicking on the icon you used to make the change.

• Using whichever method you prefer (page 204), highlight the entire second sentence. Click on the ☰ **Center** icon in the Menu Bar.

The sentence is now in the center of the page.

1. Click down arrow.

2. Use scroll bar

3. Click on desired font.

■ After you highlight text, the font can also be changed by clicking on **Format**, then **Font**.

• Highlight the entire third sentence. Click on the ☰ **Align Right** icon in the Menu Bar.

The sentence remains flush right on the page.

• Highlight the entire fourth sentence. Click on the ☰ **Align Left** icon in the Menu Bar.

The sentence is now flush left on the page.

• Highlight the entire fifth sentence. Click on the arrow Calibri (Body) ▾ to the right of **Font** in the Toolbar. This will reveal the different fonts (typefaces) available to you. Use the Scroll Bar to view the fonts. Click on whichever font appeals to you.

The sentence could look like this **My vacation was hot**, or this `My vacation was hot,` or countless other ways, depending on which font you choose to use.

• Highlight the entire sixth sentence. Click on the arrow 11 ▾ to the right of the font size box in the Menu Bar. Click on whichever size you want to see. This sentence could be My vacation was hot or My vacation was hot.

Play with the different styles and sizes of fonts. But if you've been at the computer for a long time, sit back, take a breath, and look around the room. When you've been focusing on the computer screen for a while, it's a good idea to give your eyes a break.

Repeat the exercises in this chapter as often as you can. It's only through repetition that you will become comfortable with your word-processing software.

Smarter Than the Average Bear

Your word-processing software is designed to make life easier. It even checks your spelling! Highlight the word "vacation" and retype it, spelling it "vaction." Note that when a word is highlighted and you start typing, the highlighted word disappears and the new word replaces it.

With some word-processing programs, a potentially misspelled word will have a red squiggly line under it. This is a heads-up that the word doesn't appear in the software's vocabulary list. You may also notice that some text may be underlined in green. This lets you know that the computer is questioning your grammar. Cheeky!

Let's perform a spell check on your document.

HELP

If you're ever stumped about how to do something and need help, simply move the mouse arrow onto the word **Help** in the Menu Bar and click. From there you can get all kinds of information. There may also be the option of clicking on a "?" question mark, then clicking where you need help, and the screen will show some helpful hints pertaining to what you are doing.

IMPORTANT CONCEPT
You must always let the computer know where you want it to take action (accomplished by clicking on or highlighting the area), and then you must tell the computer what action to take.

CLICK AND GO

1. Misspell "vacation" as "vaction."

2. Click on Spell Check.

3. Click change.

■ Microsoft Word (and most other word-processing programs) lets you spell check a document. Miraculous!

• Move the mouse arrow onto the ABC **Spell Check** icon in the Menu Bar and click. The spell-checker will review the document for errors. In this case it will pick up that "vaction" is not in the dictionary and it will suggest "vacation."

• Click on the word **Change** or **Replace** in the sidebar. The computer will make the change and then either continue the spell check or let you know the spell check is complete.

The computer's dictionary may not contain a word that you have typed (such as a person's name or a technical term) and will signal that it appears to be wrong and should be corrected. However, if you know it's correct and should not be changed, you would click on **Ignore** or **Skip**.

Bar Hopping

You've been alternating between using the Menu Bar (where you find File, Edit, View, etc.) and the Toolbar (where you find **B** , *I* , **U** , etc.) throughout the previous exercises. As we've seen, the Toolbar is a series of shortcuts for actions that can also be performed using the Menu Bar, but the Menu Bar usually requires more clicks of the mouse than items in the Toolbar. Use whichever bar you prefer or a combination of both—whatever suits you.

■ The Menu and Toolbars of Microsoft Word 2003.

When you're getting to know Microsoft Word, I suggest you click on every item in the Menu Bar and read each menu that drops down. You're going to find all kinds of goodies, such as page formatting, a thesaurus, and the ability to set up bullet points, to name just a few. Don't expect to remember what each menu has to offer. It's kind of like window-shopping—you can go back and look at what really appeals to you again later.

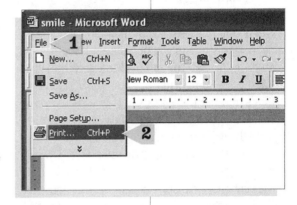

A Souvenir

The last thing we'll do in this chapter is to print your first document.

- Make sure your printer is on.
- Move the mouse arrow to the word **File** in the Menu Bar, click. and move it down to the word **Print** and click.
- There are several print options available in the Print window. You can print the current page that you're working on, all the pages of the document, or select individual or groups of pages. You can also print as many copies of the document as you want. If you want to have one copy of all the pages in your document and the print window is open, simply hit the **Enter** or the **Return** key or click on **Print**. The

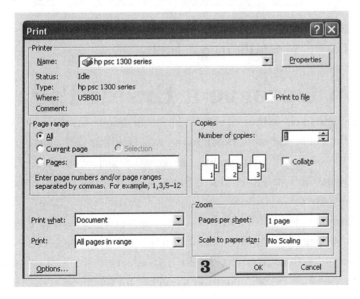

CLICK AND GO

1. Click File.

2. Click Print.

3. Click OK.

▪ The Print window allows you to choose which pages to print and the number of copies you want.

A Cautionary Tale

Here's the scenario: You've been writing for hours. So transfixed by your own words that you neglected to click **File,** then **Save** to save your work periodically. (A bad habit you must break—it's essential to save regularly.) The phone rings—it's your neighbor and she desperately needs you because her toe is stuck in the bathtub drain. (Strangely, this is not the first time you received this SOS, but that's another book.)

In your haste to attend to her, you click to close the document you've toiled over. This question is posed to you: ("Do you want to save the changes to . . .") What do you do? Hmmm . . . the right answer is stay calm, move your hands away from the computer, and read the question. If you want to save the changes, you click **Yes.** However, let's say that because you were in a rush to go to the aid of your neighbor, you clicked **No**. Tragically, all of your work you did since the last time you saved your changes is irretrievably lost. Gone. The fact is it would have

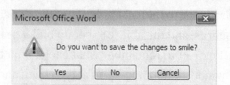

been better off to walk away from the computer and not answer the question at all, rather than to answer it without thinking it through. The option of **Cancel** would bring you back to the document, neither saving nor not saving changes. It cancels the action of you closing the document.

Here's the drill for the future: When the computer warns, notifies, or asks you about something and you don't know best how to respond, don't respond at all. If you're really flummoxed, leave the computer alone and call someone who might know the best action to take. If they aren't home, leave a message. Wait for them to call you back. The computer isn't going anywhere.

Print icon won't offer all the choices that the **Print** window does, but it is a fast way to print the entire document.

You Deserve a Break Today

I t's time to close the document. Move the mouse arrow to the word **File**, click, and move down to the word **Exit** or **Quit** and click. You will now be asked if you want to save the changes made to the document. Click on either **Yes** or **Save**. Now your document is saved on your hard drive.

These are just the basic tools that your word-processing program offers. As you work more in the program, you will get better acquainted with what else it can do. If you ever get stuck, you can try to call the software manufacturer's number for technical support. If your call isn't fruitful, ask a friend, family member, or look in the local paper for computer groups or classes.

What Can I Say?

At this juncture in the book I want you to take a break. It's been a pleasure joining you on this exciting adventure thus far. Try to get on the computer every day for at least half an hour to keep from getting rusty. There's also a lot of very helpful information in the back of this book. Be sure to give it the once-over so you know what resources are available to you. Visit my website *www.abbyandme.com* for additional guidance. If you haven't visited my website yet, please do; you can simply stop by to say "Hi," or you can check out the site that will help you get accustomed to your computer. When you're feeling at home with your computer and game for more, turn the page. I'll be waiting for you whenever you're ready.

Q: **I tried to edit a document I wrote, but when I typed, the computer kept deleting the text after where I wanted to type. What is happening?**

A: It is a simple fix for what can be a very frustrating problem. Depress and release the **Insert** key on your keyboard, and all will be remedied.

Q: **What is the Toolbar? I don't see one.**

A: At the top of every window there is a Title Bar; below it there is usually a Menu Bar and a Toolbar. If the Toolbar is missing, click on **View**, then click on **Toolbars**. Now click to the left of **Standard**. Repeat the same steps and click on **Formatting**. A check should appear by both.

Q: **Where can I get more instruction on using Microsoft Word?**

A: Unfortunately, the manufacturer does not provide a manual. You may notice the word **Help** in the Menu Bar. Help isn't always helpful, but sometime it can be. Try it. Microsoft Word doesn't typically come with a tutorial, but if your version offers one, watch it. Lots and lots of instructional books are available for purchase, but before you buy one, sit down and see if it speaks your language or that of a computer geek. If you can't understand the book, it won't help you understand the computer. Another option is to contact your local library, senior or community center, or community college to see if they offer Microsoft Word classes. Also, be brave and click on the items in the Menu Bar to see how much you can understand.

Q: My document keeps printing over and over again. Why and how do I stop it?

A: You control your computer and printer. The document is printing multiple times because you instructed the printer to do so. My guess is that when the printer didn't *immediately* spit out your document you clicked on **Print** again and, maybe, again and again. The printer is just doing what you asked it. The simplest way to stop a print job is to turn off the printer. See Chapter 25 for how to delete print jobs from the computer.

Q: Every time I print a single-page document a second blank page prints. Why?

A: If you look at the very bottom of the page you'll see a reference to how many pages your document actually is (i.e., 1/1 or 1/2—one of one, one of two). I bet your document is actually two pages, but the second page has no text on it. Click at the end of your text. Hold down the **Shift** key and the down arrow key (bottom right of keyboard). A thickish black line appeared. Release those keys and hit the **Delete** key. Save your changes. Only one page should print. Try it.

Homework Assignment

Go back over the last three chapters and repeat each of the exercises until they become second nature.

WELCOME
TO THE
NEIGHBORHOOD

CHAPTER 16

Practical Precautions

Secure your identity and your computer

Now that you've gotten your feet wet with e-mail and the Internet, I want to mention some precautions to take when venturing further on the information superhighway. As an overall guide, use the same instincts you use in your everyday life when you're on the Internet. If an e-mail you receive seems fishy, assume it is. If you're not comfortable giving your credit card information online, don't. Let your gut be the judge and caution be your guide, and all will be fine.

Settle yourself into a nice comfortable chair before you read on, and remember the scenarios below are possibilities, not probabilities. Do not be intimidated by the information; become empowered by it.

Put Up a Firewall

Before the advent of personal computers, when someone mentioned a hacker it was either someone who chopped things in to pieces or had a terrible cough. My introduction to a computer hacker was in the movie *War Games*, where Matthew Broderick plays a teenage hacker who unwittingly hacks into (i.e., gains access to) the military's computer system. In computer-speak, a hacker is a highly skilled programmer. The problem is that those skills can be used with good or bad intentions. The connotation of a hacker is usually negative and refers to someone who breaks through security codes on the computer to access otherwise protected information. Why would someone choose to hack? Some hack to gain access to a cache of credit card numbers or to gather personal data from a computer. But others hack just because they can. In the computer geek community there is a prestige to being able to break a code. Hackers don't necessarily do any damage, but they make their mark in the hackers' hall of fame.

What can you do to protect your computer from hackers? Your first line of defense is a firewall. Think of your computer's relationship to the Internet as a swinging door. It swings open when you send a request out (i.e., ask to connect to a website) and it swings open again when you receive a response to your request (i.e., you connect to the website). At both moments when the door is open, the computer is vulnerable. Uninvited guests can sneak in and view the contents of your computer or leave behind a program that may make your computer susceptible to junk mail or worse. With a firewall, these points of entry and exit are protected from intruders. (Imagine your

■ Windows Security Center. Here's where you can see the status of your computer's firewall.

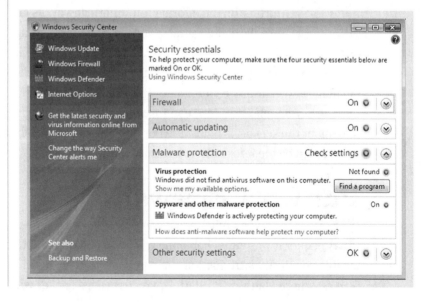

front door protected by a wall of fire.) Chances are very good that your computer came with a firewall preinstalled. Let's see if it is activated.

To check for a firewall on your computer if you have a PC:
- Click on **Start** or 🪟 in the bottom left of your screen.
- Click on **Control Panel** 🗒.
- Double-click on **Security Center** 🛡.
- If your firewall indicates that it is ON, you are protected. If it indicates that it is OFF, click on the **Windows firewall** icon 🧱 at the bottom of the screen. In the General options section, click the bullet next to the ON option to active your firewall.

To check for a firewall on your computer if you have a Mac:
- Click on in top left corner.
- Click on **System Preferences**.
- Single-click on **Sharing** 🗂.
- Click on **Firewall** tab.
- Click on **Start** to enable your firewall. Click on **Advanced** to see more options.

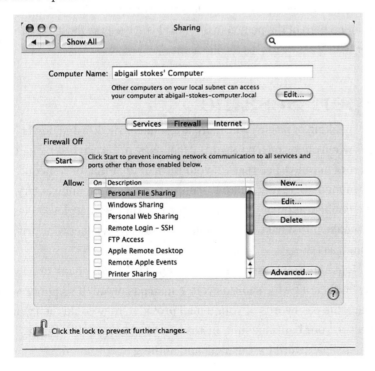

Mac Sharing window with Firewall. Here's where you can see the status of your computer's firewall.

Here you can read about firewalls and activate the one that came preinstalled on your computer. One thing to remember: If at a later date you decide to add software to your computer, the firewall may have to be turned off during the installation process to avoid interference.

Another preventive measure to take against hackers is to ask the provider of your high-speed connection to the Internet whether they offer any protection in the way of a router. A router is a device that also thwarts hackers by scrambling information needed to access your computer. If your ISP doesn't offer a router, you can purchase one on your own. If you use a dial-up to connect to the Internet, chances are your computer will be below a hacker's radar because your Internet connection will be slow.

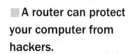

With these protections in place, it's unlikely that a trespasser will gain access to your computer but not impossible. Therefore it is wise not to store certain information on your computer. For example, do *not* have your Social Security number, bank PIN (Personal Identification Number), or any other passwords recorded on your computer. If you can't think of any place to store your password information other than your computer, at least name the document after your first pet or your childhood hero or the person in the world you trust the most—anything other than "passwords" as the file name.

■ A router can protect your computer from hackers.

Open Sesame

Speaking of passwords, there are some basic do's and don'ts when choosing a password. Most passwords can be cracked in a matter of minutes. Let's see . . . your birth date or that of someone in your immediate family, a family member's name, your anniversary, some configuration of your street address. Am I getting close? Please don't make it that easy for someone who doesn't respect your privacy as much as I do.

Most important, as I mentioned on page 171, your bank or ATM PIN should not be the same as your e-mail password. If someone were to hack the passwords of your e-mail provider, they could then gain access to your bank account. Instead, have your bank PIN be an exclusive password for the bank and nothing else.

When choosing a password for your e-mail or a website, assume the password must be at least six characters in length. It's more difficult to guess a password consisting of a combination of letters and numbers. Even better, because passwords are often case sensitive, throw in a couple of capital letters to up the ante. The trick with any of these choices, however, is *you* need to remember your password. Write down the password as soon as you choose it. Do *not* rely on your memory.

So, what to use to inspire your choice of a random sequence of letters and numbers? Think of something not in public records about yourself but that you'll never forget.

EJNJ18 = my siblings' and parents' first initials and my age when I moved out of the house.

Elephant3 = my favorite stuffed toy and the number of wisdom teeth I had removed.

7haRRiet = number of days in the week and my favorite children's book character.

Starting to get the picture?

Avoid an Identity Crisis

I dentity theft is not as attributable to computer use as we are led to believe. Most identity theft occurs the old-fashioned way—by sleight of hand. Your purse or wallet containing vital information about you is stolen. Your trash is rummaged through, revealing your credit card numbers and more. You give information over the phone to someone who sounds legitimate but is not. Here are ways you can protect yourself . . .

Guard Your Social

The key to stealing someone's identity is his or her Social Security number. You should *never* carry your Social Security number in your wallet. For some, doing so may be an old habit, but it's time to break the habit. Your full name, date of birth, and your mother's maiden name are

all public record. With a little investigation, such information can be uncovered. But your Social Security number, which is often used by financial institutions as identification, is not public record. Give your Social Security number to a thief, and identity theft becomes a cakewalk. Your Social Security number may appear on your health insurance card. If it does, contact your insurance company and have them reassign a nine-digit number that in no way resembles your Social Security number. You will not be the first person to call and ask that this be done. It is now common practice.

Keep Copies

Make a copy of the front and back of your driver's license and your credit cards. Keep the photocopies in a safe place. If your wallet is stolen this information will facilitate the calls you should make immediately to cancel your cards. File a police report. This reinforces the validity of your claim of loss to the credit card companies. Call credit-reporting organizations to place a fraud alert on your name and Social Security number.

Here are some phone numbers to get you started:

Equifax: 1-800-525-6285

Experian: 1-888-397-3742

Trans Union: 1-800-680-7289

Social Security Administration (fraud line): 1-800-269-0271

It's also a good idea to check your credit report annually to be sure you're not carrying a bad report due to fraud. Visit *www.annualcreditreport.com* for a free credit report.

Be Smart About What You Toss

When the time comes to throw away expired credit cards, always cut along the magnetic strip. The magnetic strip, when left intact, contains all the pertinent information for that credit card, making it way too easy for a thief. Then cut up the rest of the card into small pieces and distribute them overtime into different waste bins. Without sounding too paranoid, the same should be done with any correspondence revealing your credit card or Social Security numbers. Maybe this is the year to ask Santa for a paper shredder.

Mum's the Word on the Phone

What about the seemingly lovely person who calls you at home to verify information for your own protection or to enter you in a contest or to send you a promotional gift? Never, *never*, never release personal information over the phone. You have no idea who is really at the other end of the line. Have the caller give you the information to confirm, or, better yet, ask the caller to give you their number so you can call back to confirm if it is a legitimate company placing the call. You will stop them in their tracks.

None of the scenarios just described involved a computer at all, but somehow computers receive the blame for identity theft. However, be aware of dangers when surfing the net.

Whenever you want to take a break from all of this doom and gloom, do. Then come back after you've seen the silver lining on the cloud to finish up this precautionary tale.

DEFINE IT
How many times have you been stymied by a computer term? A great online computer dictionary can be found at *webopedia.com*.

Phishing Is So Very Fishy

G lad you returned. I had faith you would. Now let's learn about the world of phishing. And, no, I didn't spell that wrong. What makes phishing truly clever and deceitful is that the sender's e-mail address will read as though it came from your bank and if you click through to the website, it will be designed to look just like your bank's website.

Phishing (Webopedia Definition)

(fish´ing) (n.) The act of sending an e-mail to a user falsely claiming to be an established legitimate enterprise in an attempt to scam the user into surrendering private information that will be used for identity theft. The e-mail directs the user to visit a website where they are asked to update personal information, such as passwords and credit card, Social Security, and bank account numbers, that the legitimate organization already has. The website, however, is bogus and set up only to steal the user's information.

Here's an example of an e-mail that looks legitimate but is actually phishing.

So, what are you to do? Know that *no* bank and any other financial institution will *ever* ask you to confirm critical information through e-mail. It just isn't secure enough. Banks try their best to protect their customer's information. They know e-mail is not the place for such sensitive content.

If you think you've received a phishing e-mail you can forward it to *reportphishing@antiphishing.org*. They will review the e-mail and the links and post it on their website to warn others.

Spam—It's No Picnic

Is your home mailbox flooded with mail-order catalogs? How do you think the catalog companies got hold of your mailing address? Yup. You ordered a little something from one catalog, and that catalog in turn sold your mailing address to another and another and another. Suddenly, yours is the most popular mailbox in town.

Spam is electronic junk mail and now accounts for half of all e-mail. The proliferation of spam occurs in the same way as junk snail mail. However, with e-mail you actually have an option not offered by the U.S. Postal Service. When you create your primary e-mail address, you can also create a second e-mail identity to use when you shop online, join an online

UNSUBSCRIBE

I hesitate to even suggest that you open junk mail, but if you repeatedly get mail from certain senders you can try to unsubscribe from their lists. At the bottom of the e-mail there is sometimes an "Unsubscribe" link that you can click on. It's worth a try.

newsletter, or in any other instance where you're asked for your e-mail address by a commercial enterprise. You'll only give your primary e-mail address to friends, family, and business associates. This will significantly decrease the spam received at your primary e-mail address. For example,

janedoe@yahoo.com = address exclusively for friends and family

janedshopping@yahoo.com = address for shopping, newsletters, etc.

Beware that some spammers are so stealthy, spam can appear in your inbox with your e-mail address as the sender. Not to worry. Your e-mail address has not been hijacked. The spammers disguised their information targeting you specifically to entice you to open the e-mail. Once you've opened the e-mail and clicked through to whatever is being pitched, your e-mail address is certain to be sold to other mailing lists. Rule of thumb: If you don't recognize the sender's e-mail address (or it is suspicious) and the subject is not something very specific to you, do *not* open the e-mail. Don't let your curiosity get the better of you; there is no satisfaction found in spam. Promptly trash the e-mail.

SPAM ... A LOT?

The debate continues about the derivation of spam. It could be a tribute to the Monty Python song "Spam spam spam spam, spam spam spam spam, lovely spam, wonderful spam . . ." A nonsense word repeated over and over again with no point. Or it could be mocking the lunch meat. Spam by any other name would still be unwelcome.

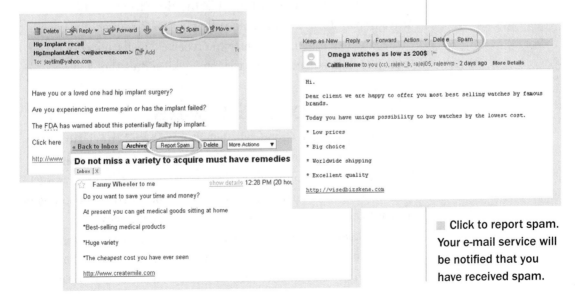

Click to report spam. Your e-mail service will be notified that you have received spam.

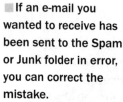

If an e-mail you wanted to receive has been sent to the Spam or Junk folder in error, you can correct the mistake.

Click to remove item from Spam or Junk folder.

Most e-mail providers now have filters to divert spam into a junk or bulk mail folder instead of your inbox. The targeted e-mail remains in the folder for a limited time until your e-mail company deletes it. Unfortunately, these filters cannot always identify what is junk and what is not. Junk mail may still make its way into your inbox, and sometimes an e-mail you wanted to receive is misdirected to the junk folder. Your e-mail service offers a method to redirect the e-mail from the Junk folder to your Inbox. Look at the Menu bar for options to **Move** or **Not Junk Mail** or some other option to redirect the e-mail to the intended folder. To be sure you receive e-mail from people you want, add their e-mail address to your e-mail address book.

Cover Your Tracks

Like Hansel and Gretel, who left a trail of bread crumbs to follow on their way back home, cookies leave a trail for a website to find its way back to information about your activities during previous visits to the site. A *cookie* is actually a file left behind on your computer by a website that you've visited. There are advantages to a website leaving cookies behind. It allows a site to personalize your Internet experience. Here's an example: You visit Amazon (*www.amazon.com*) and buy an Agatha Christie murder mystery. The next time you open

Amazon's website, the home page says, "Hello, (your name). We have recommendations for you." It's like a doorman remembering your name or a salesclerk who remembers your favorite perfume. It was a cookie placed on your computer when you bought Agatha's book that provided Amazon with this information for your next visit.

Some websites require that you register, often at no charge, to view the website in its entirety. This is true of the website of *The New York Times*. You can read the paper online for free, but you must register first. No private information is asked of you, but by registering, *The New York Times* can inform their advertisers about traffic patterns (i.e., how often in a day, a week, or a month an individual visits *www.nytimes.com*) and some demographic information that you can choose to give or not give when you register. *The New York Times* will give you a "remember me" option so you don't have to keep signing in. It's cookies that allow for this convenience.

If you choose to bank online, more often than not the ID the bank uses to identify you will be your account number. Rather than you typing your account number every time you visit the site, your bank places a cookie on your computer so your bank ID will automatically be remembered. For security purposes, your password will be required every time you visit the site, but that is as it should be.

Cookies do not allow access to any other information on your computer besides the data the website has chosen to save. No website can view another website's cookies. A cookie is all about recognizing you and your preferences or past history with a certain website.

The only threat posed by cookies is they enable an unwelcome visitor to your computer to view information now stored on your computer by the cookies. Frankly, my shopping habits aren't anything anyone wants to know about, but your cookies may contain more significant information—possibly your credit card numbers. I don't choose to allow websites to store my credit card information. If you do allow for that, the information will be stored in a cookie. If you want to delete the cookies on your computer, you can do so without harm to your computer. The only downside to cleaning out your cookies is some websites that previously recognized you won't anymore. You'll just have to introduce yourself all over again. At that

"I used to get all hung up about the names that have been given to different things on a computer like bytes, hertz, and cookies. Now I don't give it a thought and I just have fun on my computer."
—*Paul*

point a new cookie will be placed on your computer so you'll be recognized on your next visit to that website.

When you choose to delete cookies from your computer, you could access the folder they are stored in and pick and choose what to delete, but it's difficult to always recognize what website the cookie is for and what information it contains. I prefer to delete them all and reintroduce myself to websites. (Because of the possible deletion of cookies after registration to a site, I print a document with all my registration information—website, user name or ID, and password—in case I need to refer to it later.) Let's remove the cookies accumulated on your computer.

If you use Firefox to access the Internet, follow the steps below in the Click and Go to delete cookies. If you use Internet Explorer (the big blue E icon) to access the Internet, follow the steps at top right in the Click and Go to delete Cookies. If you use Safari to access the Internet, follow the steps at bottom right in the Click and Go to delete cookies.

CLICK AND GO

1. Click Tools.
2. Click Options.
3. Click Privacy.
4. Click Show Cookies.
5. Click Remove All Cookies.

Firefox

Here is how to delete cookies with Firefox.

Explorer

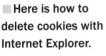
Here is how to delete cookies with Internet Explorer.

Safari

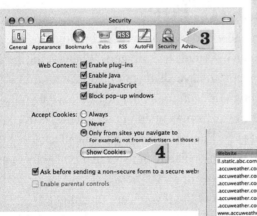

Here is how to delete cookies with Safari.

While you're in the Internet Options window of Internet Explorer there are other points of interest. Do you see to the right of **Delete Cookies** there is **Delete Files**? The files referred to are temporary files allowing a website previously visited to open up faster on your computer. Over time the contents of this folder can slow down the computer. If your computer operates more slowly than in the past, access the Internet Options window and click on **Delete Files**. Wait for the hourglass to go away before continuing on with your next computer task. You may notice things run a bit faster after you've deleted those files. Other computer housecleaning tips can be found in Chapter 25, "Troubleshooting—I Think It Has a Fever."

Below the Temporary Internet Files portion of the window you'll see History. History is where the computer stores the websites you've visited in the past. This is all well and good unless you've traveled somewhere on the Internet you'd rather not have others know about. No confessions necessary. If you don't want someone to see the websites you've visited, click on **Clear History**. This won't protect you if the Feds confiscate your computer and want to investigate past behavior, but it will prevent a curious spouse or grandchild from tracking your Internet activities.

Keep on Your Toes

Don't forget the old-fashioned techniques used by would-be thieves . . . their keen eyes and sticky fingers. When typing a password in a public place, try to have all of your fingers in motion over the keys to make it more difficult for someone to see what you actually type. Do not walk away from your computer when it is on, to protect it from curious eyes. Frankly, when in a public place I wouldn't walk away from my laptop at any time for fear that someone would steal it and make it their own.

What a terrible note to end on! But if you learn the potential pitfalls, it's easier to avoid them. There was also a lot of computer jargon to absorb in this chapter. Why not set up a tray of cookies (the edible kind) and a cooling drink for yourself and take a break before you journey to the next chapter?

Q: Is the Internet safe?

A: Yes. It is as safe as any other place you visit in the "real" world. You just have to use the same precautions and common sense when you're visiting the Internet as you would traveling someplace you've never been before.

Q: What is spyware?

A: Spyware is software installed on your computer without your consent. Spyware can monitor your computer behavior, sending that information back to advertisers, along with diverting you from a desired website to another. One way to avoid spyware is not to download (or add) any programs onto your computer without being sure of the source and certain that you need the software offered. You can install anti-spyware software on your computer. This is a topic best dealt with by asking friends or relatives in the know or a computer professional who can help install anti-spyware software and/or help remove any spyware that was found on your computer.

Q: I use a laptop computer, not a desktop. Do I need to connect wirelessly?

A: Not necessarily. You can connect to the Internet using an Ethernet cable, as you would with most desktops. (An Ethernet cable looks like a phone cable, but the cable itself is a bit fatter and the end you plug into the computer is wider.) The only advantage of a wireless connection is that you could work on your laptop anywhere in your home and be able to connect to the Internet without a cable.

Q: How will I know if someone has accessed my computer without my permission?

A: Unfortunately, you won't. It will only be after they have used that information (e.g., shopped with your credit card) that you will know. Unless they are stupid enough to change settings on your computer so it will appear different to you, but that would be like leaving their glove in your home after they've broken in. If you are suspicious that your computer has been hacked, call in a tech support person to check things out for you.

Q: **Who do I contact if I think my computer has been broken into?**

A: If you have any evidence that your credit card number(s) or your identity has been in any way jeopardized, call the police and file a report (they may want to see the computer) and call the numbers listed on page 222 in this chapter. Bring your computer to a technical support person and have them go over the computer to see what evidence of intrusion they can find. While they have your computer, be sure to have them take the necessary steps to make it as secure as possible.

CHAPTER 17

Advanced E-mail

Let's go to the next level—web links, attachments, and more

As you've discovered by now, e-mail is a wonderful way to stay in touch with family and friends. It's also an efficient means to communicate with co-workers and business associates. But surely it can't replace snail mail entirely. What if you apply for a job and your prospective employer wants a copy of your résumé? That would require the U.S. Postal Service, right? No, not really. What if you want your daughter to send pictures from your grandson's graduation? She'd have to mail them, right? Not anymore. Sit back and let me explain. But before we get into attachments, let's go over some other e-mail details you should know as you become more experienced on your computer.

E-mail Services

Web-based e-mail does not require software to be installed on your computer but instead allows you to access all of its features from a website. That means you don't have to use your own computer to get the e-mail. You could be on any computer anywhere in the world and access your e-mail. Many web-based e-mail services are free, such as Yahoo, Gmail (Google mail), and Hotmail.

Why Choose Web-based E-mail?

I strongly suggest that you don't use the e-mail provided by the company you pay to connect to the Internet. Why? If, over time, you accumulate reasons to take your business elsewhere, you may hesitate because you like the e-mail address you currently have. Better your e-mail address can be used with any company you choose to pay to connect to the Internet.

As I said in Chapter 14, your computer may have come with e-mail services already installed, such as Outlook, Entourage, or Apple Mail. Microsoft Outlook comes bundled in the Microsoft Office Suite software. Outlook offers you e-mail, a calendar, an address book, task and content management, and a journal. Entourage is the Mac version of Outlook designed by Microsoft. It also offers e-mail along with a task manager and a personal information manager that will organize your calendar, addresses, and notes, as does Apple Mail. The advantage of all these over web-based e-mail accounts is that you can access previously received or sent e-mails and write e-mail without connecting to the Internet. Your newly drafted e-mails will be held in your computer's memory until you connect to the Internet and send them.

Because free e-mail accounts are available to you, why not have more than one e-mail address, as mentioned in Chapter 16? Consider having a secondary e-mail address that you use when making purchases or when being added to a newsletter or desired mailing list. This will help prevent too much junk mail from being received in your primary e-mail account.

E-Manners

Netiquette was introduced to you back in Chapter 14, but here are some additional guidelines to keep in mind when you communicate by e-mail.

   • *Remember you are corresponding with a human being.* No matter how faceless and casual e-mail may appear, abrupt and curt e-mails are rude. I open my e-mails with "hello" or "dear . . ." I close with "best," "cheers," or maybe just my initials.

- *Less is more.* Not to contradict my previous point, but convey your message in sentences rather than paragraphs. A lot of people read e-mail at work, where time is limited, and a computer screen is no place to read a novel. If you must write a lengthy e-mail, use paragraphs to break up the text. Avoid indentation because the format of your e-mail may change through transmission. Indentations can make e-mail difficult to decipher.

- *Try to be specific in your subject line.* Unless you're writing a chatty hello, don't bother with a benign "hi" or "it's me" for a subject. Let the recipient know specifically what the e-mail is about. It allows him or her to prioritize and identify it at a later date.

- *Watch what you say.* E-mail is easily forwarded, and really remarkable ones can make the rounds all the way to the news.

- *Do not lose your cool.* Serious matters of the heart or workplace warrant one-on-one interactive audio projection dialogue (aka speaking face to face). As is possible with any writing, but especially in this abbreviated form, e-mails can be open for misinterpretation. If you're determined to send a scathing e-mail, send it to yourself first, and feel what it's like to receive your harsh words.

- *Discriminate about how and what e-mail you pass on.* Just because you received an e-mail doesn't mean the contents are true or worthy of passing on to your loved ones, acquaintances, the pharmacist, your milkman, and that lady you sat next to on the bus. A constant barrage of jokes isn't funny at all—it's irritating. If you must share an e-mail, be sure to tidy it up before you hit Send. Read "Break the Chain" on page 236 for instructions on the tidiest way to share an e-mail.

- *Include the portion of the e-mail you refer to.* If someone asks questions in an e-mail, sending them the answers alone may cause confusion. Either include their entire e-mail for reference or the specific text relating to your responses. You can use copy and paste as described on page 237 to bring chosen text from one e-mail into another.

- *Respect others' privacy.* Sometimes it is inappropriate for all the recipients of a group e-mail to be exposed to each other's

"It took me quite some time to get used to how casual e-mail is. Now I appreciate the lack of formality."
—*Grant*

E-MAIL IS NOT ANONYMOUS
E-mail can be traced to the computer where it was generated, even if you take on a false e-mail identity.

"I am so sick of getting e-mails that have obviously been forwarded several times before I was added to the heap of recipients."
—*Jimenez*

e-mail addresses. When there is no need for e-mail addresses to be revealed, use the BCC: area to input addresses instead of TO: or CC:.

• *Reread the e-mail address and message before you click on* **Send**. I've warned my students to be cautious about inputting the correct recipient for years and recently found my face red when a slightly bawdy e-mail I wrote accidentally made its way to an elderly student rather than the intended close friend. Oops. Check for typos and spelling errors as well. Most e-mail services offer spell-check capabilities.

• *If you feel like it, add expression to your words.* Utilize emoticons (page 250) to add a little levity or emotion to your e-mail.

DO THE MATH
You send the e-mail on to 10 people. Those 10 send it to 10 more = 100. Those 100 send it to 10 more = 1,000 and so on. By the time the e-mail has made the rounds only six times, it will have reached 1,000,000 people!

WARNING: If you or others you know use a work e-mail account for personal matters, beware. (Work e-mail can be identified by the company name as the suffix of the e-mail address, e.g., johndoe@westinghouse.com.) The employer owns the e-mail account and has a legal right to view all incoming and outgoing e-mail. Not only can this prove embarrassing, but it also reveals, by virtue of the volume of personal e-mail received or sent, time spent on one's private life and not work. Companies are monitoring work e-mail accounts more and more. Before you send an e-mail that is best kept private, ask if your friend or relative has a personal e-mail account. You should open a personal e-mail account for yourself, if you haven't, and stop using work e-mail for personal communications.

Break the Chain

At some point you will receive an e-mail warning of a terribly destructive virus or relating a tragic story of a child suffering from cancer or a chain letter that cautions if you *don't* send the e-mail on to ten friends bad luck will befall you, but if you *do*, good luck or even money will come your way. It is only responsible for you to send the e-mail on to loved ones who should be warned, may want to help, or are in need of luck or miraculous funds. Or is it?

What if the e-mail is a hoax? Most of these types of e-mails are designed to see how many people can be reached. Or, even more insidious, the e-mail addresses accumulated in the forwarded e-mails are culled by spammers to fill inboxes with junk mail. Before you decide to pass on this type of e-mail, check to see if it is a hoax at *www.hoaxbusters.org.*

If you deem the e-mail worthy of sending on, do not click on **Forward** and possibly forward all of the past e-mail recipients into the land of spam. Instead, copy and paste the important text into a new e-mail. While you're at it, let's not expose each recipient to the other's e-mail address. Use BCC: (for guidance, see page 238) instead of using TO: or CC: when addressing the e-mail.

• The technique of copy and paste was introduced to you on page 206 in Chapter 15. If you haven't yet used copy and paste, feel free to go back and review. With e-mail you've received there's only one way to highlight the text to be copied. You must click and drag over the text. The easiest way to accomplish this is to start at the end of the text.

• Open the e-mail that contains the text you want to copy.

• Place the mouse arrow, which probably now is the mouse I-beam, at the end of the chosen text.

• Click and hold down the mouse while you drag across the text to the left and then straight up until you reach the start of the text. (If you're using a touch pad, this may require both hands.)

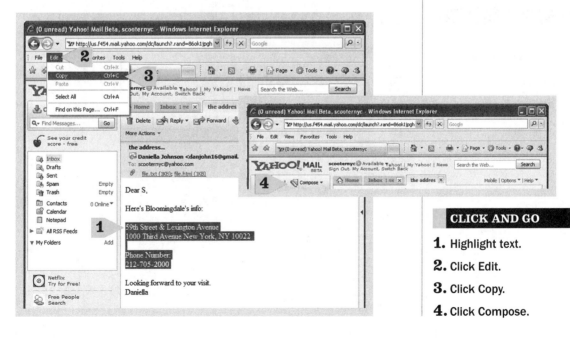

CLICK AND GO

1. Highlight text.

2. Click Edit.

3. Click Copy.

4. Click Compose.

This is a tricky operation and may take a few attempts before you get it right. Be patient. You will conquer it, I promise. If you don't succeed in highlighting the desired text, click the mouse anywhere in the window to eliminate the erroneous highlighting and try again at the end of the desired text.

- Once the text is highlighted, click on **Edit** in the Menu Bar.
- Click on **Copy**. (Most e-mail will not allow you to cut.)
- Click on either **Write** or **Compose** or **New** to open a new e-mail.
- Click inside the text area of the new e-mail where you normally type your message. A blinking line should appear.
- Click on **Edit** in the Menu Bar.
- Click on **Paste**.

Voilà! The text is now in a new e-mail with no trace of its past journeys. Well done.

Let's send this e-mail to a group without exposing the recipients to each other's e-mail addresses. Each e-mail service works slightly differently, so you may have to find where you activate BCC: instead of TO: when addressing an e-mail. You might have to click on **Add**

CLICK AND GO

1. Click in text message area.

2. Click Edit.

3. Click Paste.

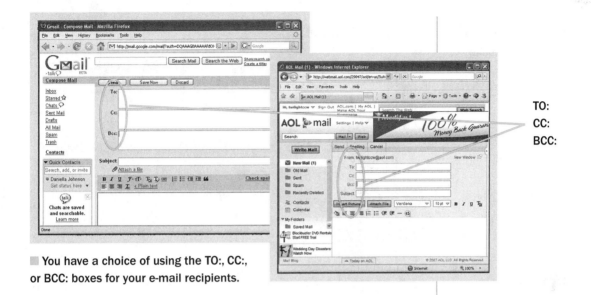

TO:
CC:
BCC:

■ **You have a choice of using the TO:, CC:, or BCC: boxes for your e-mail recipients.**

BCC: to reveal the BCC: address area. If you select recipients from your e-mail address book, you may choose the BCC: option at that time. Some e-mail services require there be at least one address in the TO: box. Why not type your e-mail address in the TO: box and then delete the e-mail when you receive it? That's also a good way to know if the e-mail went out and you won't have exposed any of your recipients' e-mail addresses to each other.

Be sure to type in a Subject so the recipients know what the e-mail is about. Off it goes!

Web Links in an E-mail

When I'm planning a trip with my mother I'll often do online research about our destination before we depart. If I come across a website that Mom will find useful, I'll send her the website address embedded in an e-mail. Because website addresses can get very long and gibberishy, I certainly don't want to have to trust myself to retype it all. Instead I can copy and paste it into the e-mail.

Try it yourself. Before going through the specific steps to embed the web link (copy and paste a web address into an

TAKE YOUR TIME

When you rent a car, the car initially appears unfamiliar and perhaps even a little intimidating. After you relax a bit you begin to identify the location of the blinker, the emergency brake, and so on. The rental car isn't really very different than the one in the garage at home. At some point, your e-mail service will update or redesign their website. This should not be a crippling event. Don't let it throw you off. Instead, take your time to get to know the "new look."

1. Click on website address box to highlight.

2. Click Edit.

3. Click Copy.

4. Minimize the window.

5. Click on e-mail window.

6. Click in text area.

7. Click on Edit.

8. Click on Paste.

WHY DO WEBSITE ADDRESSES APPEAR AS GIBBERISH?

Once you have typed in a website address you may notice that with each page of the site that you look at, the address gets longer and more confusing. That's because it is actually all coding that identifies the website and the specific page you're on. You don't have to type or remember the long addresses, just the basic web address you used to access the site.

e-mail), open up your e-mail account and have a blank e-mail waiting for the link. Shrink your e-mail account by clicking on the ▣ **Minimize Box** or ⊖ **Collapse Box**. Now, open another Internet window and go to the web page that you would like to share. I'm going to send my mother the Amtrak train schedule from New York to Boston.

• Highlight the web address by clicking once on the web address at the top of the window. (If you have a Mac, you'll have to click in the far left corner of the web address box on the icon.)

• Click on **Edit**.

• Click on **Copy**.

• Minimize the browser window and open the e-mail window that is waiting in the Task Bar.

• Click in the message text area.

• Click on **Edit**.

• Click on **Paste**.

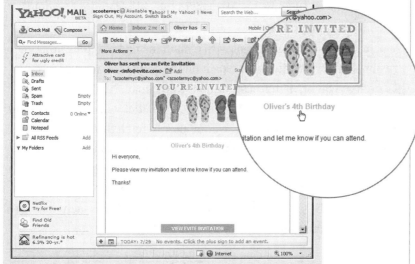

If the mouse arrow becomes a hand, it is an indication that the embedded web link can be accessed with a click of the mouse.

Voilà! Now you can finish the e-mail, type in a subject, put in the recipient's e-mail address, and off it goes!

When you receive an e-mail with a link it in, you usually should be able to simply click on the link to go to the intended website. If for some reason the link is not active or working, you can copy and paste it into the website address box at the top of the window and then visit the suggested site. Receiving an e-vite or e-card is a common way to receive a link embedded in an e-mail. An e-vite is an invitation via e-mail, and an e-card is a greeting card sent via e-mail. Visit *www.evite.com* to access free e-vite invitations and *www.123greetings.com* to access free greetings cards.

Get Attached

An attachment is anything you send along with an e-mail. It could be a document (e.g., a poem you wrote, driving directions, your résumé, your favorite recipe, etc.), a photograph, or even a movie or song. Let's go with the résumé scenario . . . In the days before computers, you'd type your résumé (then probably make photocopies of it or have a printing company produce copies for you). Next, you'd compose a cover letter either by hand or on a typewriter. Then, you would paper-clip a copy of your résumé to the cover letter.

> "I was totally intimidated by attachments until I finally opened one. I felt foolish being so timid when it wasn't a big deal at all."
> —*Nicholas*

Your résumé would now be attached to the cover letter and would become an attachment.

In theory, it's no different with e-mail. Instead of typing your résumé on a typewriter, you type it on the computer, where it's stored to print at will or, in this case, attach to an e-mail. Next, you access your e-mail account and compose the e-mail that will accompany your résumé. Lastly, you instruct the computer to fetch the stored résumé and attach it to the e-mail. All you do then is click Send and off it goes! No trip to the post office, no waiting in line, and your dispatch arrives at its destination within minutes. Don't worry, we'll go through the process step by step together. But before we *send* an attachment, let's discuss *receiving* one.

Receiving an Attachment

Check out the sample e-mail shown here. Your e-mail service may look different, but all e-mail services offer the same components. Relax, take your time, and figure out how this illustration relates to your e-mail service.

Your e-mail service uses a symbol to indicate that an e-mail contains an attachment. Nearly all services use a paper clip as seen here. AOL employs ⊠. Make yourself take notice of whether an e-mail has an attachment or not.

To view an attachment, you must first open the e-mail it was sent with. Then you open or download the attachment. Before going forward with opening the e-mail, ask yourself, "Do I know the sender?" E-mail attachments are one of the ways to unleash a virus onto your computer. If I receive an e-mail with an attachment and I don't recognize the sender, I'll delete the e-mail without opening it to protect my computer from a possible virus. (I routinely delete unopened

■ An e-mail with an attachment in Yahoo Mail. The paper clip indicates there is an attachment.

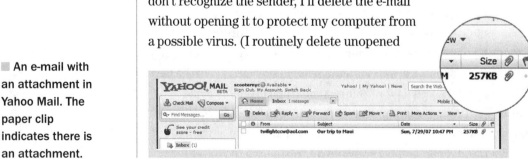

e-mails from unknown senders to lessen the spam on my computer as well.)

Here are instructions for you to follow to download an attachment received in Yahoo! Feel free to read through them now, but don't expect the information to make sense until you're in front of the computer with an actual attachment.

• Open the e-mail as you usually do.

• Move the mouse arrow onto the name of the attachment. Don't be surprised if the mouse arrow now appears as a hand. (Remember, the hand is a positive indication that if you click there something will open for you.)

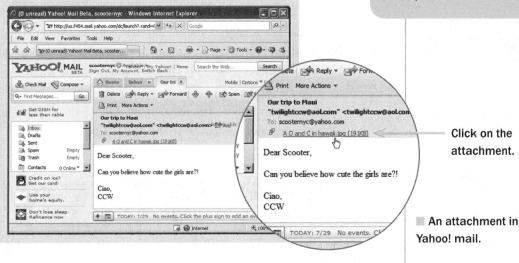

Click on the attachment.

■ An attachment in Yahoo! mail.

• In the case of Yahoo!, either click on the name of the attachment or the words **Save To Computer** to the right of the attachment. With your e-mail service, you may instead click on **Download**, **Download Now**, or **Open**. (If a single-click doesn't do the trick, try a double-click.)

• Yahoo! automatically scans attachments for viruses (a real plus) and lets you know if they find anything suspicious. If no viruses are found, next click on **Download Attachment**. You may need to use the Scroll Bar to move down the page to expose **Download Attachment**.

Click on Download Attachment.

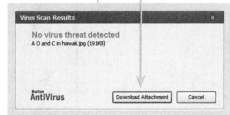

Click on Save.

• You have the choice to either open the attachment or save it. If it's an attachment you want to view once and discard, then click **Open**. If it's an attachment you want to keep, at least for a while, then click **Save**. For the sake of an exercise, I'll show you what to do to save the attachment. Click on **Save**.

• A window opens for you to decide where you want to save the attachment. (This is an important step because if you don't take command of where you put the attachment, you'll have trouble finding it later.) Click on the down arrow to the right of the location listed in the window. A drop-down menu appears; click **Desktop**. This instructs the computer to download the attachment to your Desktop—an easy place to find it later, but not where you'd want it to live permanently. Eventually you'll want to organize the documents on your Desktop into a filing system. We'll get to that in Chapter 20. Notice the name of the attachment, so you can identify it later. You can also change the name at this point to whatever you'll remember.

• Now click on **Save** and wait. Depending on the size of the attachment (photos are slower to download than most

REMEMBER TO SCROLL

If there is a Scroll Bar, use it. Otherwise you may miss out on something the page has to offer.

CLICK AND GO

1. Click on down arrow.

2. Click on Desktop.

3. Note the name of the attachment.

4. Click Save.

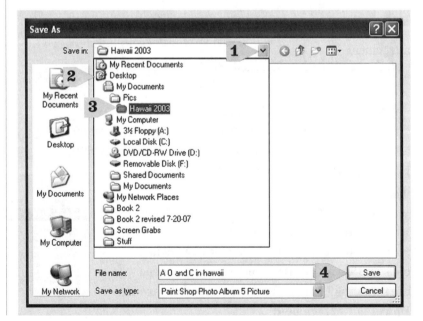

documents because they take up more space) and what type of
connection you have (a dial-up is slower than high speed), this could
take as long as a minute or two. (Unfortunately, some files can be too
big for a dial-up to handle and may not download at all, yet another
reason for you to consider a high-speed Internet connection.)

• The attachment may have opened on the screen for you to view.
If it didn't, you can shrink your e-mail window. Remember the Minimize
Box (■ for PC or ⊖ for Mac). Click to minimize the window.

• The attachment will now be one of the icons on the Desktop.

• Double-click on it to open. If necessary, maximize the
attachment (▣ for PC or ⊕ for Mac).

Fun, isn't it? When you decide you no longer want the item on your
computer, you can click and drag it into the Recycle Bin or the Trash.

Why Won't
My Download Open?

T o download or upload simply means to move something from
one place to another. Here's an example of downloading: The
weather warms up and I download my summer clothes from the top
of my closet to my dresser. An attachment gets downloaded to your
computer from the e-mail it was attached to. When you send an
attachment, you upload it from your computer to an e-mail and send it.

Sometimes, however, when people try to download an
attachment, they don't succeed and they blame themselves or their
computer. There are several possible reasons for this failure to
download, but the most likely is that the format of the attachment isn't
compatible with the computer attempting the download. This is
neither the user's fault nor the computer's. Let me explain: The word
"file," in computer-speak, refers to written documents, photographs,
music clips, or movies. Anything that contains data is called a file (not
to be confused with file folders, which contain multiple files). Every
file, regardless of whether it is text or image or sound, is created using
a particular software program. The same software program that was
used to create the file is usually necessary at the other end to view the
attachment when received. For example, if someone sends you a

document written using Microsoft Word, you need Microsoft Word on your computer to view that document. Think of it this way: Computer software programs are a language. Your computer needs to speak the same language as the attachment in order to read the attachment.

Hang in there while I show you the most common formats for an attachment. In Chapter 15 (on page 201) we talked about naming a document. You choose the name of a document or a photo (both known as a file) on your computer. Each file also has a suffix, or extension, that you don't choose, which identifies the format (designated software program) of that file. As an example, a Microsoft Word document ends in .doc. Remember the document we created and named "Smile" in Chapter 15? In fact, "smile.doc" is its full name.

Here's a list of the most common suffixes you may encounter:

.doc = Microsoft Word document

.xls = Microsoft Excel spreadsheet

.pdf = Adobe Acrobat portable document file

.ppt = Microsoft Power Point Presentation

.cwk = Apple Works document

.mov = QuickTime movie

.wav = sound file

.jpg = a graphic or image

.zip = compressed data

If you receive and download an attachment and the name of the attachment ends in .doc, the Microsoft Word software program must be installed on your computer to view the attachment. A pattern will begin to emerge for you of attachment file types you can and cannot open. If you receive an e-mail attachment but it won't open, you have the option to e-mail the sender, let them know what attachments you have successfully opened (e.g., "I can open Word, which ends in doc, and Excel, which ends in xls, and photographs if they end in jpg."), and place the burden on them to convert the attachment to a format your computer can read.

Sending an Attachment

N ow let's upload an attachment to an e-mail to send. The same instructions apply whether you're sending a document or a photo. Before we can begin the process of uploading, decide what you want to attach. Do you know where it lives on your computer? (i.e., Desktop, My Documents, etc.). Do you know the name of it? During the upload process, you must tell the computer where to find the file to upload, so you need to know where it is and what it's called. The process doesn't start with opening or viewing the item you want to attach. It starts with your e-mail. This time let's use Gmail as an example for sending an attachment.

• Open your e-mail account and click on **Write**, **New**, **Compose**, or **Create** to generate an e-mail. It's easy to put in the recipient's e-mail address, compose the e-mail, and forget to actually attach the file. To circumvent forgetting, we'll attach first and write later.

• Click on either the paper clip 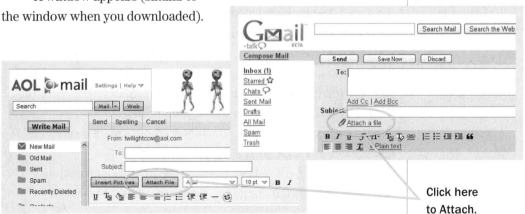, **Attach Files**, or **Attach**. The more comfortable you become with the computer, the more you'll be able to look around a window and instinctively find what you seek. Remember you may need to use the Scroll Bar to reveal what you need. Take your time, remain calm, and be patient with yourself and the computer.

• With most e-mail services, you click on **Find**, **Browse**, or **Choose File** to direct the computer to the item to be attached.

• A window appears (similar to the window when you downloaded).

STAY CALM

If what appears on these pages is different than what you see on your screen, calmly look at the window on your screen to see what allows you to attach a photo, document, and so on. I bet that you can find what you need.

Each e-mail service is slightly different regarding what you click on to attach a file.

Click here to Attach.

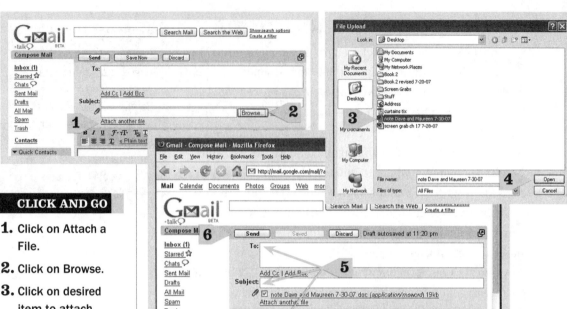

CLICK AND GO

1. Click on Attach a File.

2. Click on Browse.

3. Click on desired item to attach.

4. Click Open.

5. Fill in the address, subject, e-mail message.

6. Click Send.

Again, you'll click on the arrow to navigate to where the attachment lives. Once you find the item to be attached, either click on the name of it, then click on **Open** or **Attach**, or you can double-click on the name.

• The attachment name will appear either near the subject area of the e-mail or you may need to scroll down to see it at the bottom of the e-mail. You have attached a file to an e-mail! Congratulations!

• Now fill in the recipient's e-mail address, subject, and type a note. Be sure to mention the existence of an attachment in the subject or the message. Cautious e-mailers won't open attachments unless they know the sender consciously sent it, just in case it's a virus that attached itself without the knowledge of the sender.

How are you doing? Are attachments, both sent and received, making sense? I hope so.

Up until now, we've been dealing with a file (document) that already exists on your computer. Hmmm . . . how do you get a document or a photo onto your computer if you don't receive it as an attachment and it's not a document you wrote and saved yourself. We'll discuss using a digital camera and a scanner to get images onto your computer in the next chapter.

Time for a Little Reflection

Wow! You've come a long way. It seems like only yesterday that you and your computer met for the first time. Now here you are uploading and downloading. Please return to this chapter as often as you need when you've received an attachment or have a masterpiece of your own to send, and you want a little support. Don't forget to visit *www.abbyandme.com* for additional advice on e-mail and attachments. It would be my pleasure to be of assistance.

Q: How do I save an e-mail I want to keep?

A: Some e-mail services will store your e-mails permanently; others may only store them for as little as a month. Be aware that the service's policy may change and you might not be notified. Some e-mail services offer a way to set up a folder system to store e-mails. However, the most surefire way to know that you have a copy of an e-mail is to print it. Alternatively, you can open the e-mail and click on **File**, then click **Save As**. You can now decide where the e-mail should live on your computer completely independent of your e-mail service.

Q: How do I know that the person sending an e-mail is who they say they are?

A: You don't. It's the same as someone calling you on the phone who says they are "Bill Smith" when they are really "John Doe." You must be cautious, as you are in any situation in life, with a stranger. Use your instincts and powers of reasoning to determine if the person you are e-mailing is sincere or an imposter. Caution prevails! Be careful not to reveal any personal information, unless you are certain of who you are talking to and their intentions.

Q: Can I make changes to an e-mail before I send it?

A: Yes. Until you click **Send**, you can edit your e-mail to your heart's content. Get it just right before you decide to send it on.

Q: If I have a PC and my daughter has a Mac, can I still send her attachments?

A: Yes. It isn't the kind of computer you have that matters with attachments. What matters is if you have the necessary software on your computer for your daughter to be able to open the attachment on her computer. For example, if you send her a spreadsheet you created in Microsoft Excel, she needs Microsoft Excel on her computer to open and view that spreadsheet.

Q: Sometimes I can't even open an e-mail with an attachment. The computer seems to stall or says "timed out." What does that mean?

A: Your computer is having problems because either the attachment that was sent to you is very large or your Internet connection is slow. Are you using a dial-up? If you are, you may have problems opening up larger attachments. A document, no matter how large, will almost never be as cumbersome as a photograph, music, or video sent as an attachment.

Say It With an Emoticon			
:-)	smile	:'-(	crying
:)	also a smile	;)	wink
:-D	laughing	:'-)	happy and crying
:-}	grin	:-@	screaming
:-(	frown	:-&	tongue-tied

CHAPTER 18

Picture This

Digital and scanned photos from A to Z

Gone are the days of Instamatic cameras, drugstore runs to drop off film and pick up photos, and costly photocopies at your local copy store. I can even remember back to flashbulbs and carbon paper. Thank heavens that is all behind us. Nowadays modern technology offers us a digital answer to taking pictures and copying documents. None of that would be possible without our good friend the computer. Your computer, along with a digital camera, a scanner, and photo-editing software, lets you play professional photographer and copy shop owner at a relatively reasonable price and all in the comfort of your own home.

Plan to Scan, Stan?

You were introduced to the concept of a scanner on page 20. Now we're going to put one to use! As a refresher, a scanner works much like a copy machine. Lift the lid of the scanner, place an item on the scanner glass face down, and the scanner makes a copy. The difference is that rather than the copy being printed, it is stored in the brain of your computer. From there you can print the scan, e-mail it as an attachment, or store it to refer to at a later date. The scan lives on as a file in your computer until you decide to throw it away. If you haven't

"I no longer have to gather my newspaper clippings and make trips to the library copy machine with my change in hand. Having a scanner at home has saved me so much time and money. I can also make my own copies in color!"

—*Arlene*

A flatbed scanner (top) allows a book to be scanned. A single-feed scanner can scan individual pages only.

already purchased a scanner, keep in mind that a flatbed scanner gives you more options because it offers the ability to make copies from a book or other bulky item, not just a single sheet of paper. I'll tell you a secret, but you have to promise not to tell my publisher. I used to tear pages out of my cookbooks to scan and send recipes as attachments (a very bad habit). Now, with a flatbed scanner, my cookbooks remain intact and I can still share recipes with friends as e-mail attachments.

When you purchase a scanner or a combination scanner, printer, and copier, it comes with installation software. The machine will not work unless you install the necessary software and connect a cable from the scanner to the computer. Some stand-alone scanners do not require an electrical cord—they use the electricity of the computer. Follow the sequence of the installation instructions included with the scanner. Don't hesitate to ask a friend to help. I believe you can install it on your own, but there's no harm in having someone by your side.

Find a photograph, document, or page from a book that you would like to scan. Place the object face down on the scanner glass. There are usually arrows to guide the placement of an object to be scanned. Most scanners have a button that you push to initiate scanning. My experience is that if you have a choice between using the button on the scanner or initiating the scan through the software, you should go with the latter. (There's not enough room here to explain why, but trust me: the process is more intuitive and less problematic when I go through the software first.) An icon probably appeared on your desktop screen during the installation of the software—it is the pathway to the scanner's software.

I don't know what brand or model scanner you own, so these scanning instructions will be general to all scanners. When you open your scanner software, look at what's on your computer screen and patiently try to find the equivalent of what is in the illustration of a scanner window in the steps to follow. Remember the rental car analogy? All scanners have similar components and essentially function in the same way, but your screen may look different than what you see here. Don't let that throw you for a loop. Any time you use the computer, it's important for you to be flexible and develop intuition about how you decipher what's on the screen because there may be no consistency from one program or website to another. Adaptability and patience help you conquer something like your scanner. You're in no rush, so take your time reading everything on the screen before clicking. Take a break whenever you need one.

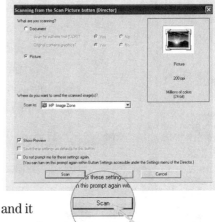

• Double-click on the icon for your scanner/printer. If there is no icon on the desktop, go to your Programs/ Applications and open it from there.

• Click on **Scan**, **Scan Picture**, or **Scan Document**. If you don't see the word **Scan**, click on **File** and it should appear in the menu. If you don't see the word **Scan** anywhere, look for the word **Import**. You'll be given a chance at some point to let the scanner know whether you're scanning a picture or a document and in color or in black and white. The scanner will scan the item differently according to the nature of the item to be scanned. Text can be scanned with less definition than a photo.

Click Scan.

• Most scanners at this point will show you a preview of the image being scanned. Often there will be a dotted line around the image. You can click and drag this dotted line to establish the edges of the item

CLICK AND GO

1. Click and drag edges to crop image.

2. Customize the image.

3. Click Accept.

■ A preview of your scan will appear.

(or portion of the item) to be scanned. You'll likely also be offered a variety of options for customizing your image (e.g., resizing, lightening/darkening).

• Be patient when scanning. The scanner may make some bumping and grinding noises while it calibrates preparing itself to scan. Don't try to speed things up . . . *wait*.

A few examples of complete scans.

• Before accepting the Preview of your image, check the resolution. Resolution is measured in dots per inch (dpi). The higher the number of dpi, the more detailed or clearer the image will be. However, the higher the dpi, the more space the image will take in bytes, and the larger size may make it difficult or slow to send as an attachment. Look for the word **Resolution** on the screen. If it isn't visible in the window you're viewing, click on each item in the Menu Bar to reveal where you can customize the resolution. I suggest you scan images at 100 dpi, especially if you want to e-mail the image.

• Now is the moment of truth. Click **Scan**, **Accept**, **OK**, or whatever else makes sense to continue the scanning process. Again, you'll have to wait because this step may take a minute or two.

• If you're asked whether you have another item to scan, click **No**. (Let's not get into multiple pages on your maiden voyage.)

• Again, *wait*. At this juncture, another part of the scanning software will open revealing your fabulous new scan, but it may take a moment to appear. Look at the Title Bar of the new window. This may give you a clue as to where to find the scan later. See if somewhere you can click on the name of this new file. (Probably it is scan.jpg or scan1.jpg.) Click on the name and see if you can change it to whatever would make sense to you. This is important so you can identify your scan later.

Congratulations! You created a scan of a photo or document.

While you're viewing the scanner's software, click on every item listed in the Menu Bar. Read the drop-down menus for each item. Even if you don't understand most of what you see, some of it will look familiar to you (i.e., Print, Save As, etc.). A little investigation goes a long way in becoming familiar and comfortable with your computer and its programs.

If your first attempt didn't work properly, don't be hard on yourself (or your friend, the computer). You are learning. It is inevitable that things won't always go your way along this journey of discovery. Don't be discouraged. Try again. Write down the steps you take so you can follow them or amend them as necessary. A week or longer may pass before you have the need to scan again. It's always helpful to have clear notes at the ready to assist you next time, in case you forget the sequence of steps that worked.

Say "Cheese"

The popularity of digital cameras is no surprise. There isn't any film to buy, you view your photos almost instantaneously, and you can share them with friends and family without a middle man. Long ago before digital cameras, I stopped taking pictures entirely because my photos always looked like they were taken during an earthquake. I'd be so frustrated because I wouldn't know for a week that the pictures were lousy, and the disappointing discovery was expensive. So, I threw in the photography towel. Now, however, I'm back in the game. If you haven't played with one yet, most digital cameras have a display screen, so you can view the photo seconds after you shoot it, to see if a retake is necessary. Amazing technology!

Instead of film, a digital camera has a memory card on which to store the photos. You can view, edit, and delete photos on the camera, but that can be a drain on the batteries. Most people transfer the photos to their computer and do the edits and purge from there. When you buy a camera, it will come with software, as the scanner did. Once the software is installed on the computer, the camera and computer communicate through a cable included with the camera that you'll plug into both pieces of equipment when you want to transfer your photos.

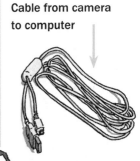

Cable from camera to computer

↑ **Software**

← **Memory Card**

Digital Camera Basics

Digital cameras come in a wide spectrum of designs, styles, and prices. Consult with friends and family who are already taking digital photos, and ask what they recommend you purchase. Thankfully, all digital cameras come with simple, but detailed instruction manuals (unlike your computer!). Start snapping away as soon as you buy the camera because you can delete any bad pictures, but promise yourself that at some convenient time, you'll sit down with the camera in hand and go through the features in the instruction manual.

There are so many options about the quality and size of the images you take as well as editing tricks when you take the photo.

Quality Counts

Do you know the size of the image you want? Are you printing it or only sending it over the Internet? Here's a guide for choosing the resolution:
- 640 dpi—for Internet use only
- 1024 dpi—Internet, as well as wallet-size prints
- 1280 dpi—Internet and any size up to and including 4 × 6 prints
- 1600 dpi—Internet and prints as large as 8 × 12

Memory Card Capacity

Your digital camera will come with a memory card, which stores the photographs taken by your camera, instead of storing the photos on film. When the memory card is full you transfer the photographs to your computer and then delete the transferred photos from the memory card, so it can be used again and again and again.

Usually the memory card that comes with the camera doesn't store very many photos and isn't adequate for your long-term use of the camera. I suggest that you purchase an additional memory card—one that offers more storage capacity—so you won't worry about filling up the smaller memory card that came with your camera before you're done taking pictures of your white water rafting trip. Think about purchasing a memory card with at least 258 MB (megabytes) of storage. You may even want to have an *additional* memory card in case something goes wrong with the first or you fill the card before you get a chance to transfer the images to your computer.

You may want to purchase a memory card reader. It is a device

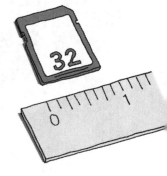

A memory card.

Be Kind to Your Memory Card

Do not remove the memory card from the camera while the camera is taking a photo or a photo is being viewed. It is best to turn off the camera first. When the camera indicates that the battery is low, believe it. Taking a picture when the battery is low can corrupt the memory card. It is always better to delete photos from your computer than from the memory card. Deleting from the memory card can cause the card to become defective.

---

that plugs into your computer by way of a USB cable. You take the memory card out of your camera and place it in the reader. Now you can transfer images from the memory card onto the computer. Transferring images from the camera to the computer directly can be a real strain on the camera's batteries.

Pixel This

Pixel is an abbreviation of Picture Element. Digital images are made up of hundreds and thousands of small squares called pixels. Pixels establish not only the quality of the photo (more pixels equal a clearer image) but the color, as well as the size when viewed on a computer.

This can get confusing, so hang in there. (Keep in mind that you can take great pictures without ever truly understanding any of this. However, the information here allows you to be more specific about the size and quality of photographs taken.) DPI (dots per inch) is the quality of how your printer prints, not the quality of the photo it is printing. Think of it this way: The more dots per inch the clearer the image. PPI (pixels per inch) will affect the quality of the image you are printing. If your digital photograph is 800 pixels wide and 600 pixels high and you print it with a PPI setting of 100 pixels per inch, your print will be 8 inches wide by 6 inches high. If you print that same image at 200 PPI, you'll get a printed photograph that is 4 inches wide

by 3 inches high. So the results at 200 PPI will be better quality, but the actual printed photograph will be smaller. In most cases 320 PPI is the highest number you'll really need. The most commonly used is 240 PPI, and even that can be higher quality than you need. I wouldn't suggest going below 180 PPI—that's when you really notice a drop in quality.

When buying a digital camera, keep in mind that the pixels of the camera itself will affect the quality of the photographs it can deliver.

A 1 megapixel camera setting delivers images good enough for e-mail, or to put on a website, or to look at on your computer screen, but they do not make good prints.

A 2.0 megapixel camera setting gives you photographs that you can use when doing desktop publishing and will produce good quality 4 × 6 prints.

A 3.0 or higher megapixel camera setting produces images in professional photo quality and offers 8 × 10 or larger photo-quality prints.

▉ **Digital images are made up of hundreds and thousands of pixels.**

Send and Receive Photos and Scans

Once you have an image living on your computer, whether it came there by way of a cable from your digital camera, from a scan you made, or because someone e-mailed it to you, you must give it a name that you'll recognize down the line. Why? Imagine how many photographs you'll accumulate over the time you have your computer. Now imagine if all of them had different numbers as their names. How on earth would you be able to quickly find that adorable photograph of Samantha with birthday cake all over her face?

In Chapter 20 we're going to create folder systems for what you have stored on your computer. That way you can organize your photos and documents to access them readily, but for now let's rename an image on your computer.

Often when you receive photographs as attachments from someone, the name of each image is a random number designated by their camera to the picture. You can rectify the situation after the image has been downloaded to your computer. (If you skipped the previous chapter, go back and read it to find our how to download attachments.)

The easiest way to rename an image is to move your mouse onto the icon for the image. Click once to highlight the icon, wait a second or two, and then click once directly on the name of the image. Now all the text below the image should be highlighted. Whatever you type will replace the current name. Once you've typed the new name, depress and release the **Enter** or **Return** key on the keyboard. May I suggest that you include in the name the subject of the image and the date (at least the year) and perhaps something about where it was taken or what they are doing? The ideal name is a name that tells you all you need to know about the photo without having to open it to see what it is.

Now that you've renamed your photos, feel free to send them to friends or family as e-mail attachments following the steps in Chapter 17. Whoever you send them to will appreciate that you have given the images a name rather than sent them on with the random numbers the camera gives each image.

WHAT'S IN A NAME?
As you've learned in Chapter 15, every file on your computer has a suffix or extension that identifies the type of item it is or the software it needs to be read. Most images end with either .jpg, .bmp, .gif, or .tif.

CLICK AND GO

1. Click on the image.

2. Wait a second and click on the name. Type new name to replace highlighted text.

3. Hit the Enter or Return key on the keyboard.

"I didn't even know I wanted to take photographs, but when I was given a digital camera for my sixtieth birthday from my grandkids a whole new world opened up for me. I'm now the official family photographer."
—*Oliver*

Save Me!

Let's talk about some safety measures for your treasured memories. After you transfer your photos from the camera to the computer, you'll want to empty the memory card so there's plenty of room for you to snap away. The camera's instruction manual will walk you through those simple steps. Now the photos you took live only on your computer. Right? What happens if your computer is stolen or breaks down? The family reunion you documented could be lost forever. It is crucial to back up your photographs (and all your important files) regularly.

We haven't really discussed backing up the computer before. You should back up your computer at regular intervals, depending on how you use it. If you only use your computer for e-mail and to surf the Internet, there's really not much to back up. If you have web-based e-mail, your e-mail service keeps your e-mails on their computers. (That's why you can access your e-mail from any computer, not just yours at home.) However, if you use your computer to write documents, create spreadsheets, and store photographs and/or music, you'll want to save that information onto a backup periodically, in case something happens to your computer.

In Chapter 12 we set the Background or Wallpaper on the desktop of your computer. Now that you have photographs on your computer, those photos can now be chosen as the background on your Desktop. Return to page 148 to refresh your memory of how to customize your Desktop. Instead of selecting from the images offered, click on **Browse** or **Choose Folder** to find a photo from your collection.

Not so long ago, floppy disks were used to back up computers, but nowadays a writable CD (compact disc) is more common because it holds much more information. You may also use a writable DVD depending on what you're backing up. A couple of different methods are available to copy data from your computer onto a CD or DVD. Here's one method:

If you have a PC:

- Open the CD or DVD drawer. Be gentle as it is a fragile piece of equipment and yet be firm enough, if you have a laptop, that the CD or DVD snaps into place. Close the drawer.
    - A window may automatically open. Close the window by clicking on the **Close Box** ⊠ in the top right corner.

• Make sure any documents or photos you want to backup are closed. You can't back up something if it's open.

• Move your mouse onto the icon of the folder or file you want to back up.

• Your mouse has two buttons, one on the left and one on the right. Up until now you've only been using the left mouse button (see Southpaw note). For the first time, you're going to use the right button. The right button on the mouse opens up an advanced menu allowing you to perform tasks in fewer steps—kind of like a shortcut. Try it now.

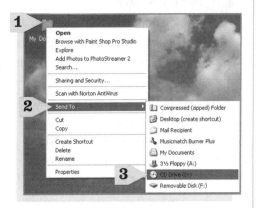

• *Right*-click on the item to back up.

• A menu opens. Move your mouse onto **Send To** and *left*-click.

• Another menu has opened to the side. Move your mouse into that menu and *left*-click on the **CD-RW Drive** or it may read **DVD/CD-RW Drive**. Give the computer a minute to copy.

• To remove the CD or DVD, open the drawer.

If you have a Mac:

• Push the CD or DVD into the slot. The computer will grab the CD or DVD from you. An icon for the CD or DVD will appear on the Desktop.

• Click and drag the folder or file you want to back up onto the CD or DVD icon. Release the mouse.

• Give the computer a minute to copy.

• To remove the CD or DVD click and drag it to the Trash.

That's all it takes to copy something from your computer onto a CD or DVD! At some point, you'll back up your entire system, but for now we'll stick with the simple method to back

---

PC USERS—TRY TO RIGHT-CLICK

You *right*-click the mouse to get the advanced menu. Once the advanced menu is available, you *left*-click from that point forward.

CLICK AND GO

1. Right-click on folder icon.

2. Left-click on Send To.

3. Left-click on CD or DVD drive.

DEAR SOUTHPAW

If you reversed the features of the mouse, as described on page 146, reverse the instructions here.

up desired files such as the first draft of your memoir or those adorable photos of Fido.

Enhance My Experience

Y ou may get so into digital photography that to take a picture, print it, and send it on an attachment may not be enough for you. You may decide you want to enhance or manipulate your photographs. What inspired me to buy my first scanner was a friend's impending nuptials. With the scanner I was able to scan existing childhood photographs of the soon-to-be bride and groom onto my computer. Once the images were on my computer I copied the bride (sitting Indian style at about age 5) from her photo and pasted her on the handlebars of the groom's picture (riding a bike also at about age 5). It was so much fun!

The scanner transferred the images onto my computer like a camera transfers images onto a computer. It was photo-editing software, not the scanner, that enabled the copying and pasting of the images. If you're interested in altering the images you've brought onto your computer, ask friends and relatives who do the same what

---

Back Me Up!

Use the same steps described here to back up the masterpieces you've written when word processing (discussed in Chapter 15). You don't want to lose your writing any more than you want to lose your photographs.

By the way, just to add a new bit of computer jargon to your vocabulary, what you just did was backup data, copy data, or "burn" data to a CD or DVD. That's all burning means—to copy onto another format, in this case onto a CD or DVD. Once a CD or DVD is burned or information is backed up, the CD or DVD should be labeled. An indelible marker like a Sharpie is the best writing tool to mark a CD or DVD because most regular markers smudge, and pencil isn't dark enough. Always date a CD or DVD including the year, and be specific about what it contains. You might not look at the CD or DVD for a very long time, and you'll want to identify the contents without having to put it into the computer. Store the CD or DVD in a safe place. If it holds vital financial information, you may want to store it in a home safe or a safe deposit box.

software they recommend. Some well-known programs are iPhoto (for the Mac), Adobe Photoshop, Corel Paint Shop, and Microsoft Digital Image Suite.

You'll be able to draw that mustache you miss so much back onto Uncle Charlie's face and erase the unfortunate one on Aunt Charlene. The sky is the limit with what you can do with photo editing. If you're really gung ho about it, you may want to track down an adult education program in your area to jump-start your photo-editing abilities.

An image can be altered once it is on the computer.

A Disappearing Act

Do you remember the original fax paper? It was shiny and thin. What a shock to discover faxes disappeared off the paper before our very eyes a few years after their composition. No one can be sure about the flaws or longevity with new technology. I say this as a warning about printing photo images at home. It's very satisfying to take a picture of a memorable event, race home, attach the camera to the computer, and transfer the image onto the computer. Seconds later, the image is printed on photo paper with your home printer. It really is incredible. But what do we know about how long that image will last on that paper? Ten years? Twenty years? It may be more, but maybe not. I tell my students if it's a really important photo, bring the backup CD to a professional photo shop and have them process a set of pictures as they would from a set of negatives. I could be wrong. Your printed image could last until the next ice age, but why take a chance?

There's another way you can save your images. Some websites offer to store and process your photos if you upload them onto their website. Again, be sure to choose a reputable company. It would be tragic if the company went out of business with all your pictures stored on their computer.

PHOTO-FRIENDLY WEBSITES

Here are three websites worthy of a visit where you can store, order, and share photos:

www.flickr.com
www.kodakgallery.com
www.shutterbug.com

Visit www.abbyandme.com to experiment together with some photos I've put on my website. I'll also bring you to flickr.com.

Q: I'm using kodakgallery.com to store my digital pictures. What happens if they close up shop?

A: Kodakgallery.com is unlikely to be going out of business any time soon. But it's important to choose a website that's been around for a while (and that will stay around) to store your images. Having said that, regardless of what website you store your images on, always burn (or copy) the pictures onto a CD or DVD for safekeeping, since there's no guarantee that a website will always be around.

Q: If I delete all the photos on my camera, is there any way to get them back?

A: Unfortunately not. If you haven't transferred them to your computer and you delete them from the camera, they are gone.

Q: Will my camera lose the photographs I've taken if the batteries run out?

A: No. The photographs are stored on the memory card inside the computer. The memory card holds the photographs regardless of the battery power. However, low batteries can affect the memory card's ability to do its job, so change the batteries as soon as you see that they are running low. Using rechargeable batteries is both environmentally and economically smart.

Q: What is the difference between a scanned image and a photo?

A: Well, they are both images in the mind of the computer. The only difference is how they got onto the computer. One is a photograph taken by a camera. The other is a photo taken by a scanner.

CHAPTER 19

Join the Conversation

Instant messages, blogs, chat rooms, and online dating

From dating to diary entries to discussions of literature, the Internet offers a whole new way to meet people, communicate, and express oneself. No more waiting for the mail carrier. Now you've got e-mail, and if e-mail isn't fast enough, you can instant message (IM). No need to head to the drugstore to buy a birthday card; you can send an e-card. Don't wait for cupid's arrow to find you; start dating online. Want to share your views? Tell the world via your blog. But before you dip your toe into these ever-evolving means of communication, let's understand how each works.

Faster Than a Speeding Bullet

Instant messaging (IM) is just as it sounds—a nearly instant way to send a message over the Internet. With pokey old e-mail you compose the e-mail, click Send, and then wait until the recipient accesses their inbox and replies. There is no waiting to speak of with an Instant Message. As fast as your fingers

"My grandson and I instant message whenever we're on our computers at the same time. I had no idea I would have so much fun IMing!"
—*Arthur*

can type the words out and click Send, your missive appears on the recipient's screen (if they are online). The slowest part for me with an Instant Message is my lousy typing! IMing takes place in real time just like a real conversation does.

IMs are quick and often abbreviated. America Online, Yahoo!, and Google offer IM services. When you sign up for IM service, which should be free, you create a buddy list or contact list of those whom you know who IM with that same service. The basic steps to set up a buddy or a contact list are pretty much the same with each service. Look for **Contacts**, **Add a Contact**, **Buddy List**, or **Add a Buddy** to lead you to where you can add to your list of IM pals.

You can only IM with your buddies (but anyone can be your buddy, if you want), and both you and your buddy have to be online when you IM. You can see which of your buddies are online when you go online (and they can see that you're online too).

You have an unlimited amount of space to write your Instant Message, but writing lengthy missives kind of defeats the purpose. IMing is all about fast instant communication. It's faster than e-mail because you bypass the formalities of clicking Write, adding the address, inserting a subject, and so on. IMing is to e-mail what a quick conversation on the phone is to chatting over lunch.

CLICK AND GO

1. **Look for blinking line.**

2. **Type message.**

3. **Click Send.**

■ An Instant Message.

IOW W/B (In other words, write back)

Due to the brevity of this form of communication, shortcuts are often used. Here are some abbreviations for you to try in addition to the emoticons found on page 250.

AYEC	At your earliest convenience	**G2CU**	Good to see you	**PU**	That stinks!
		HF	Have fun	**RUOK**	Are you okay?
B4	Before	**HRU**	How are you?	**SLAP**	Sounds like a plan
BC	Because	**IG2R**	I got to run	**SUP**	What's up?
BFN	Bye for now	**IOW**	In other words	**T+**	Think positive
BTDT	Been there, done that	**JK**	Just kidding	**TSTB**	The sooner, the better
CWYL	Chat with you later	**JMO**	Just my opinion	**TU**	Thank you
CYA	See ya	**OTL**	Out to lunch	**WAM**	Wait a minute
EOM	End of message	**N1**	Nice one	**W/B**	Write back
FC	Fingers crossed	**NOYB**	None of your business	**WU?**	What's up?
F2F	Face to face			**WUF?**	Where are you from?
GL	Good luck	**PLZ**	Please	**XLNT**	Excellent
GR8	Great	**POS**	Parent over shoulder	**YW**	You're welcome
GTG	Got to go	**PRT**	Party	**ZZZZ**	Sleeping

Try to translate this:

RUOK? WOULD LUV A F2F. CAN U GO OTL? TSTB. IG2R. EOM. ;)

Are you okay? I would love to have a face to face. Can you go out to lunch? The sooner, the better. I've got to run. End of message. Smile and a wink.

Say It Face-to-Face with a Webcam

A webcam is a video camera capable of showing video on the Internet. It's a great tool to communicate with family and friends who are far away because you can see them face to face while you speak. I have a friend here in the United States whose dad lives in Ireland. Her children sit at the computer in San Francisco while Granddad is at his computer in Belfast, and they hear and see each other by using a webcam (some webcams have sound capabilities).

Some computers come with a webcam, some don't. Some even have a webcam built directly into the monitor. If your computer didn't come with a webcam, you can purchase one at any time and connect it to your computer after the fact. You'll simply plug it in using the cable attached and follow the instructions for installing it. Most people place their webcams near or on the monitor because that's where they face when at the computer.

There are also webcams set up to capture images of particular locations as well. Here's a web address to see New York City's Times Square 24/7: *http://www.earthcam.com/usa/newyork/timessquare/*.

This is a one-way operation . . . you can view what is happening in Times Square on this website whether you have a webcam or not.

Feeling Chatty

Social networking on the Internet fills many people's dance cards, especially those who can no longer drive at night or travel great distances. The quality of conversations taking place on the Internet is as varied as the wealth of topics discussed. There are chat rooms, forums, and discussion groups where people often focus on a single topic and the conversation can go on at length. Message boards are usually a bit briefer than a chat room, forum, or a discussion group, but that truly depends on who is crafting the message or the response to the message.

My first exposure to a chat room was over a decade ago, and I was not impressed. There was plenty of adolescent potty talk and not much else going on. But chat rooms, message boards, forums, discussion groups, and the like, have evolved since then, and many offer an opportunity for groups of people who will likely never meet face to face to discuss topics of mutual interest intelligently.

It may be that your alma mater's website allows for discussions, and it's possible that the website you visit to research a particular ailment or travel destination has a message board. Or, when researching used car prices you may see a message board for visitor comments. Keep your eyes open for message board, chat, or forum in

TO POST A MESSAGE
When your words are published online in a forum, newsgroup, or message board it is referred to as a *post*.

the table of contents of a site. Visit the websites listed here for starters. The topics being discussed vary with every visit, so if there isn't anything of interest on your first foray, do give the site a second chance:

ME!!! at *www.abbyandme.com*

www.aarp.org/boards

discussions.seniornet.org
(Note: The website opens faster without www.)

www.myspace.com (The older audience for this site is growing, but it is dominated by teens and early-20-year-olds)

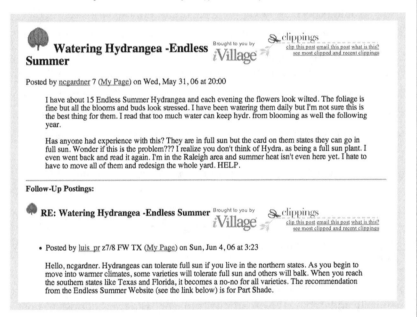

🌳 **Watering Hydrangea -Endless** Brought to you by *i*Village ✂ clippings
Summer clip this post email this post what is this?
see most clipped and recent clippings

Posted by <u>ncgardner</u> 7 (<u>My Page</u>) on Wed, May 31, 06 at 20:00

I have about 15 Endless Summer Hydrangea and each evening the flowers look wilted. The foliage is fine but all the blooms and buds look stressed. I have been watering them daily but I'm not sure this is the best thing for them. I read that too much water can keep hydr. from blooming as well the following year.

Has anyone had experience with this? They are in full sun but the card on them states they can go in full sun. Wonder if this is the problem??? I realize you don't think of Hydra. as being a full sun plant. I even went back and read it again. I'm in the Raleigh area and summer heat isn't even here yet. I hate to have to move all of them and redesign the whole yard. HELP.

Follow-Up Postings:

🌳 **RE: Watering Hydrangea -Endless Summer** Brought to you by *i*Village ✂ clippings
clip this post email this post what is this?
see most clipped and recent clippings

• Posted by <u>luis_pr</u> z7/8 FW TX (<u>My Page</u>) on Sun, Jun 4, 06 at 3:23

Hello, ncgardner. Hydrangeas can tolerate full sun if you live in the northern states. As you begin to move into warmer climates, some varieties will tolerate full sun and others will balk. When you reach the southern states like Texas and Florida, it becomes a no-no for all varieties. The recommendation from the Endless Summer Website (see the link below) is for Part Shade.

Don't be put off if a website requires you register in order to view their discussion groups. You will most likely be asked to establish an identity or ID. Keep in mind that anonymity is part of safe surfing on the Internet, so don't use your real name, but instead a nickname of some sort. It's not out of the question that with your registration you've made yourself vulnerable to spam or junk e-mail, so it's best not to use your primary e-mail address. Instead utilize the secondary address you opened for shopping and newsletters. If a password is required, the same rules we discussed earlier apply. Do not use the password you

"I thought chat rooms were a waste of time until I started to plan my trip to Guatemala. It was so helpful to be able to discuss accommodations and places to avoid with people who have been there, even if it was done online rather than face to face."
—*Crystal*

▮ A "conversation" on a message board.

RECORD YOUR PASSWORD

Please write down your selected password *before* you even type it to be sure you have the *exact* password you want. Be precise about what letters are uppercase and lowercase.

use for any financial transactions. Assume the password needs to be at least six characters and a combination of letters and numbers. To really scramble things because passwords are case sensitive, add a couple of capital letters here and there.

I encourage snooping before you join a conversation. Sign into a chat room or get on a message board and read what's being discussed before you jump on board. It may be that after a few minutes of eavesdropping, you decide this isn't the place where you want to invest time or share your thoughts. It is this sharing that makes the entire experience unique: the ability to broaden your social circle and enjoy the company of individuals you would otherwise never have encountered. Remarkable, isn't it?

As with blogging (see below), avoid revealing your home address or phone number. You also don't want to somehow let slip your birthday, where you were born, or your mother's maiden name. Those pieces of information can be used to confirm your identity with credit card companies and banks. Keep those tidbits to yourself for your own safety. And keep in mind your conversation is being read by many. Using a chat room or forum to sell your wares or force your views on others is frowned on, as is ranting and raving on a particular topic.

"Blogs have opened up my entire world. I can't get around on my own so reading blogs makes me feel like I'm in on a conversation even though we are miles apart."
—*Claire*

Blogs Don't Bog You Down

A web log, known as a "blog," is much like a diary or journal entry except blogs are shared with the world rather than kept to yourself. A blog appears on a website and is a personal web page regularly updated by the creator or "blogger." Bloggers choose to post their feelings, thoughts, and observations for millions to read rather than scribble them into a diary, turn the tiny key, and hide it under the mattress. Blogs are usually updated daily or weekly, and most offer readers an opportunity to post a reply. There is no editor, publisher, or filter for the information. So freedom of speech prevails, but the quality of writing and subject matter are up for grabs. A blog may be used to promote a project, share experiences, voice opinions, or chronicle a journey. The possibilities are endless, and to date more than 70 million blogs are on the Internet. A blog I visit daily is one maintained by a very dear friend who is battling breast cancer for the second time. She created her blog so her friends could be kept up to date on her health without her fielding phone calls all day. Most blogs are conversational and may contain photographs or other graphics and links to other websites.

To get a sense of what blogs are about, check out my blog at *www.abbyandme.com*. After you've gotten the feel of a blog at my site, visit *www.blogsearch.google.com*. Type in a topic of interest to you, and take a tour of the scores of blogs listed. Some of the most popular blogs are listed at *www.technorati.com/pop/blogs*. Or, give any of these a try:

www.boingboing.net

www.huffingtonpost.com

www.drudgereport.com

Here are some samples:

YOU ARE CORDIALLY INVITED
Visit my blog at *abbyandme.com*. I await your feedback!

One million dollar bond set this week for man who conned $20 from store in 1990

POSTED BY **MARK FRAUENFELDER**, MARCH 27, 2008 4:57 PM | PERMALINK

In 1990 Gary Weaver of Ohio was alleged to have bought $21.64 cents worth of merchandise from a store, using a roll of dimes to pay for part of the bill. After he left, a store employee discovered that the roll was filled with pennies, and that roll was capped with a dime on each end.

The long arm of the law caught up with Mr. Weaver on Wednesday and Municipal Court Judge Richard Bernat set a $1 million bond on the case.

...e jail – that officials say is overcrowded and in need of ...at is $999,978.36 higher than the amount he is ...ago.

March 23, 2008

Tara Suri
Posted: 09:29 PM ET

Bake sales and recycling are common fundraising tactics in middle school. But Tara Suri wasn't baking cupcakes for just any common cause. Her cause was hope, literally.

When Tara was 13, she was more than saddened by her trip to India with her family. From her sadness sprung the idea of trying to help the orphans in India and Sudan whom she saw abandoned by their parents, sometimes found in garbage dumps. Tara started H.O.P.E., or Helping Orphans Pursue Education. It aims to give kids the opportunity to achieve their full potential with the basics, like a sturdy roof over their heads, that Tara and her friends sometimes took for granted back in Scarsdale, New York.

Now, at 16, she has expanded her cause with an umbrella organization called Aandolan, which means "a movement for change" in Hindi. Through that fundraising group, Tara now runs **Turn Your World Around** and Connect a Kid along with H.O.P.E., and a lot of it for kids growing up who are in sad situations.

What would you ask this inspired teenager? Send your questions as comments below, or – better yet – send question on video to iReport.com. Then be sure to look for yourself during the CNN.com Live interview F March 28 at 3:30 p.m. ET.

Filed under: Under 20 • Worldwide reach

Share post | 48 Comments | Add a comment | Permalink

COURTESY TARA SURI
Tara Suri, 16, hopes to help to young children around t achieve their full potential.

P⊙gue's Posts
The Latest in Technology From David Pogue

March 27, 2008, 11:19 am

Are You Taking Advantage of Web 2.0?

At a conference for the public-relations industry a couple weeks ago, I was asked to speak about Web 2.0—those interactive Web sites where we, the public, supply the material (Facebook, MySpace, Craigslist, eBay, YouTube, Flickr, TripAdvisor, and so on, not to mention blogs, podcasts and amateur video).

Before my talk, though, an emcee warmed up the audience with an exercise. He pointed out the wireless laptops on every table in the ballroom, and explained that anything typed on them would appear on huge screens. Using this instant-feedback mechanism, he posed P.R.-related questions to the attendees and commented on the responses as they appeared on the big screens.

One of them was: "Why isn't your company (or client) taking advantage of Web 2.0?"

The audience loved that one; within seconds, there were 132 responses on the screen in a huge, scrolling list. "Not enough money." "Don't understand it." "No technical resources." "Not enough manpower." "No visible return on investment." "Fear of ridicule." "Fear of slander." "Fear of permanence." "Fear of the public running amok."

The fears are rational enough: over and over again, we've all seen blog comments devolve into juvenile, offensive bickering, backstabbing and grandstanding.

Read more ...

Comments (22)   E-mail this   Share

■ **A variety of blogs.**

If you're considering creating a blog of your own, there are plenty of free blogging websites. Visit *www.google.com* and search for "free blog," or when you visit a blog you like, see if it shows who powered or hosts that blog. Take a look at these three free blog sites:

www.blogger.com

www.livejournal.com

www.thediary.org

Each of these sites will walk you step by step through creating your own blog.

If you start a blog and few Internet travelers visit at the onset, remember Rome wasn't built in a day. It takes time for people to become aware of a blog and for you to establish an audience. Post on other blogs to introduce yourself and invite people to visit your blog.

Again, be very careful not to send private information into cyberspace. The unfortunate reality is scammers, hackers, or worse may be lurking to take advantage of your forthright exposure of who you are. Never give information on your blog revealing your home address or phone number. Also avoid hanging other people's dirty laundry out on your blog. You may be willing to tell all, but are your friends and family?

Affairs of the Heart

Y ou can use the Internet to keep up to date with people you know, but you can also use it to meet new people. Some of the people you meet online you may never want to meet face to face; others may become great friends or more. Wedding bells have rung for thousands of couples who met online, and hundreds of engagements take place monthly with the Internet as matchmaker. I know a really lovely older couple that met online and married a couple of years after. You may not be in the market to get hitched, but a dinner companion or even an online flirtation might be just what the doctor ordered.

Online dating uses the same technology as computerized dating services did in the 1960s. You answer a series of question to create a profile. Most of the online dating sites then compare your profile with

"When I first started online dating I thought I wanted to get married again. Now I'm having so much fun dating, I don't want to limit myself to one person."
—*Shelly*

the qualities you describe in yourself and those you desire in another, and, presto, matches are made. If you would rather not have someone else make your match for you, you can take your time to view the profiles that you feel fit your criteria without anyone's guidance. You can search the profiles listed based on a piece or several pieces of information given—age, physical attributes, location, education, likes, dislikes, and so on.

As you can see by the example, there is usually a photo of the prospective match. (I never bother to read a profile if the person wasn't willing to include a photo.) Most dating websites have subscribers answer standard questions about height, weight, body type, smoking and drinking habits, education, location, and so on. Then there is a choice if you want to list most recently read books, favorite musicians or songs, what five things you can't live without, what kind of person you're looking for, and what you have to offer. The questions asked may vary from dating site to dating site, but each site wants to gather as much information as possible to paint a detailed picture of who you are and what you're looking for.

Some online dating services are free, but the majority charge a fee. Fees vary and usually cover a period of time or the number of contacts

You decide what type of person's profile you want to see.

Search Members

I am/We are a
Woman

Seeking a
Man

Between the ages of
18 and 99

Country
United States

State/Province
New York

Zip Code (U.S. Only, within 10 miles)

[search] » Advanced Search

Me

Height:	5 ft 3 in / 160-161 cm
Body Type:	Slim/Petite
Hair Color:	Blonde
Hair Length:	Long
Eye Color:	Brown
Eye Wear:	Either
Location:	New York, New York (0 miles from you)
Last Visit:	vhammer is online now!
Relocate?:	Maybe/Yes
Occupation:	author, teacher
Education:	Some college
Ethnicity:	Caucasian
Religion:	Agnostic
Status:	Single
Have Children:	No
Want Children:	No
Interests:	Arts, Cooking/Baking, Dancing, Entertainment, Exercise and Fitness, Fine Dining, Gardening, Reading, Travel, Volunteering
Cigarettes:	I'm a non-smoker
Booze:	I'm a light/social drinker
Drugs:	Prefer not to say

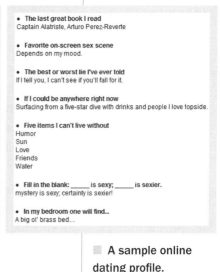

- **The last great book I read**
Captain Alatriste, Arturo Perez-Reverte

- **Favorite on-screen sex scene**
Depends on my mood.

- **The best or worst lie I've ever told**
If I tell you, I can't see if you'll fall for it.

- **If I could be anywhere right now**
Surfacing from a five-star dive with drinks and people I love topside.

- **Five items I can't live without**
Humor
Sun
Love
Friends
Water

- **Fill in the blank:** _____ is sexy; _____ is sexier.
mystery is sexy; certainty is sexier!

- **In my bedroom one will find...**
A big ol' brass bed...

A sample online dating profile.

PLAY = HANKY PANKY

You might be asked what you are looking for: Friendship, Dating, Marriage, or Play. Don't make the same mistake I did. To choose Play means an interest in fooling around and not much else. I chose it once on a dating site and proceeded to receive graphic photos from the men who were interested! Silly me; I thought Play meant have fun, not "have sex."

made. Most sites allow you a free trial or limited use before you need to give credit card information. I highly recommend you take advantage of a sneak peek before you commit yourself financially to a site. Because individuals have personalities, so do websites meant to match people. Some are based on age, religion, race, or sexual preference: *jdate.com*, *gay.com*, and *seniorfriendfinder.com* are some examples of dating websites that are very specific to the people who join. Jdate is the leading Jewish singles networking site, *gay.com* is a dating site for gays and lesbians, and *seniorfriendfinder.com* is a site where seniors can create new relationships. Some sites are racier than others. Here in Manhattan, *nerve.com* is considered a bit racier than *match.com* or *eharmony.com*. Ask around to see if you know anyone who has taken the plunge to look for companionship or more on the Internet. If you find someone, ask about their experiences.

Here are some simple guidelines to online dating:

• Never divulge your last name or home address before meeting face to face.

• If you choose to chat by phone, give a cell phone number so your home address cannot be traced.

• When arranging a meeting, agree to make it brief (a cup of coffee) in a public place, and make sure a friend knows what you're doing when and where.

• Under no circumstances should you get into a car with this person or meet in an isolated place.

• Listen to your instincts and your head. Your heart doesn't have eyes and ears.

Statistically, profiles with a photograph are viewed more often than those without a photo. In the previous chapter we talked about how to get photographs onto the computer. Once your picture is on your computer, you can post it on a website. Please use a photograph that truly and honestly represents what you look like *now*. You'll do yourself a disservice if you post a 20-years-younger or 20-pounds-lighter photo. If someone shows interest and you would like to meet, imagine his or her disappointment when you've posted a misleading photo. Your suitor will feel lied to, and he or she would be right. You would feel the same way if the person you met didn't look like the person in the photos you've viewed and taken a shine to. Have more faith in yourself than that. Put the true you online for all to see.

If you find a profile of interest, there are usually two routes you can take to make contact. You can e-mail the person through an anonymous e-mail account that is set up with the dating website. They won't know your real name and you won't know theirs until you both decide to reveal them.

Or you can send the person a "wink." This is an unwritten message but the recipient is notified of your interest. This will bring your profile to their attention and they can then decide to make contact or not.

You have no obligation to respond to everyone who contacts you and vice versa. Do not be hurt if you don't hear back from someone. You may not be their type or they may have already found someone and forgotten to take their profile off the website. If you'd rather be the date shopper and not have others window-shop your profile, you can also make your profile private. If, and only if, you find someone of interest, you can allow him or her to see your profile.

Caution should prevail, however, when you venture into online dating. A broken heart can heal, but fraud that results in your retirement

savings being swindled out from under you by a cunning Romeo (or Juliet) can take a much longer recovery. Have fun. Date and be merry. But think long and hard about what you really know about this person before you make any legal arrangements or lend money. Tragic stories

WHILE AWAY
Don't limit yourself to meeting people only in your hometown. The website you've listed your profile on may have members from all over the country (maybe even the world). If you're traveling, check out the profiles of people at your destination. It might be nice to arrange a dinner date for the night you arrive to kick off your time away.

You can decide to reveal or hide your profile from others.

of people marrying before actually meeting seem improbable, but they occur. Poetic words have been used to woo and sometimes deceive for centuries. Bask in the attention, but let your head and not your heart guide your decisions.

I've taken all the romance out of it, haven't I? Not at all! Online dating is a wonderful way to make friends, develop relationships, and, possibly, find love. I want you to have a good, if not great, experience. However, as is true with any affair of the heart, you must not be reckless. The cyber world of the Internet has just as many Gallants as it does Goofuses. Take advantage of the varied ways in which the computer and the Internet can connect you to a world few of us could imagine even 20 years ago. Just exercise a bit of caution until you're more familiar with the ways of this new world.

Q: **Why would someone participate in a blog under a false identity?**

A: Some people who add their thoughts to a blog want to remain anonymous, but their input is nonetheless valid and well intended. They just don't want to reveal their name for privacy reasons. Others contribute false information to a blog because they want to screw around with people. Remember that kid from grammar school who put the frog down your shirt? Some people never change. So be discriminating when you read something on the Internet. Not all written words are true.

Q: **Do I have any recourse if someone has misrepresented themselves on a dating website?**

A: Every online dating site offers a way to contact the people who own the site and let them know if someone's behavior should prevent them being listed on the site. But a little fibbing about height, weight, finances, and so on, probably will not get someone banished from the site.

Q: What do I do with my profile if I start dating someone and I don't want to be contacted by anyone until I decide if the relationship is going to work out?

A: You can usually hide your profile at any time and then "unhide" it when you're ready to reenter the dating market.

Q: Will I get my money back from a dating website if I meet someone and discontinue my membership early?

A: No. You can look at the money you paid as an investment or a gamble, but either way you will not be reimbursed.

Let's Review

blog

a website where the contributor(s) share(s) ideas and opinions on the Internet

chat room

a place on the Internet where people as a group can communicate live by sending typed messages back and forth

e-mail (electronic mail)

to send or receive typed messages via the Internet

forum

a meeting place online for group discussions (see chat room)

instant message (IM)

to send and/or receive typed messages via the Internet in real-time

message board

a bulletin board on the Internet where you can type messages

post

to submit text to a blog or message board

CHAPTER 20

Put It All in Order

Create a filing system, organize, and maintain all that lives on your computer

Y ou don't need to be a neatnik for the sake of your buddy, the computer. It couldn't care less whether you can find the documents you "penned." Nor does it have any investment in whether your photographs are organized in a folder on the Desktop or if they live higgledy-piggledy all over your machine. Your computer will not lose sleep over whether you've copied your photos and documents onto CDs for safekeeping or not. *You* are the sole beneficiary of an organized computer. Knowing where things live on it makes your computing experience manageable and more pleasant. Don't you deserve that?

As for the computer, what matters is that you do some regular housekeeping to help it function at its best. First, let's take care of your needs. Unless the computer is misbehaving, it can wait.

File vs. Folder

F iles and folders have been referred to several times in the book. Let's get to the nitty-gritty of exactly what the difference is between the two and how you can make use of both.

A file can be a word-processing document, a digital or scanned photograph, a video clip, an audio or music recording, a PowerPoint slide show, or a movie. It could be a multipage document containing text, graphics, and photos. In every case, a file must have a name. Ideally, that name clearly describes the contents of the file, thereby eliminating the need to open the file to reveal the gist of its contents. It's a good idea to include the date in the filename (i.e., smile May 07.doc). A file name can contain spaces, may be uppercase and lowercase but should not include punctuation. The only period used precedes the suffix, both of which are typically added by the program. If you must have a means to divide text, use the hyphen key (i.e., accountant final letter 4-14-07.doc).

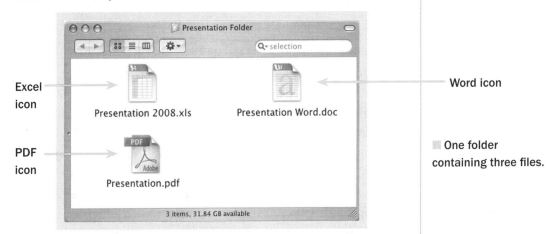

Excel icon

Presentation 2008.xls

Word icon

Presentation Word.doc

PDF icon

Presentation.pdf

One folder containing three files.

In Chapter 15, I described how to use **File** and **Save As** to name a Microsoft Word (MS Word) document. Using **File** and **Save As** as file-naming devices is not exclusive to MS Word. Both options appear in many different software programs. Feel free to click on **File** in any program when curiosity calls to see if **Save As** appears in the drop-down menu.

At the end of a file name is a suffix or extension that identifies the software program used to create the file. On the next page is the same list from our discussion on attachments in Chapter 18.

PUNCTUATION IS NOT WELCOME

Avoid any punctuation when you name a file or folder. Slashes (/) and periods (.) are a coding used by the computer to designate the location of an item on the computer. Because of this, steer clear of punctuation when you name a file (aka document, photo, etc.) or folder. Period!

File Name Extensions

 .doc = Microsoft Word document

 .xls = Microsoft Excel spreadsheet

 .pdf = Adobe Acrobat portable document file

 .ppt = Microsoft Power Point Presentation

 .cwk = Apple Works document

 .mov = QuickTime movie

 .wav = sound file

 .jpg = a graphic or image

 .zip = compressed data

"My actual desk is a mess, yet somehow I'm able to keep my computer quite organized. Who knows why I can do it with the computer and nowhere else, but it definitely eliminates computer confusion for me."
—*Daniel*

FILE OR FOLDER
Drop the phrase "file folder" from your lexicon, and it will be easier to understand dealing with a file *or* a folder.

Notice there is an icon beside the suffixes listed in the above box. The icon represents each software program. Becoming familiar with these different icons helps identify the types of files on your computer. There are many more extensions than those shown here. The ones listed are ones you'll see most often.

A folder is *not* a file. I know it's confusing, but to the computer a file is a file and a folder is a folder. There is no such thing as a "file folder" on the computer. A folder is a means to store and organize one or more files. (For example, you might have a folder called "travel" and in it a document titled "packing list" and another called "Italy itinerary." Those two items are files contained in the folder "travel.") To assist in the identification of the contents, you will assign the folder a name. Again, specificity counts. The icon for a folder 🗀 helps clarify things because it looks like a manila folder and it functions like one.

You can even have a folder system within a folder, similar to a family tree, as in the illustration here. On my computer, the main folder is named "Abby." Within that folder are folders titled "correspondence," "travel," and "recipes," to name a few. Inside the correspondence folder are folders designated by year that store the correspondence of each year. Within the travel folder are various itineraries and conversion charts. The recipe folder

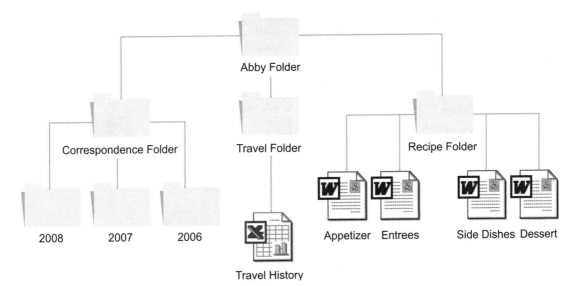

contains separate folders for appetizers, entrees, and desserts—each folder with recipes in it. Starting to get the picture?

Essentially, there is no limit to the number of files or folders a single folder can store, as long as your computer has enough memory. Here's the rule of thumb to keep things organized: If you have three or more files that can be grouped, make a folder to store them.

The Abby Folder branches out into sub-folders that contain folders and documents.

Create a Folder

Let's create a folder on the Desktop, so you can see what this business is all about.

If you have a PC:

- Move your mouse to a blank spot on the Desktop.
- Click with the *right* button of the mouse.
- *Left*-click on **New** (all other clicks will be with the left button after this point).
- Move the mouse into the menu that opened next to **New**.
- Click on **Folder** at the top of the list. A folder will now appear on the Desktop.
- Do *not* click the mouse at this stage. Instead type the desired name of the folder. For this exercise, simply type your first name. (If you did click the mouse, even though I told you not to, your folder is

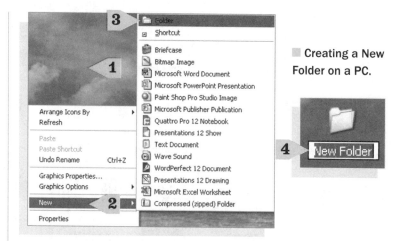

Creating a New Folder on a PC.

CLICK AND GO

1. **RIGHT-click on Desktop.**

2. **LEFT-click on New.**

3. **LEFT-click on Folder.**

4. **Do not click mouse; type desired folder name.**

5. **Hit Enter key.**

now officially named New Folder. Don't worry. We will learn how to rename a folder next. Sit tight.)

- Hit the **Enter** key to save the new name.
- Double-click on the folder to open it.

If you have a Mac:

- Click on the Desktop.
- Click on **File** at the top of the window.
- Click on **New Folder**.
- Do *not* click the mouse at this stage. Instead type the desired name of the folder. For this exercise, simply type your first name. (If you did click the mouse, even though I told you not to, your folder is now officially named New Folder. Don't worry. We will learn how to rename a folder next. Sit tight.)
- Hit the **Return** or **Enter** key to save the new name.
- Double-click on your folder to open it.

BE FLEXIBLE

Remember, the steps I go over might be slightly different on your computer. Take the instructions here and apply them to what your screen has to offer.

Well done! Repeat these steps anytime you want a new folder to appear on your Desktop. These are the same steps you would follow to create a folder within a folder anywhere on your computer. Open the existing folder where you would like a new one to appear. If you have a PC, *right*-click inside the folder where you want the new folder to appear and then follow the preceding steps. With the Mac, open the existing folder and then click on **File**.

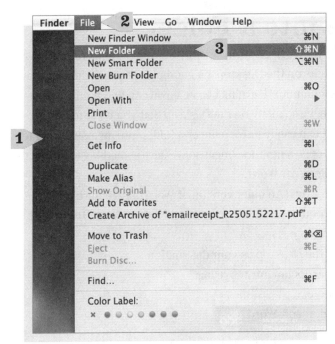

CLICK AND GO

1. Click on Desktop.

2. Click File.

3. Click New Folder.

4. Do not click mouse; type desired folder name.

5. Hit Return or Enter key.

■ Creating a New Folder on a Mac.

Rename a Folder or File

You can change the name of an existing folder or file (aka document, photograph, etc.) at any time. The same steps apply to both a file and a folder. A folder and/or file must be closed while changing the name.

• Place your mouse on the text below the icon of the file or folder to be renamed.

• Click once on the file or folder name. The computer now knows what item you want to modify.

• Click once, again, on the file or folder name. Only the name is now highlighted. You can either click within the name, if you want to modify only part of the name, or start typing to replace the entire name. For this exercise, replace your first name with your last name.

• Hit the **Enter** or **Return** key to save the change.

Pretty good, huh? If that didn't work, don't fret. Try it again slowly and carefully. You'll get it.

A PHOTO BY ANY OTHER NAME

As mentioned in Chapter 18, if you give a photograph a specific name that indicates the subject, location, and date, you won't play a guessing game as to what the image is or have to open it over and over again to find out. This is also true for any file or folder.

Move into a Folder

L et's say you've been saving all of your attachments or new documents on the Desktop. (A good place to save them at the onset of your computer learning because you can find them easily.) But now you have so many on the Desktop that you want to tidy things up. You can easily move a file or a folder into an existing folder.

First, let's open a new document so we have something to play with.
- Open Microsoft Word.
- Click on **File**. (An older version of Word may require that you open a New Document. If that is the case, click on **New Document**.)
- Click on **Save As**.
- Choose the Desktop as your destination.
- Name the document "move me."
- Click **Save**.
- Close Microsoft Word.

Great! Now we have a document on the Desktop titled "move me" and a folder with your name.
- Move your mouse onto the "move me" document (aka file).
- Depress the mouse and keep it depressed (poor sad mouse) while you drag the "move me" file on top of the folder with your name.
- When the "move me" is smack on top of the other folder, highlighting both of the icons and text, release the mouse.
- Double-click on the folder with your last name. Shazam! There is your "move me" document (aka file) inside the folder. Close the folder.
- Repeat the steps in Create a Folder on page 281. Name the new folder Bertha. Then keep reading.

Let's move the Bertha folder into the folder with your last name. It's as easy as click, drag, and drop. (You can sneak a peek at the previous instructions, if you want. They are there to help you.)

The Bertha folder should no longer exist on the Desktop. Now you can open the folder with your name.

Moving a file into a folder.

CLICK AND GO

1. Move mouse on to "move me."

2. Click and drag onto folder.

3. Release mouse.

Bertha and "move me" should be inside. Click and drag Bertha into "move me." Get it now? I thought so.

Because you can also use this method of moving items for moving files into a folder, it makes tidying up the Desktop very easy. When you're not sure where to save a photo, document, or folder, why not save it to the Desktop? You now know you can move it from there into an already existing folder or one you create.

Delete a Folder

CLICK AND DRAG
If you need a refresher on click and drag, return to page 128 and play a hand or two of Solitaire.

N ice work so far! Now, close whatever folders you have open on the Desktop.

I apologize for what you're about to do, but I'd like you to practice deleting a folder. Don't feel that all of your hard work has gone for naught because we're about to throw it away. You can repeat the preceding steps to create as many folders as you like. But what if one of your folders and its contents become obsolete? You want to be able to clean up your Desktop or any other area of your computer, don't you? I thought so.

First, find your target for where to put unwanted files and folders. On a PC, it is the **Recycle Bin** . On a Mac, it is the **Trash** . Let's get rid of the Bertha folder. Make sure it's closed. Click, drag, and drop the folder onto the Recycle Bin or Trash. Simple as that. Gone!

Be aware that there is more than one method available to create, rename, move, and delete a file or folder. As it is true with so many actions on the computer, there are several ways to accomplish each of these tasks. The more you experiment with your computer, the more easily you can decide the method you prefer. You may choose to mix and match, as I do. You can also choose to store things anywhere on the computer that you desire. There is a Documents or My Documents folder that already exists on your computer. You may want to store documents you've written there instead of creating a new folder with your name. How you decide to organize is your choice. I just strongly suggest that you *do* organize as you begin your journey rather than having to do a massive cleanup further down the line.

Two things to keep in mind:

• If you delete a folder, you will also be deleting *all* files and folders within that folder.

• If you move a folder, you will also be moving *all* the files and folders within that folder.

Trash Picking 101

What happens to the file and folders you've thrown away? They remain stored there until you or the computer, if scheduled to do so automatically, empties them. If you have a Mac, and you want to empty the Trash, click **Finder**, then click **Empty Trash**. If you have PC, *right*-click on the **Recycle Bin**, then *left*-click on **Empty Recycle Bin**.

If you feel remorse about something you threw away, you can roll up your sleeves and retrieve it from the trash unless it has been emptied. Double-click on the **Recycle Bin** or the **Trash** to open it. Click and drag the desired item out of the folder back onto the Desktop. (You may want to wash your hands afterward!)

What do you do when the message below appears on your screen?

The safest thing to do is to move your hands away from the keyboard and mouse. A hand hovering over the mouse, with its owner in an agitated state, can lead to an accidental click. The result of that click may be irreversible. In the case of this example, if you chose **Yes** and later realized your error, the item in question could be retrieved from the trash, but in other situations you might not be so lucky.

■ The computer may ask you to confirm that you want to throw something away.

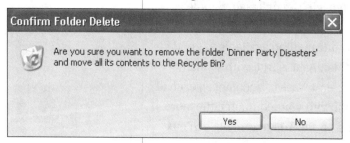

Don't Throw Out the Baby with the Bathwater!

More than one student has come to my class with the same sad story. Their computer seemed to be running slower than usual. So, they decided to delete items they didn't think were necessary in the hope that it would make the computer run more smoothly. Much to their disappointment the computer stopped working entirely. What they did was delete items they didn't *think* they used on their computer. The number of files and/or folders on your computer doesn't make a big difference in the operation of the machine, unless you have an older computer with little memory. Unwittingly, a program that works in the background of the computer can get tossed in the purging process. By deleting this necessary but unfamiliar element, you risk negatively impacting how the computer functions. Files ending in .exe, .config, .sys, .bak, and .dll should *never* be altered, modified, renamed, copied, moved, or deleted. I don't expect anyone to commit that list to memory. So, instead, here is the policy I suggest: If you didn't create it or receive it as an attachment, don't delete it. When in doubt, don't throw it out!

A SAVING PLAN
Go back to Chapter 18 to review how to copy or burn files and folders onto a CD or DVD for safekeeping.

A Little TLC Goes a Long Way

K eep your computer free of dust, animal hair, and far away from liquids. I mentioned this back in Chapter 5, but it warrants repeating. The computer will also benefit from some routine maintenance.

PCs and Apple computers differ in what regular maintenance you should provide. If you have a PC, read on. If you have a Mac/Apple, you can skip the disk cleanup and defrag section because Macs do this automatically.

Disk Cleanup

Disk Cleanup is a tool built in to the computer to help the computer remain as lean and smooth-running as possible. When activated, Disk Cleanup sweeps your computer to find unnecessary files it can safely delete to free up space on your hard drive. Rest assured the Disk Cleanup would not suggest deleting any files you added to the computer. Primarily it finds temporary Internet files and the like. The frequency that one should perform Disk Cleanup is directly related to the amount of computer use, not a calendar.

▓ The steps to take to perform a Disk Cleanup on your PC computer.

CLICK AND GO

1. Click Start.
2. Click Programs.
3. Click Accessories.
4. Click System Tools.
5. Click Disk Cleanup.
6. Click to remove any checks for files you *don't* want to keep.
7. Click OK.

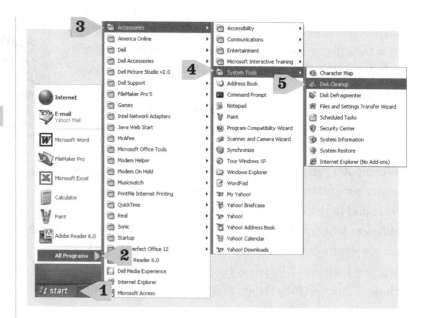

However, because that's hard to judge, you could perform a disk cleanup between once a month and once every three months. (I'll bet you a new ream of paper that most people you ask *may* do it once a year, but most have *never* done it at all!)

Here are the steps to clean up your PC computer:

- Close all programs that are open.
- Click on **Start** ![start].
- Click on **Programs**.
- Click on **Accessories**.
- Click on **System Tools**.
- Click on **Disk Cleanup**. Wait while it evaluates your computer.
- A window opens indicating what files the computer proposes to be deleted with a check mark. If there are any files you do *not* wanted deleted, click in the box with the check to remove the check.
- Click on **OK**.

Defrag

Every time you open or close a program, bits of the data used in the program move from their place of origin to another location in the computer. This is called *fragmenting*. When fragmenting occurs, it slows down the process of the computer because now the computer has to search for all the fragments scattered hither and yon on the computer. To return these bits of data to where they belong, the computer must be defragmented. Why not defrag your computer every time you perform a Disk Cleanup? Choose your computer housecleaning day to be something you can remember . . . perhaps the first of the month or when you pay your quarterly taxes.

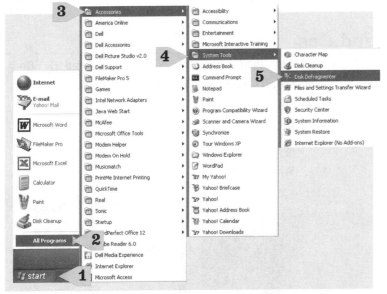

CLICK AND GO

1. Click Start.

2. Click Programs.

3. Click Accessories.

4. Click System Tools.

5. Click Disk Defragmenter.

■ The steps to take to defrag your PC computer.

Click Analyze or Defragment.

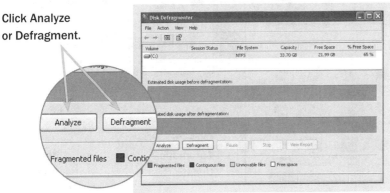

Here are the steps to defrag your PC computer:

- Close all programs that are open.
- Click on **Start**.
- Click on **Programs**.
- Click on **Accessories**.
- Click on **System Tools**.
- Click on **Disk Defragmenter**.
- Click on **Analyze**. If the analysis says you don't need to defrag, close both windows. Otherwise, click **Defragment** and *wait* . . . this could take minutes or hours.
- Eventually, it will notify you that the defragging is complete and you can close all windows.

Updates

If you have a PC, the Microsoft operating system regularly offers updates. These updates are fixes or patches from Microsoft to make your computer run more smoothly. It's a good idea to allow these updates to occur.

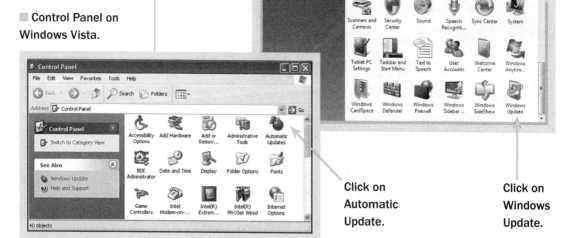

■ Control Panel on Windows XP.

■ Control Panel on Windows Vista.

Click on Automatic Update.

Click on Windows Update.

To instruct the computer to do just that, follow these steps:

- Click on **Start**.
- Click on **Control Panel**.
- Double-click on **Automatic Updates** or **Windows Update**.
- Click inside the circle to the left of **Automatic (recommended)**.
- From here you can schedule when the updates will be downloaded and installed.
- Click **OK**.

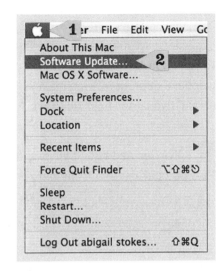

CLICK AND GO

1. Click .

2. Click Software Update.

3. Click install (not shown).

Apple also offers updates, but you access them differently.

- Click on the **Apple** in the top left of the screen.
- Click on **Software Update**.
- The Software Update program will evaluate what is on your computer. If it determines there are updates available, click **Install** to download and install what is suggested for your computer.

Remember, if you take care of your computer, it will take care of you.

With both PCs and Apples, be cautious when on the Internet you are offered to update software on your computer. How does the website know what's on your computer or what you need? Resist the temptation to download anything unless you know what it is and that you want it.

Q: I can't seem to locate documents that I've written. How can I find them?

A: If you have a PC, you can click on **Start** and then click on **Search**. Follow the instructions on where to type all or part of the name of what you're looking for. A window will eventually open with a list of items containing the keywords you typed. Take note of the **Folder** column that tells you the location of the item. If you have a

Mac, click on the **Desktop**, then click **File**, and finally click **Find**. Type in what you're looking for. The window that opens will indicate the location of the file at the bottom of the window. To prevent losing a document or file, always make a conscious decision about where it should live during the **File, Save As** stage.

Q: I've decided I don't want a folder to be inside another folder. How do I get the one folder onto the Desktop?

A: It's as easy as click and drag. Just click and drag the desired folder out of its present home onto the desktop and release the mouse.

Q: Somehow when I click and drag, the document never goes inside the folder. What am I doing wrong?

A: It's all about the aim. Use a steady hand and don't release the mouse until the target (the folder) is highlighted. Then, without moving the mouse, release your finger.

Q: I've tried a few times to rename a document, but the computer keeps refusing the name.

A: Be sure there's no punctuation in the name. Instead of punctuation, use spaces to divide up characters in a file or folder name.

Q: If I buy a new computer, how do I get all my files from one to the other?

A: After you've backed up your documents, photos, and files onto a CD or a DVD, you can then take that CD or DVD and copy all the information from the old computer into the new one. There is also a relatively new device that is perfect for moving information from one computer to another—a USB Flash Drive.

EXPLORATION
AND
DISCOVERY

CHAPTER 21

Detective Work with Your Computer

Get the most out of your searches

A milestone was reached in October 2006. That month marked the existence of 100 million websites on the Internet. To give you some perspective, in August 1995, only 18,000 websites existed. I think this thing called the Internet is starting to catch on!

There's no denying the wealth of information on the net to be researched and enjoyed. The conundrum is how to navigate, sift, and discern what is available in relationship to what you want to find. You'll find this is a process of trial and error that will improve with practice. Searching the Internet requires a sense of adventure, curiosity, and a positive attitude. Say to yourself, "I think I can. I think I can." And you know what? You can!

Search and Recover

On page 180, I introduced the concept of search engines. To refresh your memory, if you walk into the hallowed halls of your local library in search of information on heart disease, you would head straight for the "card catalog," which may now be found on a computer, or to the informative person

GIVE IT YOUR BEST SHOT

Search engines aren't the only way to find a website. Word of mouth, advertising, and sometimes guessing may get you to a website that meets your needs. For example, you love to shop at Brooks Brothers. Hmmm . . . what could their web address be? You got it: *www.brooksbrothers.com.*

behind the desk. You would use these resources to locate books and periodicals relating to heart disease. Search engines on the Internet work basically the same way. You access a search engine and type keywords pertaining to your query, and the search engine finds websites that contain those keywords. Instead of a few books on the subject, you'll likely have hundreds, if not thousands, of websites with all their information at your fingertips in your own home.

If you haven't taken a glance at the recommended websites on page 380, do so when you have a chance. Among the various categories are ten search engines for you to try. Of course, new ones can pop up at any time, and if they're really good, you'll hear about them. Even before you picked up this book, I bet you'd heard of Google. You may not have known what it was, but the buzz had probably gotten to you.

■ Do not confuse the text area of a search engine with the website address box.

Website address box where you click and type a website address.

Text area where you type in keywords for your search.

We'll use *google.com*, *ask.com*, and *yahoo.com* for our searching adventures. You can see from the windows below that although each search engine performs the same basic task, they are designed differently. Yahoo! offers many additional resources above and beyond searching on its home page. At the time of this writing, Ask and Google's home pages look very lean and at first glance appear only to offer searches. But in fact, both offer much more than just search results. Besides searching, you can find maps, blogs, news, and more if you click on the items above where you type in your search.

SHORTCUT

Can I let you in on a secret? With newer computers and software, you don't need to type "www." before all website addresses. I instructed you to type *www.* at the start of your Internet journey to form good habits, but in truth many, maybe most, websites open without the w's.

Choose Your Words Carefully

I n all three sites, the procedure is to click your mouse inside the long text box to activate it. You'll know the site is ready for you to type when the blinking line (the cursor) appears. Simply type the keywords that succinctly describe what you're looking for, and then click on **Search**. Before you type your first search, let's discuss the keywords to best find what you seek. Let's say you love visiting botanical gardens. You're thinking of organizing a vacation around the locations of botanical gardens. You might begin your search with the keywords *botanical garden*.

■ Search results for *botanical garden*.

Here are the numbers of websites I found searching for *botanical garden*:

Yahoo! = 11,200,000

Ask = 2,731,000

Google = 2,670,000

Why would one search engine's results vary in number so dramatically from another? Relatively speaking, a difference of 100,000 isn't so great when you take into account there are a 100,000,000 websites. The seeming discrepancy is because each search engine has its own system and resources for performing a search. That is precisely why you should try more than one search engine to cover your bases when seeking information.

If quotes bookend the words, the results for *"botanical garden"* are:

Yahoo! = 4,100,000

Ask = 1,001,000

Google = 1,850,000

EXCLUDE IT!

If there is a word you want eliminated from your search, add that word to the end of your search preceded immediately by the—(minus) key. For example, you want to find a website with information on hurricanes excluding information about hurricanes on the island of Bermuda. Type: *hurricane-Bermuda*. This search will render all websites that contain the word hurricane, excluding those containing Bermuda.

The difference in results between the two searches is because the second search, by virtue of the quotations marks, specifies any websites containing the phrase *"botanical garden"* in that order instead of any websites containing the words *botanical* and *garden* in any random order within the site. If you searched for *"botanical garden" Illinois-roses*, you would get all websites containing the phrase *"botanical garden,"* the word *Illinois*, but excluding any websites that have the roses.

Are You on the Internet?

Out of curiosity you might check and see if there's information about you on the Internet. No matter how certain you may be that a search for you will come up dry, you might be in for a surprise. You could appear on a website because of the political contribution made during the last presidential race or the random interview with the *San Francisco Chronicle* about busing. Try a search with your name and see what you can find. While you're at it, click on the word **Images**, and next click **Search Images**. If you or someone else with your name has any photos on the Internet you can see them! Remember to click on **Web** to get you back to your text results.

Here's something to take into consideration when formulating your search. My full name is Abigail Pemberton Stokes. (Please don't make fun of my middle name. Thank you!) I wouldn't search for my formal name because no one ever refers to me by that name, so it's unlikely I would be found by that name online. Even being addressed as Abigail is a rarity for me, unless my mother's mad at me. You may want to try a couple of different versions of your name and nickname and see what you discover.

> "When I first found myself on the Internet I didn't like it at all. It felt like an invasion of privacy. However, now I realize that the Internet offers information that is already public."
> —*Ronald*

Every Letter Counts

Every letter you choose matters. Try a search for *hanger* in the singular. Now try a search for *hangers* with an s. The difference in the number of results is significant as a result of one little letter. Interesting, right? Instead of keywords, you can also type your search in sentence form. Experiment with both. Type: *what is an eclipse*. No need for the question mark, and you can play around with whether the quotes help or hurt your results. Now try only *eclipse*.

Don't settle for the first set of results. Try different search engines using different keywords or phrases. With practice, you'll improve at zeroing in on your searches.

SEPARATE YOUR WORDS
Search engines are not case sensitive. You do not need to use capital letters. But unlike a website, you do need to separate each word with a space.

Consult Your Results

Okay. Let's try a search together.
Using either Google, Yahoo!, or Ask, type:

help the hungry

You'll see different results with each search engine, but in all cases the results will be displayed in the same way.

In most search engines, the top line of each search result is usually blue and underlined. Remember websites are usually designed

so that the links, where you click, stand out from other text. Often links are featured in blue and underlined, but not always. Each website is at liberty to make a link noticeable in any way they choose. Move your mouse over the top line, and you'll notice the mouse arrow has changed to a hand—positive confirmation that if you click there, you'll be taken to more information on the subject. This is the link to the search result.

Below the link, in black text, is a short summary of the contents of the site pertaining to the keywords in your search.

The bottom line in green is the actual website address. It's important to look at that address because it may be a deciding factor for which link you choose to check out. If one result has a recognizable website (e.g., *foodnetwork.com*) vs. an unknown entity, I'll go with the familiar website.

Our search for *help the hungry* has brought us literally millions of websites (look at the results number at the top right of the page). Each search engine shows us those results ten to a page. Generally, the order of search engine results is based on a set of rules and an algorithm that takes into consideration the number of terms matched and their relevancy. At the bottom of each page you can click **Next** or the following page number to see the next set of results. Of the websites that fit your criteria,

KEEP AN OPEN MIND

If any of these screen images look different than what's on your computer, don't fret. Websites are updated and redesigned regularly. Look carefully at your computer screen and you'll soon find the same elements referred to here. *Remember* to scroll!

generally most will appear early in the list. I rarely view more than the first three or four pages of results before I restructure my search or have found what I need.

Once you've found a website you want to view, click on the blue underlined link. Scroll down the pages of our results and read the web addresses until you find *www.thehungersite.com*. Click on the link for that site. Voilà!

This is a wonderful site where you can help the hungry, save the rain forest, donate a mammogram, and more—simply with the click of your mouse. When you click "click here to give—it's free!" a donation is made by sponsors of the website, not you. The advertisers hope you'll take note of their generosity and perhaps think of them when you shop next, but there's no obligation. Truly amazing, isn't it?

My mother and I visit this website daily and click on every tab across the top. After you click on the box you'll be brought to a page listing the sponsors. Click on the back arrow to return to the previous page, and then click on the next tab at the top to continue your support.

Don't forget to bookmark a website you may want to visit again. (See page 179.)

SPONSORED LINKS

Sponsored Links or Sponsored Results are websites that paid the search engine to appear on the site. I click on them only when I've exhausted all the other likely possibilities because the websites that open from a sponsored link often have nothing to do with the search made. They want to lure you to their site in hopes that, once you're there, you'll decide to buy what they're selling regardless of whether it was what you were looking for.

The back arrow takes you to the previous page.

Click here to give—it's free!

■ Visit *hungersite.com* every day to make donations of food and more without ever opening your wallet.

You've Got My Number

W hat if you find a piece of paper in your wallet with a phone number you've scribbled down, but no name? Visit *reversephonedirectory.com,* and be sure to use dashes when you type the number in. If the site offers you the name associated with the number for a fee, use the back arrow to return to *reversephonedirectory.com* and scroll down until you reveal the form for "white pages." Click in that text box to activate it, type the phone number, and click **Lookup**. Now, you see the information and no one is asking for money. Remember, unless a website is selling something, most make their money from advertisers. Some of these advertisers deliberately make their ads look like they're part of the website. If you find yourself being solicited for money, close the website or use the back arrow. Start your journey again and look at the entire page (don't forget to scroll!) before you click on anything.

In Google, you can also type in a telephone number to find a person. Try it with your home phone number. Use the dashes between each set of numbers—it improves the search. Click **Google Search**. Did your name and address come up? If your number is unlisted, you'll come up dry, but for those of us that are listed in the telephone book, our names, phone numbers, and addresses are public information. Try the same search in Yahoo! and Ask.

■ Reverse phone
directory website.

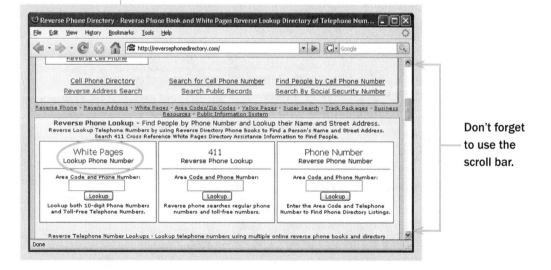

Don't forget
to use the
scroll bar.

If this revelation upsets you, keep in mind you didn't uncover anything private. A phone book would have revealed the same information (albeit by searching by name, not phone number), but I understand how it can put you off to feel so exposed. Public information is just that. The Internet makes public information more easily accessible, but it doesn't reveal anything that isn't already available.

MISSING PERSONS

If you're trying to track down that long lost someone, start your search with these websites: *switchboard.com, classmates.com, zabasearch.com, people.yahoo.com.*

Detective Work Continues...

Search engines aren't the only way to find people, places, or things on the Internet. There are websites designed to offer specific information depending on what you seek. What if you have someone's mailing address but not the zip code? Visit *www.usps.gov* (in this case and with most government-related websites use the w's). Click on **Find a zip code** at the top of the window. Fill out the form with the information you do have and click **Submit**. Handy, isn't it?

Next challenge. You have the street address of your destination, but you want to see where it is on a map. Visit *mapquest.com*. Click in the address box of the form to activate it and type the street address. Continue to fill in the form with the necessary information. Move your mouse on to **Search** and click. Amazing! MapQuest also offers driving

■ The U.S. Postal Service's website where you can search for a zip code and buy stamps.

Click on Find a Zip Code.

directions, which include length of trip, estimated travel time, and turn-by-turn instructions, along with a map. Play with this site to see all it has to offer. It's one of my favorite websites. (Accordingly, I put it into my Favorites! See page 179.) Come back to the book when you're ready for more.

MapQuest provides driving directions as well as maps.

Elementary, My Dear Watson

Let's go to *amazon.com* now. Look across the top of Amazon's home page to see if there's a table of contents, in the form of a list of topics or shopping areas, to guide you where to go. The table of contents can also appear as a sidebar on the left or right of a window. If you click on an item to see where it leads you, remember to use the back arrow (near the word File at the top of the window) to return to the previous web pages.

Some websites offer a text box built into the site where you can type keywords to search for information on that particular website. These are internal search engines. An internal search engine points you to where you want to go on that site (as opposed to the entire World Wide Web). Some of the same rules apply: Type keywords for your

Back
arrow

Table of
contents

Internal
search
engine

search. The text box is not case sensitive, so caps don't matter. Type quotes on either side of your keywords to narrow your search results.

Less talk and more search . . .

The Doctor Is In

One of my favorite websites for medical information is *mayoclinic.com* (it doesn't require the w's). My confidence in the site is based on the extraordinary reputation of the wonderful Mayo Health Clinics located in Scottsdale, AZ, Jacksonville, FL, and Rochester, MN. Their website is one of the best designed for finding information about ailments, treatments, and medications. Join me at *mayoclinic.com* to practice some searching techniques.

The home page offers three different avenues to information. Across the top is the table of contents, the search box is to the right, and "Find it Fast" (an alphabetical search) is to the left. I prefer the alphabetic search method because it doesn't require that I spell the ailment—instead I need only know the first letter. Let's look up De Quervain's tenosynovitis. (See my point about spelling?)

- Click on D in Find it Fast.
- Scroll down the page to De Quervain's tenosynovitis.
- Move your mouse onto *De Quervain's tenosynovitis* and click. (Did you notice your old friend, the hand, indicating the mouse was on a link?)

Look at the wealth of information available on this condition! They've broken down the information into manageable chunks. You can click on the section that interests you or read each

■ The table of contents gives you choices of where to visit on a website. The internal search engine allows you to search for keywords within the website, not the entire Internet.

HOME SWEET HOME
To return to the first page of a website, click on the word **Home** or **Main**. Either word could appear at the top or bottom of the page.

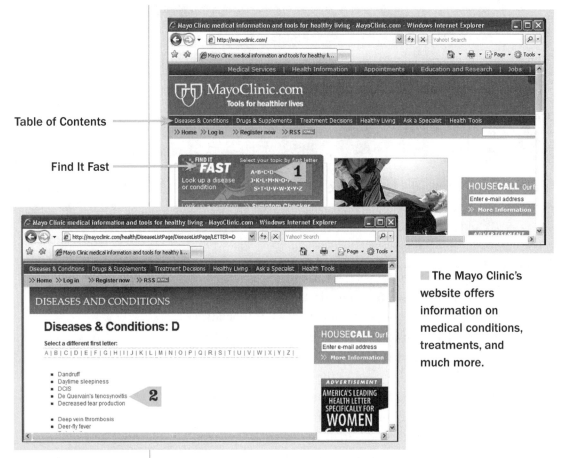

Table of Contents

Find It Fast

■ The Mayo Clinic's website offers information on medical conditions, treatments, and much more.

CLICK AND GO

1. Click on D in Find It Fast.

2. Click on De Quervain's tenosynovitis.

3. Click here to print the page in view.

4. Click here to print all the sections listed.

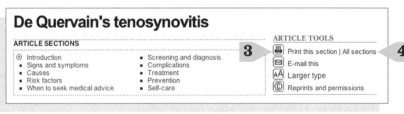

small article and click at the bottom of the page to continue. Notice that at the top of the page it lets you print either just this section or all sections, and it offers you the opportunity to view the site in larger type. Very thoughtful and practical of the website designers. If you click on **Print this section** the page is modified to have only the text of the article and none of the additional information on the page, simplifying the reading and saving you ink.

Linger on this site as long as you want. When you're ready, we'll sleuth out some more information from the Internet.

Encyclopedia Brown

Have you ever wished you had an encyclopedia at your fingertips to support your version of the facts? Just the other night at dinner my sister and I could not agree about when the first crossing of the English Channel happened by air (1909 by French aviator Louis Blériot). You don't have to always search around the Internet for what you seek. You can go directly to a known source of information, as you would if you were in a library. Feel free to access the many encyclopedias offered on the Internet.

Here are a few to start:

britannica.com

encarta.msn.com

wikipedia.com

I've always considered the text in an encyclopedia to be unquestionable and almost sacrosanct. Wikipedia, which launched in January 2001, is an exception to that rule. It is self-described as "the free encyclopedia that anyone can edit." Interesting notion, but it does make me a bit leery about what is fact and what is opinion, or even a prank.

CAN'T FIND WHAT YOU SEEK?

If you're having trouble locating a topic on a web page, click on **Edit** in the toolbar, then click **Find** or **Find (on this page)**. Type the word you're seeking and click **Find Next**.

■ Encyclopaedia Britannica's home page.

Wikipedia's main page.

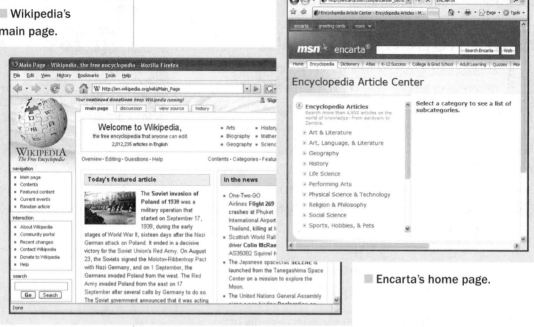

Encarta's home page.

That said, I haven't heard much about people abusing the power given to them to edit the facts, and in my experience, Wikipedia has proven a great resource every time I've visited. Still, proceed with open eyes.

Variety Pack

Whatever your interest, there's a website chock full of information for you. Start to notice and make note of interesting website addresses that cross your path. Web addresses are often referred to in newspapers, magazines, and on TV. If there's the slightest chance the site mentioned is of interest to you, jot the address down. Computer magazines, as I said earlier in the book, can be overwhelming. However, if you see a magazine cover with "100 Best Websites" or some other in-depth review of the Internet, it may be worth picking up. Because the Internet is constantly evolving, there is no single directory listing all websites. If you're considering buying a book with a directory to websites on the Internet, be sure to check out the copyright dates and buy the most recent book published.

Here's just a sampling of what's out there for you to enjoy. When you're ready for more surfing, take a look at the websites listed (by category) on page 380 or visit my website *(www.abbyandme.com)*, to see other recommended sites.

- For movie buffs, one of the best sites is *imdb.com* (Internet Movie Database). Here you can look up a movie using the names of the people involved both in front of and behind the camera, the movie title, the plot, and so on. I've found the most consistent results come from searching for an actor, director, or character name. This website has settled many a movie trivia debate!

- If words are what you seek, there are a multitude of resources. Here are a few:

m-w.com (Merriam-Webster's site)

rhymezone.com (rhyming dictionary)

www.askoxford.com (Oxford dictionary)

"As a retired librarian, I had no idea of the impact of search engines and other research tools on the Internet. It's extraordinary."
—*Rhonda*

- The sports-minded can look up scores, view schedules of competitions, and get the inside scoop on *espn.com.* From the editors of *Golf* magazine, there's *golfonline.com.* The complete TV listing of ice-skating events is available on *usfigureskating.org.*

- Foodies, make sure you spend some time at *foodnetwork.org* and *epicurious.com.* They are both excellent sites to find recipes, video cooking instruction, and party ideas.

- There are websites for every hobby and interest: For toy soldier collectors, there's *toysoldiersgallery.org.* Siberian husky owners will want to check out the Siberian Husky Club of America's site, *shca.org.* There's even a site for time travelers *(time-travel.com).* I kid you not.

- The jackpot of all research websites is *refdesk.com.* If there was only one website on the Internet to lead you to all other sites, this would be it. The amount of information it contains is extraordinary, but a bit overwhelming when you pay your first visit. Take your time and enjoy it in small bites. Anything in blue may be clicked on to lead you to more information on the subject. The home page is a very long—be sure to utilize the Scroll Bar to its fullest. During my first visits to this site (found by my mother, by the way), I would alternate

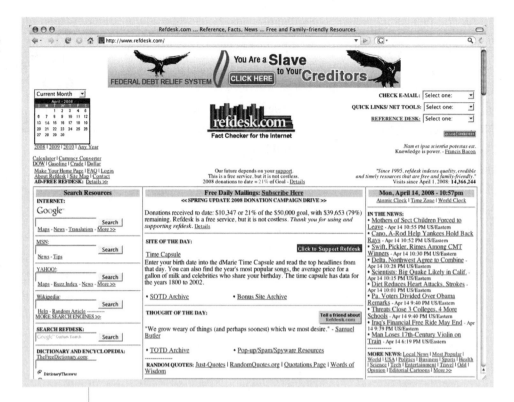

Refdesk.com's home page.

starting at the top of the page and then the bottom to be sure to take advantage of all it offers.

Are you beginning to get the picture? You name it and you'll find it on the Internet. Each of the sites I mentioned offers a way to navigate and search the site. The more you travel the Internet, the more adept you'll become at finding what you need.

The Guessing Game

Never underestimate your own powers of logic. Let's say there's an organization you'd like to find more about. Feel free to take a stab at its web address. Type *www.(yourguesshere). com*. When guessing, I would type *www.*, in case it's necessary for the website to open. Keep in mind that there are no spaces in a website address. Revisit page 175 for web address basics. If you're wrong, either a website you're not interested in will open or you'll get an error message because no website exists under that address.

(Is it possible that you could be led to a fraudulent website that registered a similar name hoping to snag viewers who made typographical errors? Yup. And beware: These websites are often pornographic.) If you really get muddled up, close everything until you're back at your Desktop, and make a fresh start. Losing your way, bungling a website address, and ending up someplace completely unexpected is part of the learning process. Every time you turn on the computer, have a research challenge at the ready so you can hone your skills. Do I have to repeat myself? Okay, I will. It is only with practice that you will tame the computer beast. Practice, practice, practice!

Homework Assignment

I'm sending you on an Internet Treasure Hunt. See if you can find the answers to the quests below (FYI: The answers are at the end, but don't peek):

1. Do a good deed—help save the rain forest. (How many square feet did you save today?)

2. Read a headline—find out what's going on in the world.

3. Check the weather for tomorrow—here or somewhere else.

4. Find yourself—remember to use the exact listing from the phone book. Are you correctly listed in the web directory?

5. Find yourself by using only your phone number.

6. Figure out if you are notable enough to be listed on a search engine.

7. Get directions—How do I get to Carnegie Hall (57th and 7th Avenue) in New York City from Faneuil Hall (75 State Street) in Boston?

8. Go shopping—look for this book.

9. Find out how batteries work or why biting aluminum foil is painful.

Suggested answers (but remember, there's usually more than one route to the information you want): 1. therainforestsite.org; 2. cnn.com or nytimes.com; 3. weather.com; 4. switchboard.com; 5. reversephonedirectory.com; 6. google.com; 7. mapquest.com; 8. amazon.com; 9. howstuffworks.com

Q: **Is there a website where I can find someone's cell phone number or e-mail address?**

A: At the moment the answer is no. Tracking e-mail addresses is particularly difficult because people register new addresses every day, and they do not always use their real names to do so. I'm not sure why there isn't a registry of all cell phones, but there isn't.

Q: **Is there a definitive website to visit for research?**

A: Of all the search engines we've discussed in the chapter, my favorite research site is *refdesk.com.* My mother found the site when I was working on this book. The site is so jam-packed with information that you have to take it in small bites or you can get overwhelmed. This is the one site to visit if you need to find a doctor by area of expertise, to contact your congressional representative, to convert a cooking measurement, to read a Tel Aviv newspaper, to see the time in Hong Kong, do today's crossword puzzle, to translate a German word . . . Are you starting to get the picture? Visit the site and don't forget to use the Scroll Bar to reveal all it has to offer.

Q: **Can someone trace what I've researched online?**

A: The websites that you've visited shouldn't be tracing your steps, but your computer keeps a history of what websites you've visited. So, if someone has access to your machine they can see where you've been. To clear the history on a PC in Internet Explorer, click **Tools**, then click **Internet Options** and, under **Browsing History**, click **Delete**. To clear the history on a Mac, when in Safari, click **History** and then click **Clear History**. To clear the history using Firefox, on either a Mac or PC, click **Tools**, then **Clear Private Data**, and finally click **Clear Private Data Now**.

CHAPTER 22

Shop Till You Drop

Shopping, auctions, airline reservations, prescriptions, and online banking

Shopping online may be one of the greatest assets the Internet has to offer. No lines to stand in, no one trying to hard-sell you, and no need to leave your home. I have a student who likes to get out of the house to grocery shop, but she has trouble managing all the bulk items like paper towels and cleaning products. She buys those items online, along with heavy canned and bottled goods, but goes to the store for fresh produce, milk, and meats. (In fact, she could buy those things online as well, but she chooses not to.)

However, if you're not comfortable shopping online for any reason, don't do it. There is no rule that mandates you must shop online merely because online shopping exists. Most of us don't climb a mountain just because it's there.

Having said that, let's investigate what's available and how to shop efficiently and safely on the Internet, if you choose to do so. Shopping online isn't limited to clothes and housewares. Anything you can imagine

is available online. My most obscure purchase was a set of shower curtains. Doesn't sound obscure, right? Well, I needed nine shower curtains in very specific colors. No, I don't have nine showers—I wanted shower curtains for my screened porch because they are waterproof and I thought they would make practical curtains. I searched dozens and dozens of websites and viewed hundreds of shower curtains before I finally found the perfect one. Unfortunately, the online store that sold it only had three in stock and they weren't able to order more. From their website, I copied the exact name of the shower curtain and product number and pasted it into Google where, with a little hunting, I found the name of the manufacturer . . . in China! The end of the story is, after the loveliest e-mail correspondence with a woman named Rain (and an invitation to visit her in China!), the shower curtains were shipped to my home directly from China. I certainly would not have been able to accomplish that task without the Internet. By the way, they look adorable.

Why Shop Online?

You can't see or touch the merchandise, so what makes online shopping so appealing? Well, the following three aspects for starters:

• Comforts of home: You don't need to leave your home (or office) to shop. Therefore, no parking hassles, no waiting in long lines, and no fighting for the last iPhone on the shelf.

• Global access: Stores all over the world are at your fingertips. A student of mine wanted an out-of-print CD that a jazz-musician friend of hers had recorded nearly 40 years ago in Denmark. She was able to track down the recording studio's website and place an order for the CD online. Even the musician himself didn't know his original recordings were still available for purchase.

• Savings: Online retailers save on personnel and other overhead costs. They often pass the savings on to you. This is especially true with travel arrangements. Shopping online should save you money— you're doing most of the administrative work!

Start with the Familiar

Get your feet wet with a visit to the website of a "brick-and-mortar" store you frequent in your area. If you shop at Home Depot, visit their website: *homedepot.com.* Is Macy's one of your shopping spots? Visit *macys.com.* Or you could pop into the website of a catalog that you patronize. Perhaps you are a Crate & Barrel *(crateandbarrel.com)* fan or a Lillian Vernon *(lillianvernon.com)* loyalist.

Right now, you and I, together, are going to visit L.L. Bean *(llbean.com)* to simulate the purchase of a canvas tote. Connect to the Internet and access *llbean.com.* Let's see what their website has to offer. Wow . . . there's a ton of information on their Home Page. It's almost too much to take in, but there is strength in numbers and together we can navigate these new waters. I spy an internal search engine. Do you? Perfect. Click inside the text box to activate and type: canvas tote. Click on **Go**.

A POLICY ON POLICIES

It's a good idea to click on and read the website's policies. You'll find out what the procedure is if you need to return an item, along with any guarantee information.

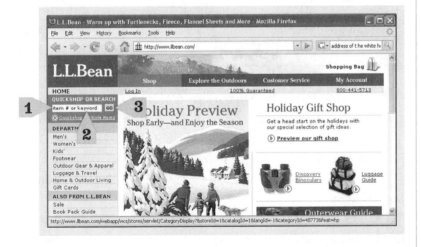

L.L. Bean's website.

CLICK AND GO

1. Click in Quickshop or Search box.

2. Type *canvas tote.*

3. Click Go.

The new page reveals a selection of canvas totes. Click on **Boat and Tote Bag, Open Top**. Be sure to scroll all the way to the bottom of the following page so you don't miss anything. When you have viewed the entire page, scroll back up and join me at

FLEXIBILITY PREVAILS

It may be that L.L. Bean redesigned their site after this image was captured for the book. If that's the case, take your time to look around the page and find the same elements seen here.

the top of the page. This site is a good example of how the same options available in the store or in the catalog are also available when you shop online. You get to choose your tote's size, color, and handle length. You can even have the bag monogrammed! Let's say you want two medium-size totes with dark green handles in the regular length.

CLICK AND GO

1. Click Medium.

2. Click down arrow, click Regular Handles.

3. Click down arrow, click Dark Green.

4. Click Quantity Box, hit Backspace to erase 1, type 2.

5. Click down arrow in box under Ship To. Type name of recipient.

6. Click Add To Shopping Bag.

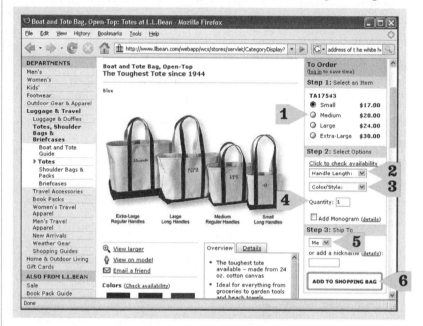

• Click inside the circle to the left of Medium. Give the window a chance to update your order.

• Click on the down arrow to the right of Handle Length; click on **Regular Handles**.

• Click on the down arrow to the right of Color/Style; click on **Dark Green**.

• Click after the number one in Quantity. Depress and release the **Backspace** or **Delete** key on your keyboard to eliminate the "1." Type the number 2.

The website will offer to ship the item to someone other than you. If that is your preference, here is where you type a nickname for the recipient of this item. Now, we're not really buying the tote; we're only practicing. Choose whomever you want to "pretend" to send a tote. I will choose my sixth-grade teacher, Mrs. Ballek. She always carried home our quizzes in a canvas tote to grade. (I can remember that but not the movie I saw last night?!)

- Click on the down arrow to the right of (Ship To) Me; click on **Other**.

- Below the text box, click on **Add To Shopping Cart**.

- Most websites, as this one does, give you the option to **Continue Shopping** or to **Check Out**. Click on **Check Out**.

You can now view the contents of your shopping cart and make any changes necessary regarding quantity.

Did you happen to notice the shipping costs? It isn't common, but some online retailers really gouge you on their shipping fees. Before you complete your purchase, decide if the shipping costs listed are reasonable. This is especially true when shopping for airfares. The lowest airfare may end up being equal to or even exceeding its competitors' fares when the taxes and fees are tallied.

- Next, click on **Check Out Now**.

- The page that opens next is an interesting one. You're offered the chance to **Log In** or **Continue as a Guest**. If this is a website you'll shop at frequently, you might consider registering with the site.

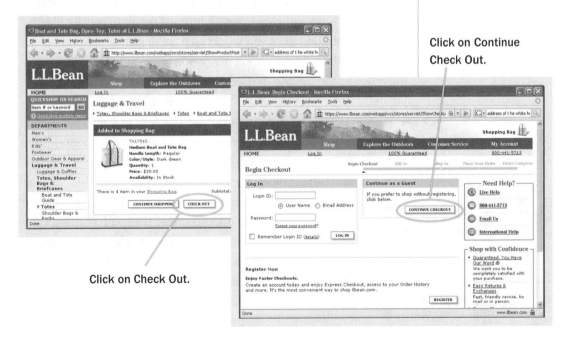

Click on Continue
Check Out.

Click on Check Out.

REMINDER
Use the Scroll Bar to view all the page has to offer.

This involves an online form you complete with your name, mailing address, telephone number (possibly day and evening), billing address, and e-mail address. The convenience of registering is that your information is kept on file and you don't need to type it every time you come back to make a purchase.

Let's not register with the website this time around. (Some websites require you to register to make a single purchase. It's a bit irritating, but you may not have a choice.)

• Next click on **Continue Check Out**.

You will need to type your billing information. Notice that any text box with a red asterisk is a required field (you must fill it in). Those areas without an asterisk are usually optional. I generally don't give any more information than necessary.

The credit card company uses the billing address to confirm that the credit card is in the hands of the authorized cardholder. Be sure you type your correct billing address—for some people that is different than the mailing address. You will be asked for the shipping address later.

Fill in the form. These forms are not case sensitive so you don't need to capitalize, unless you have a burning desire to use the Shift key. Enter the address as you would on a mailing envelope and don't use nonstandard abbreviations. When you arrive at **State:**, click on the down arrow and use the Scroll Bar to find your state. Click on your state.

Certain websites require you to type your e-mail address in twice to be sure there are no typos (typographical errors). Your e-mail address is used to send a confirmation of your purchase and to update you on the shipping status. Because this may lead to future solicitations, I use my second e-mail address—the one I created for any correspondence other than with friends, family, and business contacts. You may want to do the same.

Notice on this site there is a choice about whether you receive e-mail updates, along with an offer to store your information for future purchases. If you see a check in the box, it indicates you accept their offer. If there is a check in the box

A SHORTCUT
The Tab key moves the cursor from text box to text box, instead of clicking in each box to activate before you type.

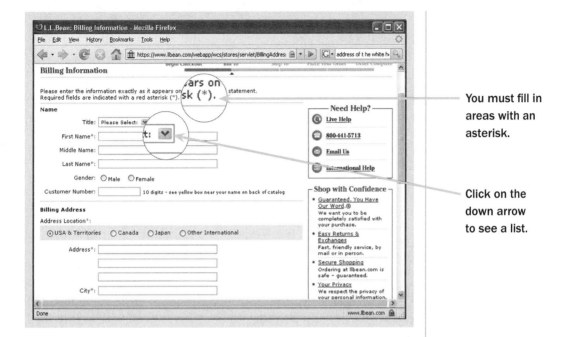

You must fill in areas with an asterisk.

Click on the down arrow to see a list.

and you don't want to accept the offer, click on the check to make it vanish. Poof! It's gone.

> • Now, click on **Continue**.

> • For the sake of practice, fill in the shipping form. You can input a fictitious address because we have no intention of completing this order.

> • Next, click on **Continue**.

You can see your entire order for review before you type your credit card information. Remove your hands from the keyboard, lest you accidentally order an unwanted tote bag! Notice where your credit card information would be typed, but remember we're not actually shopping. In the future, when you input your credit card number, ignore the spaces or dashes—type it as one long number—and examine what you typed and be sure there are no errors. You may be asked for the code on your credit card. If you use American Express it will be the four numbers above and to the right of your credit card number. If you use MasterCard or Visa it is the three numbers at the end on the back of your card. The last step after entering all the credit card information would be to click

CHOOSE YOUR STATE

Instead of scrolling from Alabama to Wyoming, click in the box and type the first letter of your state. Scroll to your state and click. Less scrolling makes for fewer mouse mishaps.

Here is where you would give your credit card information.

Purchase Now. The website then sends an e-mail confirmation of your order, which you should promptly print and keep for your records until delivery occurs.

Be on the Lookout

If, at any time, you see a customer service number, jot it down. Websites are notorious for concealing their contact numbers. For reasons of cost, most sites prefer all correspondence be by e-mail. I may be old fashioned, but when I have a complaint or question, I'd like the option to speak to a human being. If you return to the website seeking out their telephone number, look for **Contact Us**, **Customer Service**, or **About Us**. Scroll to the bottom of the page. Sometimes, what you seek (and they hide) is in very small letters at the end of the web page.

Satisfaction Guaranteed

To ensure that your credit card information is safe, websites employ SSL (Secure Sockets Layer), which encrypts data, making it safer for transmission. You'll know the page is protected by SSL when http in the web address has an added s (https) for security. A closed padlock might appear at the bottom of the browser window. An open padlock or a broken key at the bottom of the window indicates you are not on an encrypted page.

If the unfortunate happens and someone has abused your credit card (and, remember, the Internet may not have even played a role in the event), under federal law your liability is limited to $50. If a breach of security on the part of the website revealed your credit card information, the website should pay this amount for you.

The American Bar Association has created an informative website, *safeshopping.org*, for information about online shopping. (Note: It is .org, not .com.) Visit their site for more information before you start shopping on the Internet.

If something happens that warrants you bringing in the big guns, contact the Better Business Bureau at *www.bbbonline.org* (or call your local Better Business Bureau). You could also fill out a complaint form with the Federal Trade Commission at *www.consumer.gov.* Type *complaint* in the internal search engine. Another option is to contact your state attorney general. Contact information can be found at the website of the National Association of Attorneys General, *naag.org.* (Notice their website acronym almost reads like "nag"!) If your complaint crosses international lines, head to *www.econsumer.gov* and click on English.

A closed padlock indicates you are on a secure website.

Registration Considerations

When you register on a website you are required to establish an identity (ID) with the website. Some websites will use your e-mail address for your ID; others may allow an ID of your choosing. You will also be asked for a password. Do I have to tell you *not* to use your bank password? Good. You've been paying attention! A+!

If at any time during the ordering process you are uncomfortable or confused, most shopping sites allow you to complete the order over the phone. Don't be hard on yourself. If the site is difficult to navigate, it is poorly designed. You are not the ninny, the website is.

Relax while I relate a funny, and possibly helpful, story about a student of mine. Gloria, with great trepidation,

NO PURCHASE REQUIRED

If a website is really confusing or poorly designed, feel free to abandon the mission at any time. In most cases, you can find the same item being sold on several different websites.

> "I couldn't believe it when I found the American Heritage plate of my mother's that I had broken years ago. You should have seen the look on her face when I gave it to her. I love shopping on the Internet."
>
> —*Georgia*

ventured onto a website to purchase a gift for her nephew. In the course of filling in the registration form, the site asked her to type her e-mail address. She dutifully did so in the appropriate text box. Next, she was asked to type a password. She did. The next step read, "Confirm your password" with a text box beside those words. (As you may have noticed by now, when you type a password you can't see what you type. That's for your own protection, so no one can peek over your shoulder and read your password.) Gloria responded to the request for her to confirm her password. The website rejected her. She tried, and tried, and tried again. She finally gave up in frustration. In our next class together, she shared her saga. I asked, "What did you type in the box that asked for you to confirm your password?" She answered logically, "I confirm." A completely understandable mistake—the website, of course, wanted her to "retype" her password as confirmation, but the language the website designer chose made that less than perfectly clear. Shame on the designer, not on Gloria!

The burden, unfortunately, falls on you to interpret the text of a website or software program. If at first you don't succeed, try a different interpretation, then try, try again.

All Categories

Sidebar of Categories

■ **Click in either place to see more items offered from Amazon.**

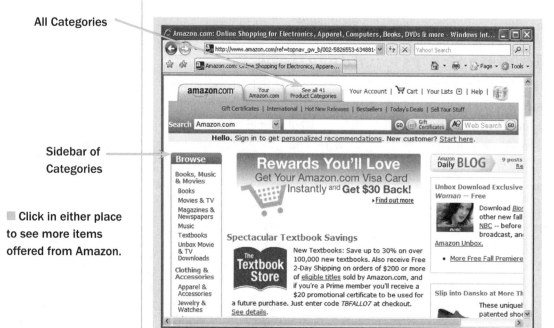

Same Moves, Different Dance Partner

T he steps we took with L.L. Bean are essentially the same as what you'll do with any shopping website you visit, whether ordering tulip bulbs, vitamins, or a bicycle built for two. Be sure to notice if the website offers, at the top or the side of the window, different categories of what they sell. Nose around the site until you find something of interest, and then click on the item for more information. Next, instruct the site to place the item in your shopping cart, bag, or basket. When

Your Prescription Is Ready

It is now possible for you to purchase prescription medication online. The most common reasons why people choose to buy prescription medications with a click of their mouse rather than a trip to the pharmacist are convenience and privacy. However, it may also appeal to you because you're able to compare prices and access more written material about the drug in question.

The steps to checking out are a little more involved than the steps to purchase a tote bag, but not by much. You will at some point be asked about allergies to medications to be sure that you can take the medication prescribed. There will also be a point where you decide how the website will verify your prescription. You can mail in your prescription, have your doctor call or fax the website, have the website walk you through the steps to transfer the prescription from your present pharmacy, or ask the site to contact your doctor directly to confirm the prescription.

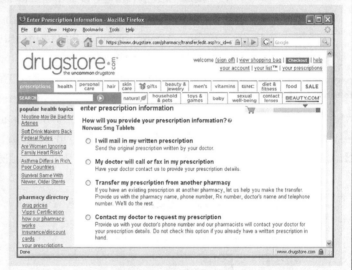

■ You decide how the website will contact your physician to verify your prescription.

Be cautious about buying prescription medication from a foreign country's website because the drug may not be exactly the same as it is in the United States. The Food and Drug Administration (FDA) regulates the quality of drugs made in the United States but not elsewhere. If you have more questions, visit the FDA's website at *www.fda.gov/oc/buyonline/*.

you're done shopping, fill in the necessary shipping and billing information. When you're certain you want to complete the purchase, fill in your credit card information. Soon after, you'll receive an e-mail confirmation to be printed and kept until your doorbell rings when the package arrives. The convenience is fantastic, and you can't deny the efficiency of the process.

The website seen on the previous page is *drugstore.com*, but ask your doctor what pharmacy site he or she recommends.

Let's Make a Deal

Before you pay top dollar for an item, perhaps you should shop around for the best deal. The same item is often sold on several different websites. Could it be that there is competition on the Internet? You bet your bottom dollar! Competition breeds competitive pricing, and that's good news for all of us. Comfort and/or loyalty may lead you to shop at a tried-and-true website. There is nothing wrong with that. But, if you want to buy a particular item and you have no website allegiances, why not find the best deal? There are search engines to hunt the World Wide Web in its entirety (e.g., Google, Yahoo!, Ask) and there are search engines that specialize exclusively in shopping.

CLICK AND GO

1. Click in box.
2. Type *hammock*.
3. Click Search.

shopping.com

shopzilla.com

pricegrabber.com

mysimon.com

Try any of these on for size. Each site allows you to type in the item you seek by name, product number, or description. The site will look up the item. If it finds it, it will let you know the different websites you can purchase from and let you see an estimate of the price.

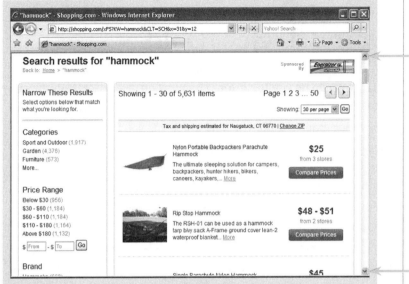

Use the scroll bar to see the results of your search for a hammock.

Scroll Bar

Feel free to also experiment with Google, Yahoo!, Ask, or any other search engine. The results, however, from a general search engine will be less specific than a search engine designed specifically for shopping. Shopping search engines usually hit on the type of product you seek (e.g., microwave) and list the various models, with a link to direct you to the websites selling that product. Remember to take shipping costs into consideration before you decide where to make your purchase.

Coupons

There are many websites with coupons for the taking. Here are a few to try:

couponcabin.com

bargainshare.com

thecouponclippers.com

learnthenetcoupons.com

Do *not* pay for coupons. That is not a coupon. That is a rip-off. If registration is required to obtain the coupons, you definitely want to give your secondary e-mail address. Registering will likely result in you being added to a mailing list which may lead to you receiving advertising and spam. Not to worry, as long as it doesn't clog up your personal e-mail account.

Going Once, Going Twice, Sold!

There is an alternative to paying a set price asked for an item. You can decide to do your shopping on an auction website such as eBay. These sites operate very much as a live auction does. If there is an object you are interested in purchasing you place a bid on the item. You watch the bidding to see if someone bids higher and then you can decide if you want to go higher, and so on. This goes on until the deadline for the bidding is reached. The highest bidder then pays for the item and it is shipped to them.

Many people buy and sell on auction sites with happy results all around, but you must have your guard up. It is extremely important that you click on and read the **Terms of Use**, **Rules**, or **Policies**. The rules of the auction site must be perfectly clear to you before you become involved in buying or selling.

Although you view an auction item on a given auction website, who is responsible if the item doesn't arrive, is broken, or is not what it appeared to be? Often that responsibility is with the seller, not the

 eBay policy
page.

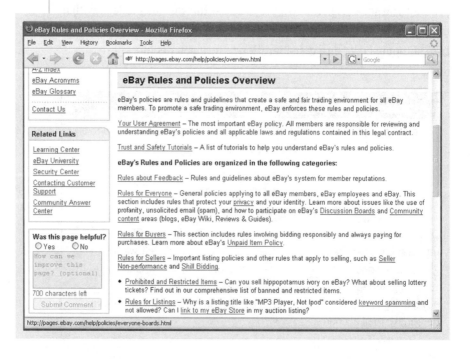

auction site. How comfortable are you with that situation? Who is this seller anyway?

These issues illustrate why it is so important to familiarize yourself with an auction site's policies and stick with reputable auction sites. Although eBay may be one of the best known auction websites, it isn't the only good one.

Here are some other auction sites to visit:

uBid.com (a general auction site)

skyauction.com (specializes in travel auctions)

biddingforgood.com (a portion of the proceeds goes to charity)

For now, let's use eBay as our gold standard. Visit *ebay.com* (no need to type the b in caps). Scroll to the bottom of the page and click on **Policies**. Take the time to read everything this page presents. The policies for whatever site you use to buy or sell should be as clear and specific as eBay's.

Standard Procedures

Auction sites usually charge a fee to the seller. The fee may apply whether your item sells or not, or the fee may only apply if the item sells. There is a time limit for how long an item is at auction. If you really want the item, get your final bid in just before the bidding closes. My heart is racing just writing about it! The reserve price, which is typically unknown to the bidders, is the lowest price, the seller will accept. Some sellers also list a buying price, eliminating the hassle and nerve-wracking auction process. Frankly, I would rather buy the item outright than play the auction game. The suspense is too much for me.

Both sellers and buyers are required to register with the auction website. (Use the same registration and password guidelines that I suggest throughout the book.) As a matter of fact, you will be using a lot of the same devices discussed previously to get the most out of your auction experience. For example, utilize the internal search engine of an auction site to compare prices on what you want to sell or buy. Also, be on the lookout for a list of categories at the top or sides of the window to narrow your search.

WHAT'S IN A NAME?

Why "eBay"? Rumor has it the founder of the site, Pierre Omidyar, wanted to name it echobay.com after his company, Echo Bay Technology Group. Someone had already registered that domain name, so he settled for eBay and the rest is history.

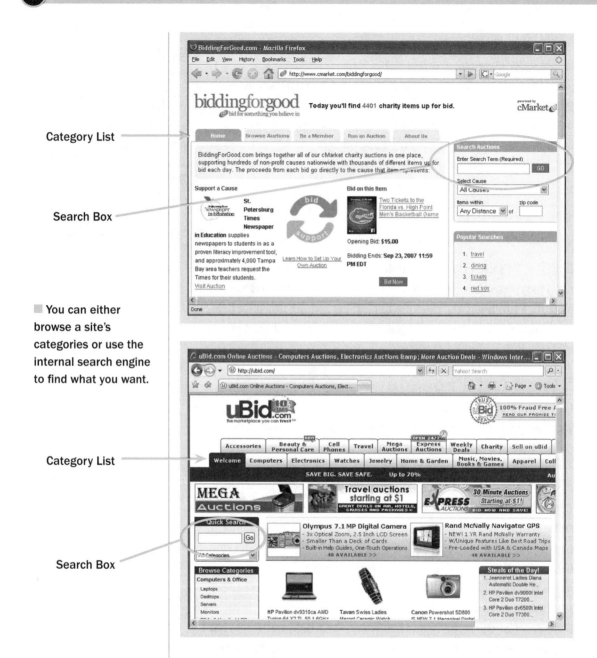

Category List

Search Box

■ You can either browse a site's categories or use the internal search engine to find what you want.

Category List

Search Box

Armed with the preceding information, find and buy the vintage Louis Vuitton handbag your mother gave away before you were old enough to appreciate it. Sell the awful lamp your sister-in-law gave you, because there is someone out there who will think it's beautiful. Bid on the missing Hummel to complete your collection. Good luck!

Advice for the Buyer

Before you decide to participate in an auction, watch a few auctions online from start to finish. Get the lay of the land. Here are some more helpful tips for buyers:

• Do not be lured away from the auction site you know and trust by the promise of that same item at a lower price by a private seller. That is called "bid siphoning." Once you leave the auction site, you leave the protection it guarantees.

• Stick with the top price you set for yourself. Sellers may have "shills" who drive up prices with no intention of buying. (Shills are a violation of most auction policies.) They rely on buyers to get caught up in the moment and overbid.

• Take heed of other people's experiences. Usually a website offers a place where people can review their experiences with a particular seller. The rating scale (another term for review) should be near the ID or e-mail address of the seller.

• Do not assume the rules are the same from one auction site to another. Some websites offer a tour of how the site works or a tutorial on how to use the site. If there is a bidding tutorial offered, take advantage of it.

• Investigate shipping costs, warranty, and return policy.

You name a collectible and you can find it on the Internet.

Advice for the Seller

Before you list your baseball card collection on an auction website, get familiar with how these websites work. There are as many shifty buyers as there are sellers. You need to have your head about you as a seller. Here are helpful tips for sellers:

• Be as specific as possible about the condition of the item. You don't want to give the buyer the opportunity to return something on the excuse that the description was inaccurate.

• A good photo will save you a thousand words about the object.

• Be clear about who incurs the shipping expense. If you're selling a large or heavy object, you may not want to be the one to pay to ship it cross country.

• Decide and post a clear return policy. The more transparent your policies, the less wiggle room for the buyer.

THE CLASSIFIEDS

Just as your local paper lists classified ads, the Internet offers the same convenient way to advertise to sell or buy a used car, rent your apartment, or find a masseur. All of the same precautions we've discussed previously should be taken here. If the website or transaction seems fishy, walk away. If it all seems right, go for it!

Some better-known classified websites for you to visit:

craigslist.com
classifieds.yahoo.com
classifiedads.com

• If the buyer suggests an online payment service that you've never heard of, check it out with a phone call or a visit to the website before you agree. Don't accept a payment arrangement that makes you uncomfortable. The standard website to facilitate payments is PayPal.

• Be on the lookout for fraudulent checks or money orders. If there is any question about a check's authenticity, bring it to your bank and ask a bank officer to have a look before you ship to the buyer. Most sellers stipulate a seven-day waiting period, to make sure the check clears, before shipping an item.

Born Free

The Internet is sort of a mixed bag when it comes to what is free and what appears to be free and ends up not free at all. Here's a good example: You want to design an invitation for Bastille Day. You search on a search engine (i.e., Google, Yahoo!, etc.) as described in the previous chapter for free clip art Bastille Day. Holy smokes! More than 49,000 websites come up. I don't want to disappoint you, but most of the clip art sites in your results aren't free at all. Sure, you can use some of the (how shall I say this and remain polite?) "less attractive" clip art, but the good stuff? That you'll have to pay for. It's a sneaky technique. Based on principle, I don't buy from a website that touts "free" and then doesn't live up to it. I find it underhanded and disingenuous.

Here's the good news . . . there are websites that offer free advice, free information, and, yes, free stuff for free. One of my all-time favorite websites is *freecycle.org*. At *freecycle.org*, you'll find all kinds of things that people want to dispose of and are willing to give away rather than sell. The whole spirit of the website appeals to me. (Although there is no law governing the use of .org, it is intended to be used only with nonprofit sites. If you type *freecycle.com*, you will arrive at an entirely different website.)

Even though the site is full of free stuff, become acquainted with their site procedures by clicking **About Us** or **FAQ** (frequently asked questions).

Freecycle.org's website.

Up, Up, and Away

The Internet offers you not only the opportunity to research where you might want to go on vacation, but what is the best way to get there, where you should stay, and how you should get around while you're there. What more can you ask?

There are several really good travel websites that you might recognize because the same companies that supply the travel books host them:

fodors.com

frommers.com

lonelyplanet.com

If you don't find the hotel you desire with the resources cited here, you can either search on *google.com* or try *hotels.com.* Most hotels have their own websites with a photo gallery, the location of the hotel on a map, and the capability of making reservations online.

One of the more intimidating transactions to complete online is the reservation and purchase of airline tickets. Almost all airlines have a web storefront where you can purchase airline tickets directly from the carrier. There are also websites that compare airline, hotel, and rental car prices for you. You can make your reservations through these websites and be offered some great discounts. However, be aware that you may be subject to the website's policies and not the airline, hotel, or rental car company's policies.

Being able to track down the flight that best meets your travel needs is miraculous. (You could stop the process there and call the airline or your travel agent with the flight information to finalize the purchase. I did that for years before I decided to take the plunge and actually purchase the airline tickets online. But now that most travel agents charge a fee to issue tickets, I almost always buy online.)

Before you take the plunge, it's best to have a printer—as likely as not you already do—because the common practice on the part of airlines is to e-mail you an e-ticket (electronic ticket), which you print and bring to the airport in lieu of having the airline mail you a ticket. You don't have to print out your e-ticket—you can pick it up at the airport—but I get nervous without some acknowledgment I can carry in my hand to the check-in desk. There are kiosks in most airports where you can use your credit card to get your boarding pass, or if you have proper identification the representative at the ticket desk will print your boarding pass for you.

There are many travel sites out there, and new ones sprout up all the time. Here are some of the better known discount airline websites:

orbitz.com

expedia.com

flights.com

kayak.com

travelocity.com

A PENNY SAVED . . .
Airline carriers usually offer you a discount if you buy your ticket online rather than over the phone.

When I shop for airfares, I experiment with several sites to compare prices and flight times. Once I decide on the flight, I usually visit the airline carrier's website to check if they can match the lowest price. Be sure to add up any fees and taxes before you decide which is the better deal.

Take your time filling in the search form. Click on **Expand Search Options**, **Advanced**, or **More Search Options** to specify one-way,

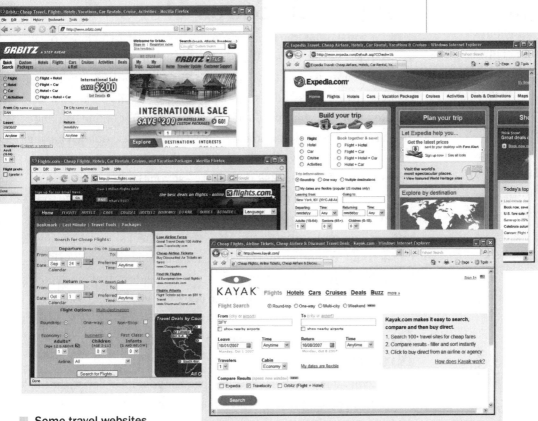

Some travel websites.

round-trip, multiple stops, and so on. When you type your destination, avoid abbreviations unless you know the airport code; otherwise, type the full name of the city, state, and country. The more specific your departure and arrival dates and times, the leaner your results.

The list of available flights can be sorted by price, departure times, and/or length of flight. Pay attention to whether there are stopovers. How long is the stopover? Too tight for the connecting flight or so long that you lose a day of your vacation?

In the event that you may need to cancel or change your reservation, the change fees with discount tickets can run over $100. If there is an opportunity to buy travel insurance at the time of purchase, you may want to consider it. Investigate travel insurance when making hotel and car rental reservations as well.

Happy trails!

"I no longer have to spend hours balancing my checkbook at the end of the month. I view my balance online every day and always know the status of my account."
—*Marlena*

The Buck Stops Here

At some point, the day of reckoning arrives and you have to pay for your purchases. That's where online banking comes in handy. No more writing checks, licking the yucky envelope, or paying postage. In one fell swoop you can pay all of your bills online in a few minutes. Contact your bank and find out if they offer online banking. You may be pleasantly surprised to learn that because online banking saves the bank money, many banks share the savings by not charging a fee to pay bills online. Ask if that's true at your bank.

If your bank does offer online banking you will be able to go to their website to view your account balance, see any recent transactions, look up past transactions, order checks, transfer from one account to another, and pay both monthly bills and onetime bills. Other than actually getting hard cash in your hands or making deposits to the bank, there isn't much that can't be done with online banking.

Do I Need the Payee's Account Number?

Whether it is your telephone company or your local florist, the bank can make a payment from your checking account to the payee online. All you need to give to the bank is the mailing address of the payee along with any account number you may have with them. You do not need any bank account information from the person or company that you want to pay online.

The bill payment window of Bank of America's website.

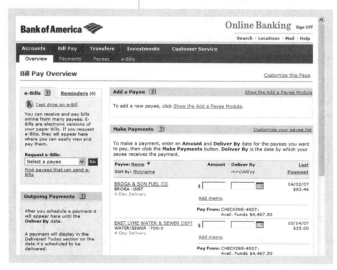

Register with Your Bank

Access your bank's website to register to view your account and pay bills, among other things. Some banks issue an ID and password. Others let you choose it yourself. (I will resist reminding you *again* about password protocol.) This is one of the rare times that you may be asked to type your Social Security number. The bank uses that number to confirm your identity. Once you have gotten past that stage, you should never be asked for your Social Security number online again. If you are, call the bank directly to be sure it is a legitimate request.

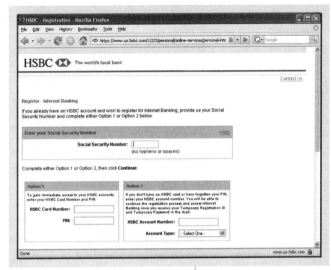

After registration, you will log on to your account with your ID and password.

Follow your bank's instructions about how to input each payee for bill paying. Double-check everything you type (account name, account number, mailing address, and telephone number) to be sure it is correct. A typo can cause a payment to go astray. Eventually the problem would be corrected, but extra care during account setup will prevent possible difficulties.

I know for some of you there is too much uncertainty with banking online. Will my payments really go through? How can I be sure? What if I make a mistake with a transaction? Do I get a receipt?

Start small. If you want to experiment with banking online, start with a utility bill or two until you get the hang of it. Once you've honed

■ The registration page of HSBC's website.

■ The Sign On window of Citibank's website.

CLICK AND GO

1. Click in box, type your User ID.

2. Click in box, type Password.

3. Click on Sign On.

your online banking skills, add your credit cards, then your mortgage payment, and before you know it, you won't be able to remember the last time you wrote a check! Continue to note transactions in your check register, however, to keep on top of your bank balance. When you make an online payment you may be given a transaction number. Note that number in your check register or on the paid bill. It will be your reference number with the bank if something goes wrong with the transaction.

Let me fess up. I still walk into the bank and wait in line for the teller to process my deposits. I can't explain why I don't use the ATM machine to make my deposits, but it's somehow comforting to me to hand my money to a live person. So I completely understand if online banking does not appeal to you. Conduct your bank transactions in whatever manner is comfortable for you.

Credit Cards Online

Consider accessing your credit card statements online. The process to sign on to your credit card accounts online is very similar to that of online banking. You can also pay the credit card company directly, if you don't mind giving them your checking account number. (I personally prefer doing all my payments from my bank site and not directly on my credit card company's site because I'm afraid I'll forget to note the payment in my check register.) You can monitor your credit card spending daily, rather than nearly passing out when the monthly statement arrives. You'll also have ample time to make up some really good excuses for your overspending before your spouse sees the statement!

You Did What?!

Your online shopping experience will probably start out slowly, with small purchases. That is as it should be. Take it at whatever pace works best for you. I hope that I've given you some tips on how to make your online shopping less confusing and safer.

However, no one can save you from your own bad shopping habits. Step away from the mouse when considering the 1980s sweater that glows under black lights. It wasn't a good idea back then, and it certainly isn't a good idea now. Do you really need *another* circular saw? Aren't two enough? Yes, I know it was a great deal, but stand firm. The convenience of the Internet can definitely feed the impulse shopper in all of us. Practice restraint and enjoy your purchases.

Q: **What if I buy something online and it arrives broken or I don't like it?**

A: Before you make your purchase, check the website's return policy. Usually you can return the item in the box it came in for replacement or refund within a certain number of days.

Q: **Is it safe to bank online?**

A: Banks have done everything they can to ensure that their websites are safe and secure. If they didn't trust the safety of their site they wouldn't have you bank online at all. Obviously if there is a breach of security that is due to the site not being designed securely enough, the results of that would be the bank's responsibility. However, if you have any hesitation about banking online, don't do it.

Q: **If I start paying my bills online can I also still write checks?**

A: Yes. There are still certain bills (like my rent) that I prefer to write a check for. You have no obligation to pay any bills online even if you access your account online. It is your decision if you only want to view your account online or actually "use it" online.

Q: **Do I get a copy of the payments made online in the mail like when I receive my checks in the mail?**

A: The truth is that many banks are phasing out sending people's canceled checks back to them. Some banks will include copies of the checks with their statement. At least you can still receive a printed bank statement in the mail. Your statement will indicate the online payments made. You can also print out a history of your payments made online from your computer.

CHAPTER 23

The Wide, Wide World of Entertainment

Finding fun on the Web

A t the end of the day, after all of the research, downloads, and prescription shopping you've done online with your computer, it's time for you to use that big plastic friend with the keyboard and mouse for fun, fun, and *more* fun! We're going to visit entertainment websites in this chapter. Some may be known to you and some may be new. Did you know you could watch DVDs, tune in to full episodes of many of the major networks' TV shows online, and buy movie tickets on your computer? Your computer, along with everything else it offers, is your gateway to many forms of entertainment.

Let's Go to the Movies

I t's Friday afternoon. How about if you hop on the Internet and see what's playing at your local cinema tonight? You may want to find out what movies have been recently released; you may know what movie you want to see, but not the show times; or you may want to purchase tickets in advance for a show that's likely to sell out. *Fandango.com* or *moviefone.com* meet most of your movie needs.

When the list of movies appears on the screen, click on the name of a film for a description, or click on the movie time you desire to

■ Go to Fandango's website to get movie information, purchase tickets, and locate theatres.

CLICK AND GO

Option 1
Click on down arrow to select a movie from the list.

Option 2
Click to type your zip code to find local movie theatres.

Option 3
Click here to type movie title or actor's name. Click Search.

■ Go to Moviefone's website to get movie information, purchase tickets, and locate theatres.

CLICK AND GO

Option 1
Click here to type movie title or actor's name. Then click Go.

Option 2
Click on down arrow to select a movie from the list.

Option 3
Click to type your zip code to find local movie theatres.

SENIOR SAVINGS
Be sure to specify if you're purchasing tickets for a child, adult, or senior. The prices vary just as they do at the cinema box office.

begin the purchase process. Next, you'll be asked how many tickets you want to buy, your e-mail address, and, eventually, your credit card information. Take note that there is a surcharge for purchasing tickets online. (This always bugs me as you've done all the work to purchase the tickets. Why should you pay extra? Oh well, *que sera, sera.*) Follow all the online buying procedures and precautions noted in Chapter 22 and you shouldn't run into any unexpected surprises.

"I always hated waiting in the lines at the movie theater. Now I can buy my tickets online, print them out, then just walk right up to the ticket taker, and get inside the theatre to pick the best seat."
—*Megan*

Home Theatre

If you bought a computer with a built-in DVD player, you have the capability to watch movies on your computer as well as on the DVD player you may have attached to your television set. Depending on the size of your monitor you might even be able to transform your computer into a mini home movie theater. The sound can be hooked up from your computer into your home stereo system for surround sound. (Visit *amazon.com* to order a hot-air popcorn popper and you've got it made!)

Search box where you can type key words.

Click on genre to see movie offerings.

■ You can rent DVDs on line using *netflix.com*

You can rent DVDs from your local video rental store, but the Internet offers you the ability to rent videos without leaving the comfort of your home. *Netflix.com* is the leading online DVD rental site. Netflix offers over 80,000 movies to choose from, and their rental plans are as low as $4.99 per month. You may also want to check out *blockbuster.com*, which offers online DVD rentals (similar to Netflix) and gives you the option of returning the movies at your local store or through the mail.

Here are the steps to sign up at *netflix.com*:

1. Register with the website by filling out an online form, choose the monthly plan you desire, and give them your credit card information for billing.

2. You can view their selection of movies by title, genre, actor, or director. They also have movie offerings organized by awards received, popularity, and recommendations by their other members and their staff.

Netflix registration page.

3. You can create a list or "queue" of movies for future viewing. Depending on your rental plan, as soon as you return a film, Netflix sends you the next one in your queue. (Some plans limit the number of movies to be sent in a month.) That way you don't have to remember what movies you'd like to see—you have a list at the ready. And you can change your list at any time.

4. Once you've watched the movie, mail it back in their self-addressed, stamped envelope.

"Every time I visit the video store I wrack my brain for what movie I wanted to see. My memory just isn't that good anymore. Now, with a movie list online I don't feel as much pressure and I can change it at anytime."
—*Jules*

CRITIC'S CHOICE
Visit *metacritic.com* for movie, DVD, book reviews and more.

It couldn't be any simpler than that! Visit *netflix.com* to view the many movies offered. Even if you don't use them as your DVD rental company, their list of movies may inspire your next movie night.

No TV, No Worries

I gave away my television set a couple of years ago and I haven't missed it since. Between watching DVDs on my computer and catching complete episodes of television online, I don't feel at all out of the loop. Yes, I said "watching television online." ABC, CBS, and NBC, along with some specific shows from cable and satellite TV, offer select episodes free online. Visit each of the network's websites (you know how to search for them on Google, if you can't guess their web address) to see what they offer online.

You may like a show enough that you'll want to purchase individual episodes (or collect the entire season) from iTunes (see page 362 for more on iTunes) or some other source, and download them onto your computer. (Remember, downloading is just moving or copying it from one place to another. In this case, you are downloading it from the iTunes website to the "brain" of your computer.) As of this writing, a TV episode sells for $1.99. Once you download it to your iTunes library, it is yours to watch over and over again. Eventually you can usually rent the entire season of a show, but those DVDs come on the market well after the season has aired.

You can purchase TV episodes on iTunes.

If I want to see the up-to-the-minute news, I visit *cnn.com* and watch their online videos of breaking news. Check out your local network's website to see what they have to offer. The real advantage is that you usually have fewer commercials interrupting the show when you watch online.

Cnn.com offers online videos of breaking news.

Do You YouTube?

Speaking of watching video online . . . *YouTube.com* allows *anyone* to upload favorite video clips onto the website to be shared with the world at large. (Upload is just like download—to move or copy files from one place to another—but in this case it's *from* your computer *to* the Web, not the other way around.) These clips aren't usually more than a few minutes long.

Be warned: YouTube can run the gamut from nostalgic clips of past television shows, to Maria Callas singing at the Met, to newsworthy current events, to juvenile, armpit-fart videos and worse. You select video clips to view based on your interests, segments most recently added to the site, most viewed, top rated, and so on. Click on the **Video** tab at the top of the Home Page to see your choices.

CLICK AND GO

1. Click on Videos.
2. Or, click and type key words in search box.
3. Click on Search.

YouTube's Home Page.

YOURS TRULY

Search for me on YouTube and you'll discover video clips of my classes! My YouTube clips can also be accessed by visiting my blog at *abbyandme.com*.

If you want to upload a digital video file onto YouTube, it's free. Just be very careful about what you choose to share. You don't want to post anything that gives away too much personal information about you or anything that might jeopardize your job, relationship, or, in the case of younger folks, chances of getting into the college of their choice. Anyone can visit YouTube, so your submission is there for all to see. Remember, Uncle Bert may not appreciate that impersonation of him being seen worldwide.

Life's a Game

As I mentioned earlier in the book, you can play mah-jongg, cribbage, and almost any other game you can imagine on your computer. You either buy software that allows you to play against the computer (unless your computer came preinstalled with the game you want to play) or visit websites where you'll actually play against other people sitting at their computers somewhere in the world. Again, Google may be your best resource to search for the game you want to play. Or look at the list of websites in the back of this book for

If you can't come up with your own diversion, visit *refdesk.com*. Scroll down to the Daily Diversions area. That'll keep you busy for a while!

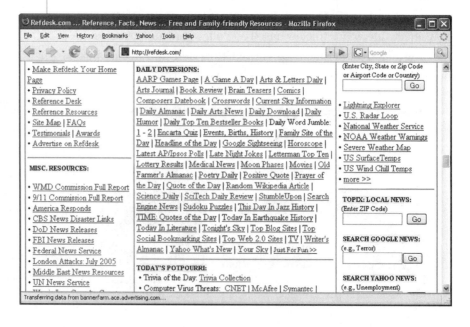

guidance. The more specific you are with your search on Google, the more specific the suggested websites. I typed in *games* in Google and the results were over 800 million websites. Good heavens, that's way too many choices. Better to type in *scrabble*, *bridge*, or *chess*. Remember, specificity counts.

Some gaming sites require a membership fee, but most don't. Most will, however, ask you to register with the site. This is when you'll decide on the name you want to be called when you're on the site. Again, be wise about how much you tell about yourself when you're on the site. That lovely elderly woman you've been playing bridge with could be the big bad wolf in disguise waiting to blow your financial house down.

> "I now play chess with opponents all over the world. Online chess has changed my life."
> —*Vittoria*

Some Entertaining Websites to Get You Started

people.com
Find entertainment news and human interest stories

espn.com
Get the latest sports scores and news

wired.com
Keep up with technology news

nytimes.com
Read *The New York Times* online

usatoday.com
Read *USA Today* online

theonion.com
A satirical look at the news

jokeaday.com
Visit for a new laugh every day

secondlife.com
A game that lets you explore a 3-D virtual world that is created by users

ew.com
Up-to-the-minute news on the entertainment industry and more

There's No End to the Fun

T he resources for entertainment on the Internet are as endless as your imagination is boundless. Whatever hobby, activity, or distraction you seek, it can be found with some detective work on the World Wide Web. And, don't forget to come to my website, *abbyandme.com*, for suggestions of where to find fun on the net!

Q: Are there websites for those of us who would like to learn how to play a bridge or other games like it?

A: Most interactive gaming websites have different skill levels, including beginner, intermediate, and advanced. The great thing about the interactive sites, as opposed to buying software, is that you can ask questions on the website and get expert guidance from other players. If you do opt to buy software instead, most either come with a manual or have a tutorial built into the software that you can watch on your computer. You can also find sites that will help teach you the strategies of certain games.

An Xbox console, PlayStation PSP, and a Gameboy DS.

Q: My grandchildren love their Xbox, PlayStation, Wii, and Gameboys. What are these things?

A: None of these game systems run on your home computer, but they all utilize computer technology to function. The Xbox, Sony PlayStation, and Wii are played on a television using a console to control your movements (games include car racing, combating villains, etc.). A PSP is a handheld PlayStation device where you can play a variety of games, not unlike the Gameboy DS. Just as with a computer, there should be a limited amount of time playing with regular breaks in between. To get a better sense of each device, visit their websites to see a demonstration.

Q: Is there any downside to playing games on the Internet?

A: It's hard to say. For some people, playing computer games increases their contact with the outside world because they can make friends living in places they may never get a chance to visit; for others, it diminishes it. Only you can judge whether the games you play online add to the quality of your life or not. The computer and what it has to offer should never replace face-to-face interaction with live human beings. Nothing beats quality time spent with friends and family. Also if you dare to gamble online, please be very cautious about overextending yourself financially.

MAKE NEW FRIENDS AND KEEP THE OLD

CHAPTER 24

Extra, Extra, Read All About It

The scoop on cell phones, PDAs, BlackBerries, iPods, and iPhones

Now that you've braved the depths of computer technology, let's venture into the somewhat murky waters of additional modern technological innovations. You may never choose to use an iPod, a cell phone, or a BlackBerry, but you should at least understand what they are and how they may or may not enhance your life. For those of you that do decide to forge ahead, before we look at the specific way to manipulate each device, let me give you some general advice.

First things first, relax, and take a deep breath. If you're nervous about something terrible happening to the device, you'll never allow your intuition to assist you with how to operate the thing. A lot of how to conquer these little beasts is to use your instincts rather than trying to memorize each step necessary to accomplish the task at hand.

The first time I have a new gadget such as a cell phone in my hand, I press all the various buttons. For example, on a phone, is there a button that has the symbol of an envelope on it? That's probably what you press to hear voice mails. Maybe there's a button that says Send or Talk. Logic says you'll use that

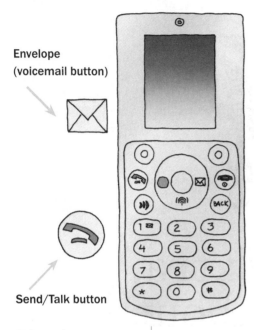

Envelope
(voicemail button)

Send/Talk button

■ Some buttons on a cell phone are marked clearly with their function.

■ Cell phones come in a variety of styles: a flip (left), candy bar (center), or slider phone (right).

button to begin a call and maybe the End button is used when the call is over. I know it sounds elementary, but when you're intimidated, the obvious is no longer obvious. So, relax . . . don't think so much. Be like a kid and just play with the thing for a while. No harm, no foul.

Buying Strategies

Buying a cell phone can be as intimidating as buying a computer, but, as with the computer, it is a mission that can be accomplished with great success when armed with a bit of research and help from knowledgeable friends and family. Before you decide which company you want to provide your phone service, ask your friends or family members to show you their cell phones; if you can, have them bring them to your home and see what kind of reception they get. Not all cell phone companies get good signals in all locations. They should, but they don't. Be sure, before you buy, that you get a strong signal so you can make and receive calls where it is most important to you.

Cell phones come in a variety of styles and sizes. Again, test out the different models of your friends and family before you decide which is best for you. Use the keypad and feel how the keys work with your fingers. Look at the display screen and be sure you can read it clearly. Make a call and see how well you can hear. Because your own ear may block the small speaker on a cell phone, move the phone around your ear and see which position gives you maximum sound.

Ask your salesperson about the battery life of the phone. At the very least, your phone should have enough steam for three hours of talk time and nearly a week of standby time. Read reviews to get an objective take on the battery life of the phones you are considering. It's a good idea to buy a spare battery, a battery booster, or a solar battery as backup when you purchase your phone. As with a laptop, you should let your phone's battery fully run out before charging it when you first get it and frequently thereafter, to help your battery last longer.

At What Cost?

Ask at the time of purchase what your monthly fee will be for calling, texting, and connecting to the Internet. A contract signed for services can be difficult to break. Do not sign anything until you know what it will cost you. In fact, there may be additional penalties if you break your contract.

"I admire all that my niece can do with her cell phone, but I just want a simple phone I can use to make and receive calls. I can't see the screen well enough to read text messages anyway."
—*Emily*

Are You a Feature Creature?

Some people want every bell and whistle available on a phone. Others just want to make a call. In either case, no one wants to pay for what they don't need or won't use, so consider the features available on a cell phone before you decide which phone is best for you. The most basic phone will probably have a calendar feature, an alarm clock, a phone book for you to store your numbers on the phone, and, perhaps, even voice dialing so you can speak a name into the phone rather than using the keypad. Other features you may want to consider are speakerphone capability, text messaging, and a camera. It doesn't end there: You can now listen to music, surf the web, and even watch movies on some phones.

BUYER BEWARE

Just because the sign outside the store is a familiar cell phone carrier or manufacturer doesn't mean they are an authorized dealer. Visit the website of the manufacturer or service carrier and seek out an authorized store.

Phone Photography

It's all well and good to be able to whip out your phone and take a photograph with it, but how the heck do you get the pictures from the phone to a computer or printer? There are a couple options. Be sure to find out if there are additional fees if you use the e-mail feature on your cell phone to transmit photographs to a computer. Suddenly, an inexpensive phone plan isn't so inexpensive. Some cell phones will come with a USB cable that allows you to download (or move) photos from the phone to a computer without use of the Internet. Ask about this feature at the time of purchase. Some phones have the capability to tape short video clips. It is a good idea to check out the website of the manufacturer of the phone you are considering. There you may find an online tour where you can see all of the features of the phone and how to operate it. Also, feel free to ask for a demonstration at the phone store before you make your purchase.

1-2-3 Go!

The first step, and often the hardest, is to find the Power button on your phone. (On my phone it is a button marked "End." Who is the genius that decided that?) Before you leave the store have the salesperson show you the on/off button. Turn the phone on and off yourself once before you exit. Be patient because it takes a few seconds for the phone to turn on and again a few seconds for it to turn off. The phone may chime or make some other noise to indicate that it is on, but the best way to know is to look at the screen. Eventually, it will show either an image, some text, or a bit of both.

At this stage, try to dial a number (your home phone number is a good one to start with) and hit **Talk** or **Send**. (Again, no two phones are alike, so consult the instructions that came with your phone to find the **Talk** button.) Once someone in your home or your answering machine picks up, say "hi" and when you're ready, hang up the phone. There is a button on the phone for this purpose, or you can close a flip phone and it will hang up automatically.

Press and release the button below the word in the screen.

Talk/Send button

The on/off button may be found in a different place on each cell phone.

Now, call someone you know, give them your cell phone number, and ask them to call you back. (Please write down your cell number and keep it somewhere convenient. It took me months to remember mine, so I was always referring to the piece of paper in my wallet when asked.) Some phone models will connect you to the caller when you lift open the phone cover, others require that you hit the **Send** or **Talk** button. Again, your instructions will tell you about your specific phone. Usually, this is a feature you can customize to your liking.

Some phones allow you to see multiple time zones, the weather, etc.

Push My Buttons

You may notice that when you look at the screen of your phone there are often words at the bottom of the screen to the left and to the right. Below each word on the screen there is a button on your keypad. If you press and release the button, the phone takes the action suggested by the word. For example, **Menu** appears on the right bottom of the screen. When you press the button below the word, a menu will open.

Your Little Black Book

Before cell phones were around, I had memorized most of my best friends' phone numbers. Now, I don't even try to remember them because they're all stored in my cell phone. All cell phones have the ability to keep your frequently called telephone numbers in the memory of the phone. Grab a bunch of phone numbers that you want to store in your phone.

Usually the easiest way to store a number is to dial the number, but instead of hitting **Send** or **Talk**, look at the screen. Is there the word **Menu** or **Store**? If there is, press the button below the word. Read what is offered, and press and release the key on your phone that allows you to save the number. This process may take a few steps because you'll probably be given the

To type the letter F, you must press and release the **3** key three times . . . once for D, twice for E, and thrice for F.

AUTOTEXT OUGHT TO HELP
Some phones automatically start to suggest or guess the word you're trying to write using the keypad of the phone. This feature is called AutoTexting and can save time and keystrokes.

chance to type in the person's name. (Of course, or how else would you identify them in your address/phone book?)

When using the keypad of your phone to type, you may have to hit a key multiple times to get to the given letter of the key. (See the illustration on page 353: To type the letter F you must press and release the **3** key three times . . . once for D, twice for E, and thrice for F.) Go nice and slow. If you make a mistake, there's a key on your phone that allows you to Backspace. It's usually either marked as Back or it may have an arrow pointing to the left. Again, experiment. No harm done. Refer to your instruction manual. Whenever you're learning an element of the phone, repeat the steps at least three times to help it stay in your memory. It's also a good idea to take notes, so you can refer back to them later. Create your own cheat sheet to use until the actions become second nature.

Leave Your Message After the Tone

Your cell phone will definitely offer you a voice mail system so you can get messages from callers when you're unable to (or choose not to) answer the phone. The instruction manual will guide you through how to access those messages, but you can probably figure it out yourself if you fool around with the phone a bit on your own. I cannot emphasize enough that fiddling with your phone makes it yours. This is the getting acquainted stage, like in a relationship. It is unnerving and exciting and you may learn more about the phone/person in the first few days of introduction than in the many years you spend together, so take advantage of this time of exploration and adventure!

My hunch is that there is an envelope on one of the keys of your phone. Am I right? (All phones are not created alike, so there may not be an envelope.) If you hold down the envelope button, the phone will dial the number necessary to listen to your messages. If you access your messages this way, you may not be required to type in a password. (But if you call in for messages from another phone you will need a password.) When you listen

KEEP YOUR NUMBERS
Newer phones have a SIM (subscriber identity/information module) card that will store phone numbers. When you buy a new phone, those stored numbers can be moved from the old phone to the new with the SIM card. Note: You must make sure that your numbers are stored to your SIM card and not the hard drive of the phone for this to work.

to your messages, be sure to listen to all of the instructions to hear what options you have when connected to your voice mail. This is where you also record your outgoing message. When deciding what to say in your outgoing message, I believe honesty is the best policy. If you know that you're not likely to answer your cell phone or listen to your messages often, then say so.

My mother has a cell phone she keeps in her car's glove box only for emergencies. I rarely answer my cell phone, unless I'm expecting a call, but some people use their cell phones all the time; some use it for all their calls, and don't even have a home phone. To each his or her own.

> **YOUR PHONE, YOUR CHOICE**
> You have no obligation to use your cell phone for more than emergency calls or as a device to make calls and not receive them, but you should let your friends and relatives know, so they don't expect you to pick up your cell phone.

Control Issues

Somewhere on your phone, you have access to a **Menu**. You may need to use the up or down features on your phone to view all the items listed in the menu. In the menu, there is probably the option to view **Settings**, **Tools**, **Customize**, **Options**, or **Preferences**. (Whenever I see any of those words, I get curious about all that the device has to offer. And, without curiosity, you'll never really take control of these gadgets because you won't uncover all they have to offer.) This is where you get to set things like your phone's volume, or if you want it to vibrate when a call comes in, the ring type, the number of rings before voice mail answers, and what appears on the screen. Somewhere in the menu is probably a place where you can set an alarm clock, see other time zone times, use a calculator, and possibly even type short notes to yourself.

Remember, we are playing, so nothing bad will happen if you change one of these settings. As a precaution, write down the current settings, so you won't forget what they were. Then, if you change something, you can change it back. This is a good rule of thumb when learning any technology. Always take notes along the way to help you remember what you did so you can either repeat it or correct it.

Text Messaging

Many cell phones also allow you to send text messages. Text messaging is not very different from Instant Messaging (IM) discussed in

TEXTIQUETTE
Please do not think that text messaging is less intrusive in the theater or movies than speaking on the phone. It is a still a rude distraction for those around you.

Abc1	Msg	450

How r u? C u soon. xo

_____

_____

_____

_____

_____

_____

Delete	☰	Send

A text message about to be sent.

Chapter 19. It allows you to contact someone without actually speaking to them; instead, you type a brief message on your cell phone. Your phone sends the message to theirs, they receive an audio and/or visual alert that they have a new text message, then they see your text message on their screen, and the correspondence continues. Because text messaging takes place on the tiny screen of a phone, people tend to abbreviate things in a way that's similar to IM. Use the reference guide on page 267 for shortcuts.

Look at the keypad of your phone and see if you can figure out what key to hit to get a space between words. It may say **Space** or it may have this symbol ⎵. The same key you used to correct errors when inputting phone numbers will be used here to erase unwanted text. (Probably **Back** or an arrow pointing left.) You may discover that you don't like text messaging because of the clumsy way you have to hit a key multiple times to get to the desired letter. Alternatively, you may fall in love with the technique when you see how instantaneous and fun it is. Or, having read this you may decide that a cell phone isn't your cup of tea at all. All decisions are right, if they're right for you. Either way, after a brief discussion about cell phone courtesy, safety, and civility, we're going to forge ahead and discuss some other gadgets and gizmos.

Phone It In or Out, But Please Don't Shout

Mobile or cellular phones (most often referred to as "cell" phones) can be a lifesaver or a public nuisance depending on whether you're in control of the phone or the phone is in control of you. Unfortunately, for many it is a daily event to overhear personal conversations on the street, in the grocery store, or on a bus that we should never be privy to and, frankly, probably wished we had never heard. There are also countless cell phone users who've decided to conduct their business dealings al fresco and we have no choice but to hear what a lousy boss they have or are. My only explanation is that Loud Larry and Shouting Shelly seem to think the cell phone is a paper cup and a string without a mechanism to project their voice to the person on the other end. Wrong! I have tested the microphone built into my cell phone, and whispering is just as effective as shouting and no one is subjected to my conversation.

Behavior Issues

Before we move away from cell phones and onto Smart phones and PDAs, there are safety and civility issues that you should keep in mind when using a cell phone.

Using a cell phone while driving, whether it is handheld or hands-free (using a headset rather than holding the phone) is proven to be a driving hazard. Cell phone use is a cognitive distraction to drivers. Unlike other driving distractions (e.g., conversations with passengers, radio listening, etc.) phone conversations can cause a kind of "tunnel vision" where the driver's brain is not actually registering what their eyes are seeing. A 2006 report sponsored by the National Highway Traffic Safety Administration (NHTSA) and conducted by the Virginia Tech Transportation Institute labels cell phone use as the most frequent behavior distracting drivers. Simply said: Hang up and drive! If there is something so important that you must call someone, then pull over and make the call.

> **HANG UP AND DRIVE**
> It is estimated that drivers talking on cell phones are four times more likely to be involved in a car accident. A Harvard University study concluded that cell phones are the cause of over 200 deaths and half a million injuries each year.

Keep in mind the following cell phone civilities:

• No one (other than your suspicious spouse's private detective or your business competitor) wants to hear your conversation. Keep it to a dull roar. A quiet purr would be even better.

• During public performances (yes, even at the movies) turn your cell phone "off." Not on "vibrate" where your purse seems about to take off when the phone is activated, but *OFF.* And refrain from text messaging on your phone. We may not be able to hear your conversation, but your typing gyrations are a distraction nonetheless. Why did you come to the performance anyway?

• For the sake of your dinner partner, decide you can live without the phone at the dining table. An hour or two without being disturbed by the phone should be a relief, not a punishment.

• When choosing a ring type, keep in mind that those around you are hearing it too, especially if you are slow to pick up. There are only so many times we really want to do the macarena.

■ Turn off your cell phone at public performances, please.

A Cell Phone vs. Smartphone vs. PDA

A few years ago, there was a big difference between a Smartphone and a cell phone. Smartphones are really swanky cell phones that function not only as phones, but also offer a connection to the Internet for web surfing and e-mail, along with photo and music features. Nowadays, Smartphones are not just a plaything for the technologically savvy—almost every cell phone has the features of a Smartphone. For example, the Motorola MotoRokr is a cell phone, but it also is capable of taking photographs, sending photos to e-mail addresses, and exchanging information with a handheld device (a PDA, which stands for Personal Digital Assistant) or a computer, and it also allows you to store and listen to your entire music library. Wouldn't you call that pretty smart?

The next step up from a Smartphone is another gadget called a PDA, which can do all of the functions named above and then some. Again, a few years ago there was a big difference between a Smartphone and PDA, but now they are very similar. Not only are they similar, but, there are certain models (Palm Pilot's Treo, for instance) that are referred to as both a Smartphone and a PDA! The real difference now between some "smart" cell phones and some PDAs is the size. Generally, a cell phone is smaller than a PDA. Because of the size limitation, a cell phone (whether very smart or sort of smart) only offers a phone keypad to type your messages, notes, and so on, as opposed to a PDA where you have a full keyboard (although small) and a writing tool (a stylus) to enter characters. The screen to view your e-mail and web pages is also larger on the PDA, so your viewing experience is more pleasant. The decision about whether you can manage the keypad and small screen on a phone or on a PDA is a personal one. No one can answer that for you. If you're considering either, play with one in the store or ask a friend if they can take you for a test-drive. Make sure you can really read what appears on the screen.

BUYING ADVICE

Most of what you take into consideration when you buy a Smartphone, a PDA, a BlackBerry, or an iPhone is the same with the purchase of a cell phone. Reread the cell phone section at the start of this chapter and apply those buying suggestions to whatever you decide to add to your shopping list.

I apologize if I haven't given you a definitive stance on what is a Smartphone as opposed to a PDA, but frankly the water is pretty murky and these gadgets' capabilities are changing and improving all the time.

Is It Handy?

Pick up a cell phone. Put it to your ear. How does it feel to talk on it? Pick up a PDA. Put it to your ear. How does it feel to talk on it? The PDA is a bit clunkier in the hand than a cell phone, but the large screen and keyboard may be worth it to you. As buyer you are both judge and jury.

Lowdown on PDAs

Let's discuss the features on a PDA (also a Smartphone), using a Palm Treo as an example. A PDA has a screen that's about 4 inches square. The main menu on the screen allows you to access all the various offerings of the device (called applications). You can either use the buttons on the Treo to access the features of the handheld or tap the screen with the stylus.

On most PDAs there is a button with a house on it 🏠 that will return you to the main menu (also referred to as the "applications page"). There will be an envelope ✉ not unlike the one on a cell phone that you press and release to hear your voice mail. Use your instruction manual, or your instincts, to figure out what you press to make a call and end a call.

A PDA should come with software you install on your computer to sync information you've input onto the PDA into your computer and vice versa. (Sync is an abbreviation for synchronize or to make exactly the same at the same time.) So, you can input your addresses using the standard-size keyboard on your computer and sync that information onto the PDA. If you then input a date in the calendar on the PDA, you can

Home button

A PDA menu screen.

The stylus on a PDA allows you to control the device along with the keyboard.

Calendar

Bluetooth

Contacts

Messaging

Tasks

Voice Mail

Camera

Memos

Phone

Web

Not all of the applications on a Treo can be seen at one time. You use the Scroll Bar to reveal them all.

go home and sync the computer and the PDA, so the date you booked will be on both the PDA and your computer.

Information can be synched from the handheld device to the computer either by placing the device in a cradle also attached to the computer by a cable or there will be a USB cable that goes directly from the device to the computer. Alternatively, there is now a wireless way using Bluetooth technology to transfer data from one to the other without ever having to connect them.

By now, we all have a general idea of what a cell phone is and can do. The next step up in technology is a Smartphone and/or PDA, and then there's the BlackBerry. In truth, there's very little difference between the capabilities of a PDA and those of a BlackBerry. But this topic, like religion and politics, is best avoided.

"I could never really see the screen on my cell phone very well, but my PDA is a dream to look at. I even text-message now."
—*Irena*

Lowdown on the BlackBerry

Okay, pull out the boxing gloves . . . Do you remember very early in the book when I talked about the feuds between Mac/Apple and PC computer users? Well, no great piece of technology is any good unless there is controversy and competition. It can be argued that a BlackBerry is a PDA (but for heaven's sake, don't say that to someone who uses one!).

As a scuba diver, I'll use an underwater analogy to illustrate the difference between a PDA and the BlackBerry. A PDA is like a tiger shark. It is efficient, sleek, and a magnificent beast. A BlackBerry is like a white shark. It is efficient, sleek, a magnificent beast, and elicits a bit more awe than the tiger shark. Curiosity draws people to both and yet, they can both cause some fear and anxiety. Are you starting to get the picture? The fear and anxiety part is as unnecessary with PDAs and BlackBerrys as it is with sharks. Generally, if you respect them, they will respect you.

As with a PDA, the BlackBerry has a button you push to return to the main menu. Refer to your manual to find the home key, as it is designed differently with each model. Essentially every feature I described earlier about a PDA is on a BlackBerry, and it can all be synched with your computer using Bluetooth technology.

There are some differences between a PDA and a BlackBerry, but they are mostly physical and not operational. The BlackBerry screen is inactive. There is no stylus used to activate or type. This can be seen as making it simpler to use or more difficult. 'Tis six of one, half dozen of the other. The screen is clearer than most PDAs and the keyboard larger. Again, a hands-on demonstration is necessary for you to make an informed decision.

TAKE THE BITE OUT OF BLUETOOTH

Bluetooth technology offers a cable-free connection between cell phones, computers, (desktops, laptops, and handhelds), and other peripherals (such as a printer). It allows all of these devices to speak to each other without any cables attaching them, and it works with virtually every new model of cell phone.

■ You get to decide which applications appear on the menu of your BlackBerry, which means they will not appear in this order on all BlackBerrys.

On to iPods

We're going to shift gears a bit here and talk about the iPod, so we can then come full circle and marry everything into an iPhone. An iPod is a storage device that can hold music, photographs, videos, TV shows, movies, podcasts, and audiobooks for your listening and viewing pleasure. (At the time of this writing, some iPods can hold up to 20,000 songs, 25,000 pictures, or up to 100 hours of video, or a combination of each!)

Not all iPods offer the same features. A full sized iPod with all the bells and whistles can store anywhere from 1,000 to 20,000 songs depending on the memory. The Nano can only store between 240 and 2,000 songs, but its compact size may be just right for your needs. Smaller yet is a Shuffle, which stores a maximum of 240 songs and can't play videos. But it is perfect to slip into your pocket or clip onto your sleeve while you work out.

Tune Into iTunes

You'll need to use your computer as the bridge between your iPod and what you want to store on it. iTunes is the software that speaks both to your computer and your iPod. Although the iPod and iTunes are Apple products, they can both be used on a PC computer.

iTunes can be downloaded (moved onto) your computer for free if you visit *www.apple.com/itunes/download/*.

Follow the easy instructions on the screen to download iTunes. Apple will offer to add you to their mailing list. You can opt out of being on their mailing list if you click on each check to remove it.

The iPod Family

Mini

Nano

Video

Shuffle

"I never thought I would want an iPod. My kids insisted on giving me one and now I love it. I listen to audiobooks and have lots of pictures to share when I get together with my friends."
—*Marty*

When the download process begins, you must wait. Downloading could take several minutes. Be patient. (If you have a dial-up connection, this process will either take a long time or it may not succeed at all. It's another reason to upgrade to a high-speed connection.) Eventually, an iTunes Installer will open on your screen. Follow the instructions step by step.

Once you have iTunes on your computer, you can copy ("import") your CDs to it. iTunes also has a store which you can access from the software, where you can purchase individual songs, albums, TV shows, and movies, all of which will be downloaded (transferred) to your iTunes software upon purchase.

When you're ready to transfer songs from iTunes to your iPod, open the iTunes software if it isn't already open on your screen.

• Plug your iPod into your computer using the USB cable provided. Initially, iTunes will recognize your iPod. You may have to answer a few questions during this process. If you do, take your time. There is no need to answer in haste; the computer isn't going anywhere.

• Eventually, you will be asked if you want to sync your iPod. If you are not asked automatically, click on **File** in the Menu Bar and click on **Sync**.

Plug your iPod into your computer to sync or charge.

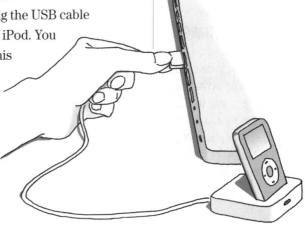

■ Here's how to download iTunes onto your computer.

1. Go to apple.com/itunes/download/.

2. Do you want to receive offers and updates? If not, click to remove checks.

3. Enter your e-mail address, if you wish.

4. Click to start Download.

5. Click Run.

6. Click Next to continue.

BATTERY CHARGING

The iPod battery charges from the juice of the computer when it's plugged into the computer. At present, the battery lasts for about 20 hours of music listening and about 6 hours of video watching.

You can sync songs from iTunes onto your iPod.

CLICK AND GO

1. Click on File.
2. Click on Sync.

• Sit back and don't touch anything while the computer and the iPod are synching. If you unplug anything at this stage, the process will be halted midstream and it is possible that will cause problems later.

• Once the iPod is synched, unplug it from the computer. (Squeeze both sides of the plug that is in the bottom of the iPod and then pull.) Be very careful not to unplug the iPod when the screen display says "Do not disconnect." It is safe to disconnect the cable when it indicates it is charging, however.

PODCAST
Podcast is the blending of the words iPod and broadcast into one word. A podcast is an audio or video file that can be transferred from the Internet onto another device (e.g., an iPod, a PDA, etc.) to be enjoyed at your leisure.

iPod Operations

The iPod has very few buttons to push. In the center on the front there is a circle called the **Click Wheel**. In the center of the Click Wheel is a button.

If you press **Menu**, it will bring you back a page until you return to the main menu. Move your finger clockwise over the wheel and you will move down the list; move your finger counterclockwise and you will move up the list. You press the center button to choose something (i.e. albums). To play something, you press ▶ **Play**. You can also press the

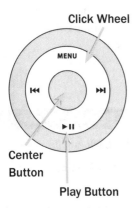

Click Wheel

MENU

Center Button

Play Button

CLICK AND GO

1. Press Menu.

2. Press center to choose a song.

3. Press Play.

THE EARS HAVE IT

You can either listen to your iPod with the earbuds (Apple's name for the unique earphones it designed for the iPod) provided or you can plug in to various speaker systems available. There are accessories available that allow you to listen in your car or through a radio. Visit Apple's website to see all the possibilities.

center button to play a song. To stop, you press that same image again to pause. Play toggles between **Play** and **Pause**. If you press the center of the circle, it's like clicking the mouse—you'll have activated something. Plug in the earbuds (earphones) and let's listen.

To turn the iPod off you can hold down the Play button. To turn the iPod back on, press the center button. The iPod will remember if you were listening to a song and will allow you to resume where you left off. There is also a lock feature on the top of the iPod so you won't accidentally turn it on when it's in your pocket or purse.

The instructions that come with the iPod are very clear, but you can also get a lot of your questions answered on the Apple website or by asking almost anyone. It seems that just about everyone has an iPod nowadays, so you have lots of resources for advice.

The iPhone, Ta-Da!

Eventually, there will be other devices that can do all the iPhone can, but at the moment the iPhone is the "it" phone. It functions as a cell phone, a camera, a TV screen, a connection to the Internet, an iPod, and whatever else you can think of in one easy-to-use, very sexy unit. The screen is made of glass, which makes the images remarkably clear. That's why photos and video are more compelling on an iPhone—the resolution from the glass screen is far superior to the screen on most PDAs and the BlackBerry. You can also view things vertically, as well as horizontally. All you have to do is turn the iPhone horizontally and the screen will adjust the image automatically. Also, there are no keys to speak of on the device. Instead it is all operated through a touch screen that allows you to tap on the screen along with dragging your finger across the screen to activate programs or move items stored on the iPhone. Visit *apple.com*, click on **iPhone**, and then click on **Watch Video**. They say it all much better than I can.

There is a Home button on the iPhone that will return you to the Home Screen.

The iPhone's capacity for storage and viewing of videos, movies, and songs is extraordinary. But if you don't have interest in any of those features, the iPhone (no matter how "it" it is) may not be for you. My guess is that the iPhone will keep improving and the price will keep dropping, so you may want to wait a bit to make the plunge anyway.

Home button

All of the applications on an iPhone can be seen on the Home Screen: Text, Calendar, Photos, Camera, YouTube, Stocks, Maps, Weather, Clock, Calculator, Notes, Settings, Phone, Mail, Safari, iPod.

Until We Meet Again

Before we move on to the Troubleshooting chapter, I just want to let you know what a pleasure it's been to go on this journey of discovery with you. If you can believe it, there was a time when you didn't know what a computer could do, let alone understand the basics of a BlackBerry or know what the heck an Xbox is! You've come long way, baby!

I hope that I've helped get you over the hurdles. You should know by now that you're completely capable of mastering all of the hardware and software mentioned in this book. Now you can choose the technology that's best for you.

Please do take the time to visit and revisit me at my website *(abby andme.com)* and I'll keep you up to date while you keep in touch.

Bon voyage!

Q: **What is Bluetooth in regard to my phone?**

A: Bluetooth technology allows your phone to send and receive signals to both your computer and you. Have you seen people with those *Star Trek*–like devices in their ear? There is no wire going from the earpiece to the phone, but a signal is sent so the caller can use the phone through that earpiece. The technology that allows this is called Bluetooth.

A wireless cell phone earpiece.

Q: **What is an SMS message?**

A: SMS stands for short message service. SMS allows for a text message of up to 160 characters to be sent to a phone or computer. Messages will be stored until the recipient turns on their phone or computer.

Q: **Is it possible that I will run out of space on my computer because of the songs in iTunes or my photographs?**

A: Music, video, and photos take up much more space on a computer than documents, so it is possible to run out of space on your computer if you have a large library of songs or many albums of photos. Rather than buying a new computer, when everything else on your computer is running fine, you can buy an additional hard drive to store these things. Remember that the hard drive is a storage facility. The new added hard drive will plug into your computer and you can direct your songs and photos to it.

CHAPTER 25

Troubleshooting

I think it has a fever—what to do if something doesn't seem right

Error messages that appear on a computer screen can cause the bravest souls to quake in their boots. These messages are generally as harmless as a spooky movie, but they can be just as frightening.

It's a good idea to keep a diary of any problems you have with your computer. Make a note of the date, time, and what happened. If an error message shows up, write it down exactly as it appears. In the unlikely case that you bought a lemon, it will also be helpful information when you return the computer.

This chapter will go over some of the problems that you *might* come across with your computer. I want you to be aware of them and show you that they can be solved. Be assured that most of these problems *will not* happen. There is even the possibility that none of them will ever happen (although the chances of that are about the same as you winning the Publisher's Clearinghouse Sweepstakes).

I don't expect you to understand the logic behind the solutions; just read along to get a feel for how to troubleshoot problems. Consider this chapter your first-aid kit for your computer experience.

Take Advantage of Technical Support Services!

Technical support is yours for the taking, based on your warranty agreement. There is no question too big or too small to be asked. Read through the scenarios in this chapter, but know that you can always call for technical assistance instead of trying to troubleshoot on your own. You paid for the service—take advantage of it!

When I turned on the computer, the screen remained black.

Most monitors have a small light that indicates if the monitor is on. If this light is not lit, it means the monitor is not getting electricity.

- Is the monitor turned on?
- Is the computer plugged in?
- Is the monitor plugged into the computer?
- Is the computer plugged into a working outlet?
- If it's plugged into a surge protector, is the surge protector plugged in and turned on?
- There is a dial to increase or decrease the brightness of the screen somewhere on the monitor. Perhaps that is turned to the darkest choice. Find that dial and see if you can adjust the screen.

These solutions may seem too obvious to solve the problem, but that is often the case with computers. Because computers seem so complex, the simple solutions are sometimes overlooked. If only I had a dollar for every time a client called in distress and the culprit was a part of the computer that had been unplugged by accident.

My keyboard or mouse doesn't work.

Again, chances are something isn't plugged in correctly. Trace the path of each cord. Unplug the cord from its port and then replug it into the port. Sometimes even I find myself wondering why a document won't print, and then I remember I unplugged the printer the last time I took my laptop on the road. Oops.

If it's still not working, try restarting your computer.

My mouse, keyboard, or screen is frozen.

This remains one of the great mysteries of the computer. Sometimes it just freezes up on you. It's a bit like when a part of my brain can't come up with the name of a person I've known for years. Something stops working momentarily. The computer might fix itself in a few minutes, but if it doesn't, you can bring it back to life.

Option 1. Rather than continue to click the mouse or hit the **Enter** key (on a PC) or the **Return** key (on a Mac), just get up from your desk and walk away. Some people get very frustrated when the computer freezes up. Be warned—computers cannot withstand the Samsonite stress test. Do not pound on your keyboard or your mouse. It will only make matters worse. If you need to take five, do so. By the time you come back to the computer, it may have adjusted itself.

Option 2. You can try gently depressing the **Esc** (Escape) key a couple of times (the Esc key is usually at the top left of the keyboard). The Esc key is used to get out of a program or to stop an action before it is completed.

Option 3. If the Esc key doesn't help, you will need to "soft boot" (or "force quit" in Mac speak) the computer. To soft boot means to close a program that isn't responding or, if that doesn't work, to force the computer to restart or shut down without pulling the plug. To "hard boot" the computer is a last resort and involves cutting off the electricity (by shutting off the computer or unplugging it) rather than following the proper shutdown process. My interpretation is that you're giving the computer a swift kick with a soft boot as opposed to a hard boot. We won't hard boot the computer unless absolutely necessary. Of course, you should never really kick the computer, with or without footwear!

To soft boot a PC:

• Find the **Ctrl** (Control), **Alt** (Alternate) and **Del** (Delete) keys on your keyboard.

BOOTSTRAPS

Are you familiar with the saying "to pull someone up by their bootstraps"? That's what inspired the term "to boot" the computer. When you "boot" the computer, you're either straightening out a problem, restarting the computer, or shutting it down.

Soft Boot = to close a program or restart the computer without shutting it down completely.

Hard Boot = to shut down the computer by either turning it off or cutting off the electrical supply.

Boot up = to turn on the computer.

When a PC freezes, first try the Windows Task Manager window to close a program that is not responding.

- Hold all three down simultaneously, and then release.

- A Windows Task Manager window will appear. It will list all the programs that are open or running.

- Hit the **Enter** key on your keyboard. That instructs the computer to **End Task**. That means the computer will close the program that is highlighted in blue. (This program may have the words "not responding" next to it.) You'll then be asked to confirm this choice. Hit the **Enter** key again to confirm.

- If that doesn't work, hold down the **Ctrl**, **Alt**, and **Del** keys again and release.

- The **Task Manager** window will reappear. If you can move the mouse arrow to the words **Shut Down**, do so and click once. If your mouse is also frozen, then hold down the **Ctrl, Alt**, and **Del** keys one more time and release again.

- This will instruct the computer to restart. It's a more gentle solution than hard booting the computer, which involves turning the computer off by cutting off the electrical current.

To soft boot a Mac:

- Find the ⌘ (Command), **Option Alt**, and **Esc** (Escape) keys on your keyboard.

- Hold all three down simultaneously, and then release.

- A Force Quit Applications window will appear. It will list all the programs that are open or running.

- Hit the **Return** key on your keyboard. That instructs the computer to **Force Quit**. That means the computer will close the program that is probably causing the problem.

- If that doesn't work, hold down the ⌘ (Command), **Option Alt**, and **Esc** keys at the same time and then release.

- This will instruct the computer to restart. It's a more gentle solution than hard booting the computer, which involves cutting the electrical current by turning the computer off.

NO NEED TO RUSH

When an error message appears on your screen or your machine does something you don't understand, there's usually no need to rush to fix it. Write down the error message, if one has appeared, then just leave the computer on (error message and all) until you get help. You won't do it any harm.

The computer may have frozen because the program you were in had a hiccup of sorts, not because the computer has any real problems. That's why we first look at the programs that are open and see if closing one of them will unfreeze the computer.

Option 4. If a soft boot fails, you have no choice but to hard boot (shut down) the computer. You do this by turning the power switch off on the computer. If that doesn't work, you'll have to unplug the computer or turn off the surge protector. Count to 20 and then turn the computer back on. Everything should be fine now.

Note: When you close a program through a soft or hard boot, you can't save any of the changes that you've made. For example, you are writing a letter to your son and the computer freezes. You soft or hard boot the computer to unfreeze it. The parts of the letter that you had not saved probably won't be there when you retrieve it. Yet another reason to save often.

■ When a Mac freezes, the Force Quit Applications window will help you to "soft boot" the machine.

My PC screen has a strange disk error message.

Don't worry! This window will only appear if your computer has a floppy disk drive on it (which most new ones will not). If you have a floppy disk drive and you see this message, you simply forgot to take your floppy disk out of the A: drive. Remove the disk and press any key (whatever key that your little heart desires) on the keyboard. Your computer should continue the startup process without a glitch.

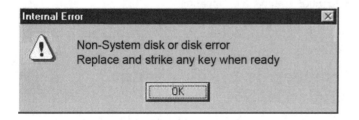

MY COMPUTER IS POSSESSED!

I had student unplug her computer as a last resort and it *still* wouldn't turn off. She called me completely spooked that the computer was still on even after she had unplugged it. It turned out the computer was a laptop. When she unplugged it, the computer remained on because it was running on the battery!

A "Microsoft Windows Startup Menu" appeared on my PC screen.

This window will appear on a PC if something went wrong during the startup process. For right now, we don't care what went wrong. We just want to get the computer back on track. In this case the first thing to do is to hard boot (turn off) the computer, count to 20, and turn it back on.

- If the box appears again, choose Option 3, Safe Mode, by typing the number 3 and hitting the **Enter** key.

- Now let's shut the computer down by moving the mouse arrow to the **Start** button (on the bottom left of your screen) and clicking once.

- Move the arrow up to the words **Shut Down** and click once.

- A **Shutdown Window** will appear in the center of your screen; move the mouse arrow to the word **Restart** and click once.

- Next, hit the **Enter** key. This will allow your computer to restart and all should be cured.

I'm sure all of this sounds a bit unappealing, but it really isn't that bad when you're doing it. Trust me.

Microsoft Windows Startup Menu
1. Normal
2. Logged (/BOOTLOG.TXT)
3. Safe Mode
4. Step-by-step conformation
5. Command Prompt Only
6. Safe mode command prompt only
7. Enter a choice: 1

My PC screen is black except for this: C:\DOS>.

On a PC this is called the DOS prompt. Try typing in the word "win" and hitting the **Enter** key. This may bring the desktop screen up. If that doesn't work, then turn off the computer (hard boot), count to 20, and turn it back on.

My screen says an error has occurred.

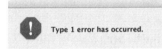

This Mac error message leads one to believe that identifying it as a Type 1 or 2 or 10,000 error would help solve the problem, but that isn't the case. For us civilians we can only glean from that message that we should restart the computer.

- Hold down the ⌘ Command, **Option/Alt** and **ESC** keys at the same time and then release.
- This will instruct the computer to restart.

This error message shouldn't happen often, if at all. Keep a record of when it occurs. If it happens frequently, it would be wise to have the machine serviced.

My computer won't let me delete a file or document.

Chances are the document or folder you want to delete is still open. Make sure that you've closed the document or folder and quit the program that it lives in.

My printer won't stop printing.

Your printer hasn't gone mad. The most likely explanation is that you actually asked it to print and print and print, by repeatedly clicking on the Printer 🖨 icon. The printer now has several print jobs in its queue and wants to print them all.

If you have a PC, follow these steps to stop the print jobs:

- Click on **Start** 🟢 in the bottom left corner of your screen.
- Click on **Control Panel.**
- Double-click on **Printers** (or Printers and Faxes) 🖨.
- Double-click on your printer's icon.

▨ Gulp!

UP WITH UPDATES
Your computer may notify you that there are updates available. As I mentioned earlier in the book, these updates are corrections, adjustments, and improvements to the operating system of other programs you run on your computer. Accept the updates and your computer may run more smoothly.

- Click on **Print** in the menu bar top left.
- Click on **Cancel All Documents.**

If you have a Mac, follow these steps to stop the print jobs:
- Click on the Printer icon in the Dock 🗑.
- Click **Stop Jobs** 🖨.
- Click to select the print jobs listed in the bottom area of the window.
- Click on **Delete** in the top left corner ⊘.
- Click **Start Jobs** ▫.

It may take some time for the printer to obey your commands and stop printing. Be patient. If you've followed the steps above and it still won't stop printing, turn everything off, unplug the printer from the computer, and count to 30. Then plug everything back in and turn everything on again. Everything should be back to normal now.

Better Safe Than Sorry

As I mentioned in Chapter 5, computers have several enemies.
- A magnet held over a floppy disk can delete everything stored on that disk. Magnets can also damage the screen and other components in your computer case. My advice: Keep your magnets on the fridge and nowhere near your computer.

- Liquids should be kept far away from your keyboard. As you may recall, it was just a few drops of milk from my cereal spoon that caused a huge amount of damage. Don't take that chance. Instead, take regular breaks from the computer and enjoy your refreshing drink away from the machine. Any excuse to get up from the computer helps prevent bleary eyes and fatigue anyway.

- Little kids are the Wunderkinder of computers. However, they may not be gentle with your keyboard or mouse. Never let young children use your computer unsupervised.

- Static electricity is another villain. I recently read an article that a woman's computer at work conked out every day at 4:45 P.M. Several technicians tried to find the problem but to no avail. Finally, a technician decided to observe her at that hour. What he discovered was that as her workday came to a close she would get more and more anxious about finishing her work on time. She would cross and recross her legs, conducting static electricity from the thick carpet below her desk, which in turn fouled up her computer. For this reason, it isn't wise to have the computer in a room with a heavy pile carpet.

• Be sure to protect your CD and DVDs from any extremes. They don't respond well to direct sunlight or heat. The safest thing to do is to store them in a box or on a bookshelf. I used to keep mine on a shady windowsill until a friend accidentally sent them on a four-story Kamikaze drop. Splat. Now I have them safely stored under my desk.

Achoo! Is It a Cold or a Virus?

A computer can have a virus (see Chapter 16), and that virus can reproduce itself inside the computer or move from one computer to another via an e-mail attachment or a CD.

The nasty truth about viruses is that they are created by humans. They are the result of some computer geek's wanting to see how insidious his or her virus can become. Viruses can be debilitating, but they can also be detected and destroyed with virus software. Your computer probably came with virus detection software. If not, ask your salesperson about it.

You are the first line of defense against a virus. The most likely way to infect your computer with a virus is by opening an e-mail attachment that is carrying a virus. Be sure your e-mail service offers virus scanning with attachments. If you receive an e-mail with an attachment and you don't recognize the sender, immediately throw the e-mail away.

A virus can manifest itself in a variety of ways. You may notice that your computer functions more slowly than usual or that certain tasks aren't being carried out properly. Unfortunately, a virus can also destroy information stored on your computer.

UPDATING YOUR VIRUS DETECTION SOFTWARE
Because new viruses are being created everyday, you will need to update your computer to protect it from the newest incarnation. The virus software that you buy will offer this feature. Be sure to take advantage of it by either sending in your registration card or accessing their website.

If your computer begins to misbehave (i.e., it suddenly turns off repeatedly, programs shut down without your instruction, the computer moves at a snail's pace when it used to be a jackrabbit, etc.), get thee to a technician and have them run diagnostics it on it to see if it has been infected.

Doom and Gloom

I just threw a lot of "ifs" and bad scenarios at you. Rather than make you anxious, this is all meant to empower you, knowing that you have the resources available should something go wrong with your computer.

I would love to tell you that your computer will never have a problem, but I would be lying to you. Computers were made by humans and they have flaws. I hope that, between this book and the instructional book that came with your machine, a solution is never too far away.

APPENDICES

Over 200 Recommended Websites

(If I have included *www.*, it means that website still requires the prefix.)

Antiques
antiques-oronoco.com
antiquesroadshow.com
goantiques.com
icollector.com

Auction
biddingforgood.com
ebay.com
ubid.com

Blogs
blogsearch.google.com
boingboing.net
drudgereport.com
huffingtonpost.com
livejournal.com
pogue.blogs.nytimes.com
technorati.com/pop/blogs
thediary.org
ypwr.blogs.cnn.com

Cars
autobytel.com
cars.com
invoicedealers.com
kbb.com
nada.com
nhtsa.gov

Classifieds
classifiedads.com
classifieds.yahoo.com
craigslist.com
loot.com
wantadpress.com

Community
facebook.com
friendster.com
linkedin.com
myspace.com

Dating
gay.com
jdate.com
match.com
nerve.com
seniorfriendfinder.com

E-mail (free)
aol.com
google.com
hotmail.com
yahoo.com

Entertainment
blockbuster.com
fandango.com
imdb.com
metacritic.com
moviefone.com
netflix.com
playbill.com

Family
ancestry.com
brainpop.com
careguide.com
family.com
fastweb.com
mamamedia.com
parenting.ivillage.com
yucky.com

Finance
ameritrade.com
bankrate.com
bloomberg.com
irs.gov
lowermybills.com
morningstar.com
worldbank.org

Find Someone
classmates.com
people.yahoo.com
pipl.com
reversephonedirectory.com
switchboard.com
zabasearch.com

Food
americastestkitchen.com
cooking.com
cyberdiet.com
epicurious.com
extratasty.com
foodnetwork.com
gastronomer.com
menupages.com
topsecretrecipes.com
whfoods.com

Fun(ny)
howstuffworks.com
jokeaday.com
secondlife.com
theonion.com
thesims.com
youtube.com

Good Deeds
globalvolunteers.org
heifer.org
hungersite.org
kiva.org
literacyvolunteers.org
makeitrightnola.org
mowaa.org
thegreatestsilence.org
therainforest.org
unitedplanet.org

Greeting Cards (free)
123greetings.com
egreetings.com
evite.com

Grocery Shopping
netgrocer.com
peapod.com
shaws.com
stewleonards.com

Health
clinicaltrials.gov
healthfinder.gov
mayoclinic.com
medscape.com
nlm.nih.gov
quackwatch.com
realage.com
webmd.com

History
ellisislandrecords.org
footnote.com
historynet.com

Household
foodfunandfacts.com
householdtips.org
replacements.com
setyourtable.com
toiletology.com

Magazines
ew.com
houseandgarden.com
people.com
tvguide.com
wired.com

News
abc.com
bbc.co.uk
cbs.com
cnn.com
nbc.com
npr.org

nytimes.com
thepaperboy.com
usatoday.com
weather.com

Photo
flickr.com
kodakgallery.com
shutterbug.com

Research
annualcreditreport.com
britannica.com
encarta.com
hardtofind800numbers.com
hoaxbusters.ciac.org
legaldocs.com
m-w.com
refdesk.com
rhymezone.com
usps.gov
webopedia.com
wikipedia.com
www.askoxford.com

Science
exploratorium.edu
nationalgeographic.com
popsci.com
sciam.com

Search Engines
altavista.com
ask.com
dogpile.com
google.com
hotbot.com
ixquick.com
lycos.com
pandia.com
webcrawler.com
yahoo.com

Seniors
aarp.org
elderhostel.org
grandmabetty.com

nsclc.org
seniornet.com
seniors.gov
ssa.gov
thirdage.com

Shopping
bargainshare.com
bbbonline.org
consumerreports.org
couponcabin.com
freecycle.com (free)
learnthenetcoupons.com
mysimon.com
naag.com
pricegrabber.com
safeshopping.org
shopping.com
shopzilla.com
sothebys.com
thecouponclippers.com
www.consumer.gov
www.fda.gov/oc/buyonline

Sports
espn.com
golfonline.com
sportingnews.com
usfigureskating.org

Travel
amtrak.com
expedia.com
flightarrivals.com
flights.com
fodors.com
frommers.com
kayak.com
hotels.com
lonelyplanet.com
mapquest.com
roadfood.com
skyauction.com
travelocity.com
tripspot.com

Glossary

A: drive the part of the computer where you insert a floppy disk (*see* disk drive)

antivirus program software that helps detect and destroy viruses

Apple a brand of personal computers (also referred to as a Mac or Macintosh) that has a different operating system than a PC

application software software that allows you to perform specialized tasks, such as word processing

arrow keys keys on the keyboard that allow you to move the cursor around the screen

attachment a file sent along with an e-mail

bits per second (bps) measurement of a modem's data-transmission speed

blog (web log) a website that is a personal journal

Bluetooth a short-range radio technology between communication devices and between devices and the Internet

bookmark a website address saved to be revisited (also referred to as "favorite")

boot up to turn on the computer

broadband high-speed communication network that allows for multiple transmissions simultaneously

browser a software program (such as Mozilla Firefox or Microsoft Internet Explorer) that allows your computer to communicate with the World Wide Web

bug an error or defect in software or hardware that usually results in the computer not working properly

byte a measurement of space; a byte equals a single alphabetic or numeric character

caps lock key a key on the keyboard that allows you to type in upper case without holding down the shift key. It is deactivated by depressing and releasing the key again.

CD-ROM a type of disk that holds files or software that can be transferred onto your computer; CD-ROM stands for "compact disc, read-only memory"

CD-RW (compact disc re-writable) a blank CD that is used to copy information to/from your computer

central processing unit (CPU) the part of the computer that serves as the pathway for all information

chat room place on the Internet where people communicate live by sending typed messages back and forth

click depressing and releasing the mouse button to initiate an action onscreen

click and drag an action taken with the mouse to move items on the screen, such as a file or an icon

clone an old term that referred to non-IBM PCs

close box the box in your title bar where you click to close a window

collapse box the box in a Mac title bar where you click to shrink a window

computer case the part of the computer that houses the CPU, hard drive, RAM, modem, and disk drives

copy an editing tool that allows you to copy text and place it elsewhere in a document

crashing an overly dramatic reference to the computer unintentionally shutting off

cut an editing tool that allows you to remove text from a document

cyberspace a figurative reference to the intangible world of the Internet, such as the World Wide Web and e-mail, visited by a computer user

D: drive (or E: drive) a part of the computer where you insert a CD or DVD to read, listen to, view, or install its contents (*see* disk drive)

desktop (1) a non-laptop computer (2) the name for the main screen display on the computer (whether it is a laptop or a desktop)

digital certificate an attachment to an electronic message used for security purposes

disk drive a part of the computer that reads information or software from a disk

domain name a person's or organization's chosen website name, including the suffix that identifies the type of website (for example: www.whitehouse.gov)

double-click quickly depressing and releasing the mouse button twice on an icon or text to take an action, such as to open a document or a software program

download transfer data or files from one location to another (for example: from a website to your computer)

dpi (dots per inch) refers to the resolution of an image. The more dpi, the more detailed the image.

drag *see* click and drag

DVD (digital versatile disc) holds 26 times the data of a CD; most commonly used to view movies

e-mail (electronic mail) to send or receive typed messages via the Internet

e-mail address a person's or organization's chosen address where they would receive e-mail (e.g., abby@abbyandme.com)

emoticon a playful use of keyboard characters and symbols to represent emotional responses (also referred to as smileys), usually used in e-mail or in chat rooms, i.e., >: -(means angry

encryption a secret code added to data for data security

Enter or Return key a keyboard feature that performs actions; also can be used like a return key on a typewriter when typing a document or e-mail

error message a message from the software indicating that an error has occurred; sometimes a code or number is given in the message so a technician can identify the problem

Ethernet port used to connect a computer to a DSL or cable modem as well as another computer or a local area network

external modem a modem that is housed separately from the computer case and is connected by a cable

favorite *see* bookmark

file a collection of information stored in one named grouping. There are many different kinds of files (example: data files, text files, image files).

firewall a security measure that can be turned on to protect a computer from unauthorized users

floppy disk a disk that either holds information to be installed on the computer or is used to copy information from your computer

font a style of type

freezing when the mouse and keyboard become temporarily inoperative

function keys a set of keys on the keyboard, rarely used nowadays, that carry out special commands

gigabyte (GB) a measurement of computer hard-drive space; roughly 1,000 megabytes

hacker a highly skilled computer user who gains entry to information on computers not intended for them by "cracking" the programming codes

hard boot to shut down the computer when it is frozen, either by switching it off or by cutting off the electrical supply

hard drive (C: drive) a place in the computer where information is permanently stored

hardware the physical pieces of a computer (i.e., monitor, mouse, keyboard, computer case)

hertz a measurement of computer processor speed

Home Page the first page of any website on the Internet

hotspot a location providing public wireless connection to the Internet

http (hypertext transfer protocol) a prefix to a website address (which no longer needs to be typed in) that helps direct your browser software to the website

I-beam one of the many faces of the mouse; a cursor that fits between the characters of text to make changes

icon a small picture or image seen on the screen that represents a software program, a document, or a command

information superhighway a reference to the seemingly limitless information of the World Wide Web

installing a process where the computer reads and stores software onto the hard drive

instant messaging (IM) a real time communication with an individual on the Internet that allows faster transmission than an e-mail and is often briefer in content

internal modem a modem that is housed inside the computer case

Internet a huge worldwide, ever-growing system of computers linked by telecommunications network that share data

Internet service provider (ISP) a company that provides access to the Internet

keyboard used to type information into the computer

laptop a portable non-desktop computer that combines the drives, keyboard, mouse, and monitor into one much smaller unit

link a website feature that allows you to click on text and be transferred to another page with information on the subject indicated

login name a unique name chosen by a user to identify him- or herself while on the Internet

login password private set of letters or numbers used to confirm the identity of the computer user

log off disconnecting from the Internet (also referred to as signing off)

log on connecting to the Internet (also referred to as signing on)

Mac or Macintosh *see* Apple

maximize box the box on a PC title bar that allows you to increase the size of a window

megabyte (MB) a measurement of computer space

megahertz (MHz) a measurement of computer processor speed

menu bar the bar that appears below the title bar in a window and offers menus to different commands

message board *see* chat room

minimize box the box on a PC title bar that allows you to shrink a window

modem the part of the computer that allows you to connect to the Internet through a phone or cable line

monitor the part of the computer that houses the screen; measured diagonally from top corner to opposite bottom corner

mouse handheld device to move the pointer on the screen

mouse buttons controls on the top of the mouse that you click to carry out a command (*see* click)

mouse pad a pad that sits underneath the mouse and helps you to control its movement

netiquette network etiquette; a protocol for how to communicate your ideas or feelings via e-mail or chat rooms (e.g., USING CAPS INDICATES THAT YOU ARE SHOUTING)

newbie a person that is new to using the Internet or a particular program or website

notebook computer *see* laptop

online service provider *see* Internet service provider

operating software the system (such as Windows Vista or Mac OSX) that organizes and manages your computer

paste an editing tool that allows you to place text that you have cut or copied

patch computer code created to correct a problem (i.e., bug) within an existing program

PC compatible software or hardware that works with a PC (vs. a Mac)

PDA (personal digital assistant) a handheld device that combines computing, telephone, Internet, and networking features

peripherals additional pieces of hardware, such as a printer or scanner, attached to the computer

personal computer any computer intended to be used by an individual (rather than, say, a large business)—includes PCs and Macs

phishing a scam e-mail sent to elicit private information from the recipient to be used for identity theft

pirated software the illegal practice of copying software purchased by someone else

pointer an arrow that appears on the screen and moves according to the manipulation of the mouse; also referred to as the arrow, mouse arrow, or cursor

port a place on the computer where the cables from the different computer parts are plugged in

ppi (pixels per inch) relates to the resolution of an item as seen on the computer screen

printer allows you to print text and images from the computer

RAM (random access memory) temporary memory used when the computer is on

resolution describes the sharpness and clarity of an image

right-click a function offered on the PC mouse that allows for more advanced tasks

router a device used to route information to/from the computer and to connect networks; it also provides a firewall

scanner copies images and text into the computer

scroll bar a feature that allows you to move a page up and down in order to view all its contents

scroll box a part of the scroll bar that allows you to control the movement of the page

search engine a website where you can search for information on a given topic

shift key a key on the keyboard that performs several functions, including typing in uppercase or highlighting text

SMS (short message service) similar to paging, SMS sends short text messages to mobile phones

snail mail a nickname for mail delivered by the postal service that negatively refers to the time it takes to be delivered in contrast to the speed with which an e-mail is sent

soft boot to close a program or restart the computer without completely shutting it down

spam unsolicited commercial/junk e-mail

spyware software that covertly gathers user information when connected to the Internet without the user's knowledge

SSL (secure sockets layer) a format for transmitting private documents over the Internet; it uses a cryptographic system that involves two keys

surfing the net traveling the Internet from site to site

surge protector protects the computer from irregular electrical currents

task bar the bar that appears at the bottom of a PC screen that contains the start button as well as access to other programs and features

title bar the bar that appears at the top of a window and indicates the name of the software program and the document; also contains the close box

touch point type of mouse used on a laptop that uses a small rubber button for control (*see* mouse)

trackball type of mouse that uses a ball for control (*see* mouse)

Uniform Resource Locator (URL) a technical name for a website address

upgrading hardware increasing the memory capacity or functionality of the computer

upgrading software installing a new and improved version of a software program already installed on the computer

upload to transfer data or files from a computer to a network (for example: transfer photos from your computer to a website)

USB (universal serial bus) the most common type of port on a computer; used to plug in a printer, scanner, etc.

user name *see* login name

user password *see* login password

virus a problem on the computer created by malcontented computer geeks; viruses are meant to damage computers and are spread by opening e-mail attachments or using someone else's floppy disks

virus protection software *see* antivirus program

web page any page that follows the Home Page of a website

welcome page *see* Home Page

wi-fi (wireless fidelity) a wireless component which connects your computer to other wireless products (i.e., Internet, printer, etc.)

window a term describing the visual frame that appears on your computer screen

Windows Vista the operating system used on more recent PCs

Windows XP the operating system used on older PCs

World Wide Web (www) a cyberspace library of information organized by website

worm a program, not unlike a virus, that replicates itself over a computer network and usually performs malicious actions

WPA (wi-fi protected access) data encryption to protect wireless communication, often utilizing a password

wrist pad a pad placed in front of a keyboard or mouse pad that helps position your hands in a way that prevents wrist strain

"writeable" CD-ROM functions like a CD-ROM, but you can also copy information from your computer onto it

zoom box the box on a Mac title bar where you click to increase the size of a window

Resource List

Here are phone numbers you may find useful. Unfortunately, these numbers are subject to change, but not to worry . . . if you can't find the 800 number you seek, simply visit: *hardtofind800numbers.com*

Computer Manufacturers and Technical Support

Acer 800-816-2237

Apple 800-676-2775 (customer service)

Apple 800-275-2273 (technical support)

Compaq 800-474-6836

Dell 800-624-9897 (customer care)

Dell 800-624-9896 (technical support)

Hewlett Packard (HP) 800-474-6836

IBM 800-426-7378

Keytronics 800-262-6006 (ergonomic keyboards)

Toshiba 800-457-7777

Printer Manufacturers and Technical Support

Brother International 800-276-7746

Canon 800-848-4123

Epson 562-276-7202

Hewlett Packard (HP) 800-474-6836

Online Services

America Online (AOL) 800-227-6364

AT&T 800-967-5363

EarthLink 800-395-8425

Microsoft Network 800-426-9400

Software Manufacturers and Technical Support

Word-processing Suites

Microsoft 800-426-9400

Perfect Office Novell 800-453-1267

IBM SmartSuite — Lotus 800-465-6887

Financial Management Software

Microsoft Money 800-426-9400

Peachtree 800-247-3224

Quicken — Intuit 800-446-8848

Virus Protection Software

McAfee 972-963-8000

Symantec—Norton Anti-Virus 800-441-7234

Mail-Order Houses

Dell 800-999-3355

MacWarehouse 800-255-6227

Mac Zone 800-248-0800

PC and Mac Connection 800-800-0005

Zones 800-258-8088

Magazines

PC Magazine 800-289-0429

PC World 800-234-3498

Macworld 800-288-6848

Test-Drive Form

1. Store: _____

  Salesperson: _____

Note the address and phone number of the store and the name of the salesperson you spoke with.

2. Brand & Model of Computer: _____

Include any numbers that follow the brand name—this will indicate the model. For example: Dell Dimension 966.

3. Cost: _____

Note the basic cost and any additional costs. For example: $499 plus $50 for RAM upgrade = $549.

SYSTEM INFORMATION

4. Computer Case:　　☐ Standard　　☐ Tower

Is the computer case a standard model or a tower model that will go on the floor?

5. CPU Speed: _____ Upgradable ☐ Yes ☐ No

Remember, the central processing unit (CPU) speed is measured in gigahertz (GHz). You will need a CPU with at least 1 GHz, but if you want to splurge, you could go as high as 2 GHz, or even higher.

6. RAM: _____ Upgradable ☐ Yes ☐ No

The Random Access Memory (RAM) size is measured in megabytes (MB). You will want a RAM size of at least 1 GB—but 2 GB is more fun.

7. Hard Drive: _____ Upgradable ☐ Yes ☐ No

The hard drive size is also measured in megabytes or gigabytes (GB). I recommend that you start with at least 40 GB. There is no need to exceed 160 GB, since that will suffice for almost anything you could think of doing on the computer.

8. Monitor Size: _____

Monitor size is measured in diagonal inches from a top corner to the opposite bottom corner of the screen itself. For most, a bigger screen is better, but you can judge what suits you best by checking out several different sizes. A flat-panel screen takes up less space on your desk and has better resolution but is more expensive.

9. CD-RW Drive: ☐ Yes ☐ No

CD-RW stands for "Compact Disc Re-Writable." Information can be brought onto the computer using a CD. You can take information off the computer as well—it could be that you want to have a backup of all the information you have on your computer. With a CD-RW drive, you can copy, or "burn," information onto a CD from your computer.

10. DVD-RW Drive: ☐ Yes ☐ No

DVD stands for "Digital Versatile Disc" and/or "Digital Video Disc." Whatever the name, you may want to strongly consider having a DVD drive. For most of us layfolk, we'll use a DVD drive to watch movies. If you don't already have a DVD player in your home, now is your chance to be able to watch DVDs on your computer! Another compelling reason to consider a DVD drive is that some software comes on a DVD rather than a CD, so you won't be able to install it without a DVD drive. With a DVD-RW drive, you can copy, or "burn," information onto a DVD from your computer.

11. Number of USB ports: _____

USB stands for "Universal Serial Bus." It is today's most commonly used type of computer port to plug in a mouse, keyboard, printer, or scanner. You want to be sure your computer has at least two USB ports. With one USB port you can purchase a USB hub, which offers additional USB ports off of the hub, but a computer with additional USB ports would be preferred.

12. Ethernet: ☐ Yes ☐ No

This port is used to connect your computer to an external DSL or cable modem for a high-speed Internet connection. An Ethernet port looks like a regular phone jack, but it is slightly wider. Even if you aren't interested in a high-speed Internet connection at the moment, you'll want your computer to have the option for it down the road.

13. Wireless Network Card: ☐ Yes ☐ No

A wireless network card allows your computer to connect to the Internet without needing to be plugged into anything. It works in a similar fashion to a cell phone, which doesn't need to be plugged into a phone jack. Again, this may be technology that doesn't interest you now, but you want to keep your future options open.

14. **Speakers Included:** ☐ Yes ☐ No

15. **Type of Mouse:** _____ **Notes on Feel:** _____

If you are buying a desktop, it will come with a standard mouse. If you are buying a laptop, note which kind of mouse it comes with (trackball, touch pad, touch point). Jot down some notes on the feel of each. Remember, you can't be expected to master the mouse at this point, but you will have an impression of how it feels. Is the mouse positioned in a place that seems easy to access or is your hand cramped while using it? Your mouse will be your constant companion when you're on the computer, so it must be comfortable to access and control. But generally speaking, control will come with practice.

16. **Notes on Keyboard:** _____

Note the feel of the keyboard. Do the keys feel mushy? Are they too resistant? Or are they just right?

17. **How Will It Fit in Your Workspace?** _____

Take notes on how you picture your computer system in your home.

SUPPORT

18. **Warranty:** _____

The length of the warranty will be in months. What parts fall under warranty?

19. **Extended Warranty:** _____ **Cost:** _____

It's more than likely that the computer store where you make your purchase will offer you an extended warranty. This is an agreement with the store or mail-order company, not the manufacturer. The agreement is valid only if the store is still operational for the duration of the extended warranty—a good reason to make sure you are shopping at a reputable store. Because a single repair on a computer can run into the hundreds of dollars, consider a warranty.

20. **Money-Back Guarantee:** ☐ Yes ☐ No

This may be an agreement with the manufacturer that you have a certain number of days to return the machine—kind of like the lemon law. Beware: Some manufacturers will not exchange a computer even if it is defective. They may only offer to repair the machine. In that case you may want to engage your credit card company as an advocate for you. Or, before contacting the manufacturer, call the store you purchased it from and ask if it is willing to exchange the defective computer.

21. Technical Support: ☐ Yes ☐ No

This is crucial. You want to make sure that the store or mail-order company you purchase from has technical support. The last thing you want to have to do is pack up your computer and mail it to the manufacturer. It is irritating enough to have to bring it to the store for repairs. Ask specifically about telephone technical support. A lot of questions or problems can be answered by a telephone call to a technician.

You should be getting free support for the length of your warranty, whether you have a problem with your computer or you have a question about how to use the machine.

If the manufacturer, not the store, provides the technical support, ask your salesperson for the technical repair number of the manufacturers you are considering. When you are home, call the number and see how long it takes for you to speak to a technician. I've been on hold with some for over 20 minutes. This could be a deciding factor in determining which computer you purchase.

22. On-Site Repair: ☐ Yes ☐ No **Cost:** _____

Can someone come to your home to repair your computer? How much will it cost if it is still under warranty? What if the warranty has expired?

23. On-Site Installation: ☐ Yes ☐ No **Cost:** _____

Can someone come to your house to install your system?

SOFTWARE

24. Operating System: _____

Preinstalled Software: _____

Note the operating system in your computer (Windows Vista, XP, Mac OSX, other) and any preinstalled application software.

25. Additional Software: _____ **Cost:** _____

Additional Software: _____ **Cost:** _____

You may want to buy word-processing software or some other software based on your interest. We talk about this choice in Chapter 8.

PRINTER

26. Brand Name & Model: _____

Include any numbers that follow the brand name—they will indicate the model.

27. Cost: _____

28. Type of printer: ☐ Ink-jet   ☐ Laser-jet

An ink-jet printer is less expensive at purchase time, but a laser printer proves cheaper over the long term because it uses toner cartridges, which last much longer than ink cartridges purchased for the ink-jet. However, that only proves true if you're doing a large volume of printing. Most individuals opt for an ink-jet printer, and most businesses purchase a laser-jet.

29. Features: ☐ Color   ☐ Black & White Only
     ☐ FaxCopy   ☐ Scanner

You will choose features based on your specific needs. A color printer and scanner might be helpful if you decide to do something like a family newsletter or making your own greeting cards. Color is definitely fun if you're printing from a website or want to print pictures. With a color printer, you have to purchase both a black ink cartridge and a color ink cartridge. Be prepared; cartridges can be pricey.

30. Paper Loading: ☐ Top   ☐ Front

It is important to note whether the printer is front or top loading so you can arrange your workspace accordingly.

31. Wireless: ☐ Yes   ☐ No

Some newer printers don't require a cable between computer and printer.

32. Number of Pages Printed per Minute: _____

If you are anticipating a lot of printing, how quickly the printer works may be quite important to you.

33. Number of Pages Printed per Ink Cartridge: _____

This is an important issue. I have a student who was interested in having a small portable printer. She was unpleasantly surprised when her ink cartridge ran out after fewer than 50 pages were printed and a replacement cartridge cost over $20.

34. Cost of Ink Cartridge Replacements: _____

35. Length of Warranty: _____

36. **Extended Warranty:** _____ **Cost:** _____

To repeat point 19, it's more than likely that the computer store where you make your purchase will offer you an extended warranty. This is an agreement with the store, not the manufacturer. The agreement is valid only if the store is still operational for the duration of the extended warranty—a good reason to make sure you're shopping at a reputable store.

37. **Money-Back Guarantee:** ☐ Full refund ☐ Store credit
☐ Other

Again, this is an agreement with the manufacturer that you have a certain number of days to return the machine. Ask the store if you get a full refund or just a store credit.

38. **Toll-Free Support:** ☐ Yes ☐ No

Remember, this is crucial. You want to make sure that the store you purchase from has technical support. You should be getting free support for the length of your warranty.

39. **On-Site Repair:** ☐ Yes ☐ No **Cost:** _____

Even with the printer, ask if someone can come to your home to repair it.

40. **Did you ask if all of the peripherals are compatible?**

Make sure that all the parts you are buying are friendly with each other. Have your salesperson confirm this and note his or her name in case the person is wrong.

Index